Praise for *Buyer Aware*

"In her wide-ranging book, Marta Tellado empowers consumers by detailing how unregulated corporatism produces systemic racism. By further explaining what is technological discrimination against the minority, low-income consumers struggling for economic justice, Tellado deftly connects consumer rights with civil rights."

—RALPH NADER, consumer activist, founder of Public
Citizen, and author of *Unsafe at Any Speed*

"With great clarity, passion, and a personal touch, Tellado convincingly argues that 'consumer' issues are not just about dollars and cents—they implicate civil rights, freedom, and democracy itself. She offers a blueprint for an innovative, nimble, and empowered consumer-rights movement for the digital age. *Buyer Aware* is a must-read for any advocate seeking to make systemic and cultural change."

—GIGI SOHN, cofounder, Public Knowledge

"Tellado is both one of the most respected consumer voices in the country and a leader in the Latino community, and her new book *Buyer Aware* is both informative and incredibly timely. It's a much-needed guide to help consumers, including Latino and Latina consumers, take back control of their personal data, overcome today's predatory practices, and ensure a better economic future."

—JANET MURGUÍA, president and CEO, UnidosUS

BUYER
AWARE

Harnessing Our Consumer Power for a Safe,
Fair, and Transparent Marketplace

MARTA L. TELLADO

PUBLICAFFAIRS

New York

PublicAffairs
Hachette Book Group
1290 Avenue of the Americas, New York, NY 10104
www.publicaffairsbooks.com
@Public_Affairs

Printed in the United States of America
First Edition: September 2022

Published by PublicAffairs, an imprint of Perseus Books, LLC, a subsidiary of Hachette Book Group, Inc. The PublicAffairs name and logo is a trademark of the Hachette Book Group.

The Hachette Speakers Bureau provides a wide range of authors for speaking events. To find out more, go to www.hachettespeakersbureau.com or call (866) 376-6591.

The publisher is not responsible for websites (or their content) that are not owned by the publisher.

Print book interior design by Linda Mark.

Library of Congress Cataloging-in-Publication Data
Names: Tellado, Marta Lourdes, author.
Title: Buyer aware: harnessing our consumer power for a safe, fair, and
  transparent marketplace / Marta L. Tellado.
Description: First edition. | New York, NY: PublicAffairs, [2022] | Includes
  bibliographical references and index.
Identifiers: LCCN 2022019171 | ISBN 9781541768574 (hardcover) |
  ISBN 9781541768567 (ebook)
Subjects: LCSH: Consumer protection. | Consumers.
Classification: LCC HC79.C63 T45 2022 | DDC 381.3/4—dc23/eng/20220617
LC record available at https://lccn.loc.gov/2022019171

ISBNs: 9781541768574 (hardcover), 9781541768567 (ebook)

LSC-C

Printing 1, 2022

To the incredible staff of Consumer Reports,
whose dedication inspires me every day.

Contents

Foreword

Latanya Sweeney
Former CTO of the Federal Trade Commission

GROWING UP, MY DREAM WAS TO BUILD A "THINKING MA-chine," a computer that could think like people. I embraced the wide-open promise of computer technology as a way to right society's wrongs. No longer would the personal prejudices of flawed human beings fog decision-making and perpetuate bias. The pure science of numbers would open vast opportunities to people who had been shut out of political and economic systems simply because of who they were. Technology was to be the great equalizer.

As Marta Tellado reveals in the pages of this powerful book, the kind of level economic playing field that I and many other computer scientists dreamed of won't materialize without a fight. The struggle is ongoing and the question of what vision will prevail is far from inevitable.

We are at a crossroads in our country, and our ability to grow consumer power—or not—will decide our future. Today's technology fails to protect the hard-earned resources of everyday people. Our networked data-driven society fuels itself at the expense of purchasers, buyers, shoppers, users, end users, clients, patrons, or more broadly, the consumer of consumers—the public.

One of my many awakenings to this reality occurred in 2012, soon after I became a Harvard professor. A journalist came to interview me, and in the course of the discussion, I wanted to illustrate a point by showing him an academic paper I'd written. The quickest way to find it was to google my name. Up popped a list of websites, and one of them was to my paper. But on the side was an offer: "Latanya Sweeney Arrested?" with instructions to find out more. Forget the paper, the journalist said. Tell me about your arrest record. I told him I'd never been arrested. Then why, he insisted, does Google say you have?

Google possesses the aura of absolute certainty that most technologies pose. It seems impartial and factual, so we often assume it's accurate. The reporter was relentless. I needed to defend myself, so I clicked on the ad, paid the fee, searched my name, and showed him I didn't have an arrest record and no one with my name in their database had an arrest record. He said, "I know what's going on here. You have one of those 'Black-sounding' first names. The search engine is assuming you have an arrest record because of your race."

What an interesting—and concerning—theory. I searched for "Latanya," and Black faces appeared. When I searched "Tanya," all white faces stared back. The journalist and I searched more and more names and learned it wasn't first names that generated the ads. The ads only appeared on the full first and last name of real people. Still, the search engine algorithm—the set of rules that govern the computer's decision-making—seemed to be distinguishing between those who had first names given more often to Black babies than white babies and delivering ads implying an arrest record to those with "Black" names, even if no one with the name had an arrest record. It also delivered neutral, meaning "find more information," to those who had first names given more often to white babies, even if a person with the name had an arrest record. Because I'm a scientist, I needed more evidence. A lot more. I did hundreds of thousands of lookups across the United States and discovered the reporter was exactly right. A search of a person who had a "Black" first name was 80 percent more likely to have one of the ads implying an arrest record pop up when someone googled them, even if there was no such arrest record in their name.

As *Buyer Aware* shows with clarity, what happens online often has devastating real-world implications. Mine was just one example of many that shows how the historic growth of technology paired with minimal updates to consumer protections threaten our country's values. People's rights and interests are up for grabs, and the only answer is informed consumers willing to demand better.

That's increasingly more difficult to do. We can expect less help from the government than in the 1990s, before the expansion of the internet. Back then, more state and federal attorney generals' offices were strong advocates for consumer protection. Consumers had more places to turn to where people understood their problems and had dealt with many of them before. We didn't worry as much about hidden fees on our monthly bills because authorities had issued a series of punishments for that, pushing the companies into compliance.

Nowadays, a lot of those government avenues for aid have weakened or disappeared. Too few leaders find consumer issues worthy of their time. Especially in the digital realm, where harms can occur from a vendor located in another state or country, it feels like the only consumer protections we get today are those that companies like Amazon are willing to give us. Often there's no one to call or no real person to talk to. Just a complaint drop-down menu, a list of preapproved problems, and a submission form you'll maybe hear back from in fifteen to twenty business days. Some companies provide an option to chat with a representative, where an employee—or a bot—will let you know whether your complaint is valid. And even if you can call to complain, you're met with a robotic voice providing a list of dial options that only take you in circles. If you talk to the typical consumer, they're aware of this dynamic. They've lived it. And they know the system isn't designed to prioritize them.

Another reason it's harder for consumers to assert themselves is the ubiquity of technology. The biggest tech companies have transformed users into the commodity they sell. Advertisers are the real customers. Our attention (and the personal data that comes with it) is for sale. The conveniences, like iMessage, Instagram feeds, and two-day free delivery, are how they keep us hooked and monetize our attention. A generation of consumers has been lost, as we've become accustomed to being the products rather than the customers.

We shouldn't be treated this way, and we don't have to. When it comes to reining in powerful companies, government can hold them accountable and set the systemic standards that protect consumers' rights and interests nationwide. But there are also actions we as individuals must take to push leaders to act, give consumers a bigger say in the marketplace, demand action, and create a more equitable and fairer world.

As *Buyer Aware* will show you, it's still possible for consumers to demand that government and companies put people before profits. That's how our "thinking machines" will begin to work for us—how they'll cease being the problem and start helping us right society's wrongs.

CONSUMER RIGHTS ARE CIVIL RIGHTS

O N A WARM AUGUST MORNING IN 1961, IN THE DARK BE-
fore dawn, my parents packed me and my three brothers,
all under the age of six, into the car. We headed to the airport,
to leave our home in Cuba for the US. My father was so worried
about neighbors reporting us that he rolled the car past their
houses before he turned on the engine. I was two years old.

My father, the only child of two domestic workers from
Spain, and my Cuban mother, who had dropped out of school
to sew garments in a sweatshop, were embarking on an im-
probable journey together. They'd been sympathetic at first to
the changes that Castro's overthrow of the Batista government
promised to bring. But it became clear to them after about a
year that the revolution meant replacing the Batista dictatorship with the Castro dictatorship, and if they supported the

1

new regime they would have to abandon their values of democracy and religious freedom. They couldn't do that. They wanted to control their own destinies, and they wanted their children to have the same freedom. That couldn't happen in Cuba.

It was partly a question of dignity. Castro's guards had raided our modest home, and neighbors, who either feared or supported the revolutionaries, kept track of our comings and goings, ready to report any questionable activity. Being watched all the time was tough to endure. Any faith my parents might have had in the institutions that once existed to enforce fairness had eroded, and without the rule of law it became difficult to trust anyone. My mother and father felt haunted by an unpredictable political movement that demanded unquestioning allegiance. There was no middle ground.

Leaving Havana broke their hearts. They never truly got over it. But their mission to live in a free and open society became the opening chapter of my story. It shaped the person I grew up to be. All my life I've been committed to ensuring that my parents' heartbreak wouldn't be in vain, and to do all I could to make the country they brought me to a place where democratic freedoms and economic equity would coexist and thrive.

The irony is that the nation I live in, once a beacon of democracy for my parents, is now dominated by corporations that value profit over people, safety, and well-being. Tech titans have built a new gilded age by spying on their customers, the very thing my family fled Cuba to avoid, with the human dignity so cherished by my parents crushed by the companies' drive to make legendary amounts of money. The Big Four—Amazon, Apple, Facebook, and Google—treat consumers like commodities, exploiting people's personal data and trying their best to keep what they do hidden. We can't trust them. Their size and their influence defy the democratic values that drew my family here.

A fifth tech titan, Microsoft, is just as big as the other companies, and its operating system is everywhere. But I'll be focusing on the Big Four, because their business models and conduct have attracted the most attention to how the digital marketplace can cause real harms and how the practices within that marketplace need to be exposed.

The problem is not just with tech companies. Deaths, injuries, and property damage from consumer products cost the country more than $1 trillion annually, with government agencies handcuffed by laws that help manufacturers dodge accountability. Financial firms cheat their customers with near impunity, secretive computer models determine how much we pay for things like home loans and car insurance, and lower-income and minority Americans slip further behind. If my family had arrived in the US in 2021, our ability to climb the economic ladder would have been even more difficult. During the first year of the COVID-19 pandemic, three million children, many of them without internet access, simply quit attending remote school. Life expectancy in the US dropped more than it had since World War II. Misinformation has divided the country, leading to violence and even death. And though we rely on government to be our watchdog, the leaders we need to pilot our democratic institutions through rapid marketplace changes have too often responded with lackluster action or no action at all.

I've painted quite a picture, I know. The challenge of standing up to powerful business interests and an uncaring government to create a marketplace that puts consumers before profit can seem overwhelming. But there are plenty of reasons to be hopeful. We don't have to accept the way things are, no matter how entrenched it seems. We can fight back. We *have to* fight back. Our democracy can flourish only if the marketplace, in which all of us have a stake, reinforces the social and economic rights that provide the opportunities to reach our potential as individuals.

The goal is to create a consumer-first marketplace where each person can be the navigator of their own destiny, able to trust companies and institutions to deal fairly, and able to feel secure in the knowledge that their opportunities are not limited, their personal privacy is respected, their safety is assured, and their dignity is valued. It can be done. Throughout the book I'll offer solutions for individuals and for society that can get us there. I'll describe some of the battles that are already being fought and many inspiring victories already won. I'll rip aside the veil that hangs between us and corporate America, shielding us from the truth that needs to be confronted if we want to engage the world as it is. Along the way, you'll see how Consumer Reports is working tirelessly, with you and for you, to bring about the day when consumers can assume their rightful role as drivers of the marketplace.

One thing I love about democracy is that it's always a work in progress. Nobody has the last word. A democracy by its definition means we must actively champion safety, fairness, and equity, and we have to work to ensure that those values are reflected in the marketplace. If we want American democracy to survive—if we want to assure our own survival and the survival of our children—we must be able to trust one another. That means continuing the difficult work of advocating for people over profit.

It's impossible to make the world perfect for consumers, but there's a lot we can do both on the societal level and from a personal standpoint to make our lives safer and the marketplace more responsive to our needs. We can live in a digital world where the roving eye of surveillance is shut, where loan applications and credit scores are truly unbiased, where everyone can drink clean water and enjoy access to the internet, where the fine print on financial contracts is big enough to read and written in plain enough language to understand, where internet users don't have to worry about intimate personal information being stolen, where government agencies have clear enforcement mandates to guarantee our food is safe, where laws place responsibility on manufacturers to ensure their products won't injure users, where incentives encourage companies and trade associations to become partners in transparency, where victims of shoddy merchandise are no longer blamed, and where consumer-friendly car-safety experts have a voice throughout the process of a vehicle's design.

It will take business, government, and consumers working together to make meaningful change. We should celebrate the many companies that act with integrity, that listen to their customers and respond by improving their products, but we should also insist that they be the norm and not the exception. We need to support the watchdogs that expose flaws so we have a chance to fix them, while at the same time demanding that government become a force fighting for all Americans, not just the wealthy and powerful.

We also need answers to many questions, both everyday and profound: Is my water safe to drink? When I'm not watching TV, does my TV watch me? How can I tell which messages in social media are true? How safe is the bed where I put my baby to sleep? Can I trust that the lettuce we eat won't make my family sick? Are the inputs that determine my credit score accurate? How do I know my car has the latest in livesaving features? Does my internet search reflect reality? Do I understand the terms of my student loan, or are there some details in the fine print I missed? How do we prevent problems with products so we're not always rushing around trying to solve them? Where do I get pure advice from sources that aren't just trying to sell me something? We all need to feel that we can make smart decisions, and we have more information at our fingertips than ever. Somehow, however, it's harder, not easier, to know where to put our trust.

Many of us feel powerless in the face of all there is to confront. I know the feeling. It was part of being a refugee, struggling to make my way in a new country. After we left Cuba, my family, along with my grandparents, ended up crammed into a third-story walk-up apartment in the Clinton Hill neighborhood of Newark, New Jersey's largest city. My brothers and I slept in bunk beds in the dining room. My parents worked in warehouses and assembly plants. In the evenings, we children did piecework for the local Clairol factory while we watched TV, stuffing hair-dye instructions into boxes. I thought all families did that after dinner. As immigrants, we felt powerless in schools that expected little of us; lost at the doctor's office, where we struggled to know what questions to ask about my grandfather's health challenges; and overwhelmed at the grocery store, where we strained to figure out which choices were best while reading labels in another language. Every decision we made, we made alone.

In a lot of ways, my family's immigrant experience influenced many of my life choices and passions: a commitment to higher education; a reverence for democracy; a desire to follow a career in public service; a passion for fairness, human rights, and the rule of law; and empathy for people who struggle to find opportunity.

In 2014, after years of working for my home-state senator, Bill Bradley, and at the Ford Foundation, I became president and chief executive officer of Consumer Reports. I'm immensely proud of its eighty-five-year history. The organization has accomplished so much: Consumer Reports exposed the consequences of nuclear fallout and was one of the first voices backing researchers who insisted that cigarettes were a health threat. Consumer Reports pushed for a law requiring the installation of seat belts in all newly manufactured vehicles, which was enacted in 1968. The organization advocated for the removal of lead from gasoline, a goal accomplished in 1976, and pushed for guidelines governing child-safety car seats that became the rule in 1981. We advocated for the creation in 2011 of the Consumer Financial Protection Bureau, which has returned nearly $13 billion to consumers since its inception. In 2014, we helped persuade carmakers to install backup cameras as standard equipment in the belief that lifesaving technology ought to be available to all drivers, not just those with enough money to choose it as an option. *Consumer Reports*, partnering with the news organization ProPublica, found in 2017 that drivers living in minority neighborhoods were charged higher car insurance premiums than drivers with similar safety records in white neighborhoods. We've also taken on irritations such as robocalls and hidden cable TV fees, while continuing the legacy of Rachel Carson—whose 1962 best seller, *Silent Spring*, revealed the environmental hazards of chemical pesticides—by fighting for clean water, safer plastic, and baby food untainted by poisonous heavy metals.

When I tell people I'm a consumer advocate, they nod quaintly. I wait a few beats and then I get questions about

products, quality, and ratings. I rarely get questions about fairness, about bias in pricing, about trusting companies, about
justice or the lack of it in the marketplace. Many people don't
realize those are issues that Consumer Reports works on. When
I mention them on social media, I sometimes get a tweet back
along the lines of "Why are you getting involved? Stick to cars
and appliances." My feeling is we have to do both. We'll continue
to rate individual products and keep manufacturers honest, but
at the same time the marketplace needs a strong advocate for
consumers in Washington, DC, in state capitals, and in the national media, and Consumer Reports has been playing that role
since 1936.

Another question I get from time to time is "What's a person
like you doing in this movement?" I'm a Latina. I grew up in
Newark in the 1960s. I might've gone into broader civil rights
work or tackled racial or gender justice. My family came to this
country from Cuba. Why didn't I build a career around immi-
gration reform?

The fact is, consumer rights are all these things. Economic
freedom is a civil right. A fair marketplace is essential to democracy. If a person's ability to secure a home loan depends on the
color of their skin or their birth country, that's not democracy;
that's discrimination. If a company can decide that any dispute
it has with a customer must be settled by an arbitrator hired by
the company and not in a court of law, that's not democracy;
that's coercion. If a company can hide the deadly effects of its
products, and the government by law must take the side of the
company against the consumer, that's not democracy; that's
injustice. Democracy is not about discrimination, coercion, or
injustice. The only way to have free choice is to have informed
choice, but that means demanding a fair exchange governed by

effective rules and standards that encourage competition and innovation and prioritizes people.

To be honest, consumer rights has never been the most well-known movement. The public doesn't associate us with a Selma, a Stonewall, or a Seneca Falls. We don't have watershed events that animate the national conscience by the mere mention of a word or phrase. We don't have a hashtag that explains everything in two or three words that are able to unite people around the world.

What we do have are focused, passionate people who've fought for consumer rights in the past and who gave us a voice. Many became household names, many more never did, and some were parents whose child was harmed, or they were grown children whose elderly parent was taken advantage of. Their courage stirs us to continue their heroic work in a new frontier of consumer challenges. At this turning point, when the obstacles and opportunities are so great, we can stand on the shoulders of many giants who've shown us how to stand up for ourselves.

ONE CONSUMER HERO WHO NEVER BECAME A HOUSEHOLD name was Ellen Swallow Richards. In the 1870s, she was refused an advanced degree she'd earned from the Massachusetts Institute of Technology because she was a woman. She helped create the first water-quality standards and the first modern sewage-treatment plant in the US, establishing the practice that survives to this day of using scientific inquiry to protect ordinary people. In 1899, Florence Kelley, another unfamiliar name, founded the National Consumers League, which launched consumer boycotts to improve factory working standards and help abolish child labor.

The consumer movement began when families shifted from producing the goods they used to purchasing them. New organizations, formed at the turn of the last century, won battles that at the time must have seemed a lot more difficult than what we face today. Congress cracked down on hucksters peddling worthless snake oil as remedies for everything including death, and Upton Sinclair's harrowing account of a meatpacking worker being swallowed alive in a vat of lard in his book *The Jungle* led to the first laws establishing government safety oversight.

In 1927, Stuart Chase, a well-known author, and Frederick Schlink, an engineer, took a stroll down Main Street America in their book *Your Money's Worth: A Study in the Waste of the Consumer's Dollar*, which detailed the potential opportunities for fraud that waited behind every shop door. Colston Warne built on their work to establish Consumers Union, which would become Consumer Reports, an independent, nonprofit organization that harnesses science to improve people's lives by taking on manufacturers who make faulty products and advertisers who make false claims.

A. Philip Randolph, a pioneering labor leader and civil rights icon, organized a March on Washington in 1941 to end discrimination in the defense industries and was an originator of the 1963 March on Washington for Jobs and Freedom. As a founding board member of the organization that became Consumer Reports, he recognized that economic fairness was integral to achieving racial equality. "A community is democratic only when the humblest and weakest person can enjoy the highest civil, economic, and social rights that the biggest and most powerful possess," Randolph said.

In the middle of the twentieth century, a number of consumer leaders exerted their influence to make the marketplace fairer. Esther Peterson spent her life fighting for American families in numerous roles, including as the first special White House assistant for consumer affairs, as assistant secretary of labor, and as a United Nations representative to the International Organization of Consumers Unions. Ralph Nader was another advocate. His 1965 book, *Unsafe at Any Speed*, helped usher in a wave of car-safety reforms. Ralph introduced me to the consumer movement when I was a college intern at his consumer-advocacy group, Public Citizen. There are so many more people I could name whose commitment has had a lasting impact on our health, our safety, and the marketplace in general. They engaged and won many hard-fought battles to reverse market failures and redress harms. Their greatness came in part from their ability to marshal others to join them in pushing for the right things because, as welcome as small acts of well-informed individuals can be, they're insufficient to accomplish feats like mitigating carbon emissions, getting deadly products off the shelves, bringing accountability to usurious lenders, and enforcing data-privacy rules. Individual action does shape the market, but it's collective action that makes for lasting change.

Through the decades, the consumer movement has continued to evolve by responding to a marketplace that's been transformed in the last twenty years. That's certainly true for Consumer Reports. For a long time, the organization was best known for its monthly magazine, which serves as a signpost for consumers looking for guidance making buying decisions. The magazine remains a vital piece of our advocacy, for and with consumers. But we need to get the word out to a new generation that Consumer Reports isn't a magazine with a mission— we're a mission with a magazine.

In this book, I'll talk a lot about trust. I'll identify threats to consumers in today's marketplaces and prescribe remedies.

I'll tackle the digital world, where so much of our commerce has migrated, and show how everything from fitness trackers to doorbells has given the biggest technology companies open passageways to our most intimate personal information, which they sell to companies that can use it to manipulate and profit from us. I'll show you how this manipulation divides Americans, breaks up families, and puts democracy in jeopardy.

Borrowing money has gotten more complex in the last few years, with lenders taking advantage of loose usury laws and using mathematical calculations performed by artificial intelligence to determine creditworthiness. We need to level the playing field for all consumers, so I'll examine the widening gap between rich Americans and poor Americans, and between Americans of different races and ethnicities. I'll discuss face-recognition programs that misidentify nonwhites and algorithms that show their developers' bias against certain people when it comes to things as varied as insurance, credit scores, and housing.

Safety, whether it's related to infant sleepers, romaine lettuce, or cars, has always been a central defining mission of Consumer Reports, and I'll reveal how existing protections have let us down while we shine a light on a path to better manufacturing methods. We'll talk about how the consumer movement is changing to keep up with the digital marketplace, and how our community of experts is working to develop new ways to test digital products, to advocate for putting data ownership back in consumers' hands, and to facilitate research to uncover emerging digital threats. I'll also tell you how we can work to improve products and services upstream, before they go to market. Consumer Reports has always helped consumers make better choices, and now we're helping make the products themselves better.

I'll also give you a snapshot of the world we have the potential to achieve, where the onus is not on consumers to check or uncheck a myriad of boxes to secure our personal data, where algorithms will be free of the biased assumptions of the people who build them, and where a lack of internet access and other critical needs won't be the difference between success and failure in America.

Improving child-safety seats, baby food, broadband access, college loans, and internet privacy and doing away with predatory lending, biased algorithms, internet misinformation, retirement scams, and inadequate government oversight—the entire consumer life cycle—are worthy of our hard work. But realizing these goals is going to take more of us exercising consumer power. It's going to take buyers becoming aware of the tricks and traps, the exploitation, and the shirking of corporate responsibility. We don't have to put up with any of it anymore. Consumers who are active, watchful, vocal, and who flex the right muscles will make sure the government and corporate America hold up their end of the bargain.

Many of the solutions I mention throughout the book require companies or government to take action. Some changes will come about faster than others, but nothing will change at all if consumers aren't involved. That's why, at the end of each chapter, I've included steps you can take to begin exercising your power as a consumer to make the marketplace fairer. Following these tips won't necessarily lead to the larger societal changes that we have to continue to fight for, but they can help you and your family right now. We've also built a resource website (BuyerAware.CR.org) to help connect you with organizations and government agencies you can turn to for help.

Our movement is all about harnessing, extending, and forti-
fying consumer power. Consumer rights are civil rights. Fairness
in the marketplace reflects dignity, humanity, and equality in society. It's essential to democracy. Every day, consumers vote with
their wallets. We have the power to reshape the marketplace.
Some of the lessons my parents took away from Cuba—that institutions can collapse if they fail to respond to the needs of the
people they're supposed to serve, and that progress is impossible
without accountability—are our lessons too. Right now, we can
push for consumer-first solutions that bring greater economic
opportunity to more Americans. We aspire to partner with big
business, big tech, and our elected officials and government institutions. But we're the ones who need to demand change. It's
up to us. Let's start now.

CHAPTER ONE

YOUR LIFE, THEIR PROFIT

YOU WAKE UP IN THE MORNING AND CHECK YOUR PHONE. You received an overnight text from a number you don't recognize, asking you to send money to a political candidate you don't know. You remember signing an online petition urging your town to turn a vacant lot into a park instead of a strip mall. Maybe that's how the candidate got your number, but you're not sure. You check the weather, and a pop-up ad fills the screen. It's for lawn furniture. That's peculiar. You've never been interested in lawn furniture. Why are you getting this ad? Then you remember buying a gas grill recently at a big-box store. Somehow that information found its way to an advertiser who figured you might be in the market for an outdoor table and chairs. Now you can't see the weather forecast on your phone until you find the X to click away the ad. In searching for the X, your finger accidentally grazes the photo of the lawn furniture, and it sends you to a website. You resign yourself to weeks of lawn-furniture advertisements popping up on your phone.

You put on your fitness tracker and go for a run. The tracker monitors your vital signs as you fall into a rhythm. It also sends the information to a database that updates its profile of you. The database sells your information to an advertiser, so you'll start seeing ads for running shoes, cholesterol blockers, and dubious nutritional supplements. On your run, you pass dozens of doorbell cameras, all recording you. The video will be available to police, who can combine it with faulty and racially biased face-recognition software to try to determine who you are and whether you might have committed a crime.

You finish your run in excellent time, so you celebrate with a selfie in front of your favorite coffee shop. When you post it, a social network uses your location to detect someone nearby whom it thinks you may know, so it recommends that you connect with the person. The person turns out to be a neighbor you recently had an unpleasant altercation with and would prefer not to see again. But the person's photo will pop up three dozen times in the coming weeks, and each time the network will recommend that the two of you connect.

Before you order a coffee, you do a search for the difference in calories between a mocha and a cappuccino. Your search subject is shared with ad brokers, who will conduct an auction that takes a fraction of a second to determine which advertiser wins the right to send you another ad. The winning ad comes with a coupon for a chai tea latte you don't want, which you can drink while you sit on the lawn furniture you're not interested in buying, alongside the neighbor you don't like.

As you walk away, sipping your drink, a hacker causes a data breach at one of the countless companies you've interacted with, and now personal information you didn't know you'd shared comes spilling into the open. Suddenly the world can see your social security number, your credit score, and your credit card numbers. Police, your boss, even a stalker can learn that you dropped in on your ex-spouse one night, joined a political demonstration, or sneaked off during your lunch break to meet a rival company's recruiter.

Pretty scary stuff, right? Tomorrow, you can do it all over again.

At some point early in the internet revolution, we lost control over our digital lives. When the biggest tech companies decided to move away from the ideals of Don't Be Evil in favor of an internet best designed for making them money, our personal information—everything from what furniture we buy to what kind of coffee we order—became the world's most valuable currency. But we don't own it. It belongs to the companies that harvest it from us before we realize exactly what they're doing. Because we haven't agreed as a society on standards for companies' digital behavior, ownership of our data catapulted Amazon, Apple, Facebook, and Google to such prominence that they've become the American marketplace. While they can see things about us we might never have intended to share, we don't always know where they're selling our secrets and to what purpose the buyers are acquiring them. What we do know is that the extreme wealth they've accumulated comes from narrowing our online choices. They got rich by putting us in boxes. Based on our past preferences, they limit our knowledge by dictating what we see in search engine results, manipulate the list of products available for us to buy and how much we pay for them, and restrict what political attitudes we're exposed to. In this chapter, I'll show how the biggest tech companies have taken advantage of their oversized market power, how we invite little spies into our living rooms, and how we can minimize our losses in a data breach. I'll take you through some of the results of our devil's bargain, which we never agreed to, and show you achievable ways consumers can wrest back control over what's rightfully ours.

HOW FREE IS FREE?

In the modern world, your internet searches may seem free, but they're not. Same with the convenience of shopping in your pajamas or connecting with far-flung friends. You pay for those things by sacrificing intimate pieces of yourself. Your value is narrowed to the data you provide and the money you spend. So much that's deeply personal about you is sold to the highest bidder, whose goal is to manipulate you into buying something, believing something, or persuading you to do something you might not otherwise do.

The big tech companies have been at this for a while, and their spying operations are sophisticated and everywhere. We don't think about them much because we're busy posting, searching, texting, working, and shopping, and the companies aren't keen to open up about their activities because it pays for them to operate behind a curtain. Research has found that if sites tell you they're tracking you across the web, you're far less likely to click on their ads. And once we yank aside the curtain, the glimpse we get isn't pretty.

We never signed up for the spying, but our devices follow our every move, tally every keystroke, and keep, catalog, and sell everything we do. This process isn't a side gig for the big tech companies. It's their main business plan—what professor and author Shoshana Zuboff calls surveillance capitalism. If Facebook had stayed merely a digital way to brag to your friends and family, founder Mark Zuckerberg wouldn't be a billionaire. The company is worth in the neighborhood of $1 trillion because it collects our personal information and uses it to make it easier for folks like lawn-furniture sellers and other businesses to hook us. Jeff Bezos built Amazon's $1.6-trillion-and-growing empire not on the book sales of *Harry Potter and the Sorcerer's Stone* but on data wizardry. After the dot-com collapse of the early 2000s, Google was near financial ruin. Founders Sergey Brin and Larry Page looked in vain for a way to squeeze revenue from internet searches. Then they realized that the bits of customer data Google collected from the searches were bread crumbs leading them to riches. The data-industrial complex is such a gold mine that car companies have gotten in on it. So have the manufacturers of TVs and doorbells. Companies have sold us cool gadgets that offer unprecedented convenience, but the devices aren't just products to make our lives easier; they're also data-collection systems. Google and Amazon are money-making machines, and it was the secretive business of handling customers' personal data that got them both where they are today. Facebook is the world's biggest advertising broker. Apple is history's first $2 trillion corporation, wealthier than Saudi Arabia's state-run oil conglomerate. Its revenue for years has been boosted by the relentless engine of data capture.

The Big Four are also monopolistic in ways that have confounded conventional legal enforcement. Their business models are opaque. They shape what we see and don't see when we explore cyberspace. And they've turned the internet—which scientists, engineers, artists, and educators once dreamed would be a limitless universe of communication, learning, and sharing—into an endless shopping mall cluttered with surveillance cameras.

The process of exploiting our personal lives without permission or apology for monetary gain feels entrenched, as if it's baked into the internet's infrastructure. It seems like an unavoidable trade-off we endure in order to gain admission to the magical world of technology, a price we have no alternative but to pay in order to enjoy near-instant global communication, next-day delivery, and all the knowledge in the world searchable in the palms of our hands.

Understanding the extent to which these companies have intruded into our lives is an important first step. Next comes action. We do have choices, and we do have ways to build devices and tech platforms that respect people. We can get product advice free of commercial distortion. We can learn to be smarter about how we navigate the internet. We can pester lawmakers by phone, email, or visits to stick up for consumers, and we can do it state by state if Congress dawdles. We can alter our approach to antitrust. We can form groups that will fight to rebalance the relationship between the world's biggest companies and the consumers who got them there. We can take small, doable steps today to better protect ourselves while we push for big-picture change. And we can express our outrage, because most businesses have to listen to their customers or eventually they'll fall behind. Consumer spending has been estimated at between two-thirds and three-quarters of the total output of the US economy, which is the biggest in the world.

That's power. We need to use it—and we need to use it now.

"WE CAN'T HAVE BOTH"

Here's the thing about the accumulation of market power. The longer it goes unchecked, the tougher it is to rein in.

Each of the four companies that dominate our current version of Big Tech are American success stories. They changed the world. They each rode a great idea, visionary leadership, engineering brilliance, and investor love to the top of the heap.

What they did to stay on top, however, should be troubling to those of us who view oversize corporate dominance as a threat to democracy.

Market domination might benefit consumers in the short term, with lower prices due to scale, one-stop shopping, and an ease of website navigation that comes with routine visits. Eventually, however, the Bigfoots quit worrying so much about customer service. They can dictate terms, quality, and prices. They get away with bullying suppliers. They lack the true competition that would push them into the kind of innovation that made them successful in the first place. They've amassed enough muscle to snuff out rivals and co-opt ideas from start-ups that, if allowed to survive, might have brought the same kind of energy and fresh thinking to the marketplace that the behemoths once did, before they funneled so much of their efforts into staying big. In the long run, consumers lose.

The Big Four are not above using dubious tactics to maintain their top-dog status. They have the means, motive, and opportunity to at least flirt with anticompetitive behavior. For years, the government did next to nothing to curb their increasing influence even as consumer advocates raised alarms. Although legal attention to the Big Four's conduct has picked up, the companies have been allowed to grow into titanic market forces without much resistance from government regulators.

It's not like prosecutors couldn't have made cases in the recent past if they chose to. Each of the Big Four has gotten aggressive with rivals. Apple has always had sharp elbows in defense of its App Store, as shown by its legal battle with Epic Games, maker of the internationally popular Fortnite. Apple required a 30 percent cut from Epic for every game it sold from its App Store, and when Epic started bypassing Apple and selling Fortnite directly to customers, Apple kicked the company out of its store. That hurt Fortnite sales, owing to the fact that Apple controls products and services used by more than one billion people. Epic sued, saying that Apple was unfairly stifling competition. The September 2021 verdict was a split decision. The judge found that Apple engaged in anticompetitive conduct under California law and may have to allow developers to charge customers directly, slicing into sales from Apple's App Store, which grossed an estimated $64 billion in 2020. The judge also ruled that Apple was not a monopolist, saying that "success is not illegal," and ordered Epic to pay Apple its cut for Fortnite apps sold during the time Epic withheld them. Appeals are expected, but for now the iPhone maker continues to reign.

Facebook has also been accused of throwing its weight around to hobble competitors. According to an October 2020 antitrust report from congressional lawmakers, Facebook has employed a "copy, acquire, kill" strategy to bleed rival companies. The Federal Trade Commission and forty-six states sued the social network in 2020, claiming that Facebook's acquisition of Instagram and the messaging platform WhatsApp amounted to monopolistic behavior that harmed consumers.

Three government antitrust lawsuits in 2021 claimed that Google unfairly disadvantaged rivals. Among the complaints: that Google and Facebook agreed not to compete against each other for digital ads, which is illegal. Another complaint alleged that Google's multibillion-dollar deal with Apple to be its default search engine hurts smaller, more specialized searches, such as Yelp for restaurants and Expedia for travel. Google handles an astonishing 89.5 percent of internet searches, and the advantage of being a default application helped get it there.

Whispers of "break up Google" have gotten louder, not only because it's so big but also because its businesses are so diverse. Its parent, Alphabet, owns close to two hundred products and services, including YouTube, the web browser Chrome, Google Maps, self-driving-car pioneer Waymo, the Fitbit fitness tracker, and Nest, which can control a home's functions from an Android phone—which is also a Google product.

As web developer and social critic Maciej Ceglowski has pointed out, it's fairly common to use the Google search engine on a Google device to access a Google website full of Google ads, using Google servers and a Google browser. "It's virtually impossible to get online now without dropping a coin into Google's pocket," according to Alex Kantrowitz of the *Land of the Giants* podcast.

If there's a corporate colossus to rival Google, it's Amazon. The company's success has made its founder, Jeff Bezos, one of the richest men on Earth and, if he has his way, in space too. More than forty cents of every dollar spent online in the US goes to Amazon, making it more than seven times bigger than number two Walmart in terms of online sales. Amazon ballooned during the 2020 coronavirus lockdown, with annual net profit rising 38 percent from 2019, an increase of more than

$100 billion. Amazon has expanded far beyond its book-selling roots. It has become a marketing platform, a delivery and logistics network, a payment service, a lender, an auction house, a book publisher, a TV and film producer, a broadcaster of live sports events, a doorbell-camera manufacturer, a fashion designer, and a leading host of cloud-server space.

Amazon's critics say the company has deployed unorthodox strategies to crush competition. One example is Quidsi, the parent company of Diapers.com. In 2009, it was a fast-growing online seller of baby care products. Amazon offered to buy it. Quidsi declined. After the rejection, Amazon slashed its own prices for baby products by as much as 30 percent and rolled out a service it called Amazon Mom, with amenities such as free shipping. Quidsi calculated that the price war cost Amazon $100 million over three months in diaper sales alone. The low prices bled Quidsi, and it eventually caved to Amazon's overtures. After absorbing Quidsi, Amazon raised its diaper prices and discontinued the Amazon Mom program.

The US Justice Department took no action against Amazon. In a 2017 article for *Yale Law Journal*, "Amazon's Antitrust Paradox," antitrust scholar Lina Khan wrote that it was as if Bezos and his team had studied the government's successful 2000 antitrust verdict against Microsoft and did everything they could to make sure Amazon didn't commit Microsoft's mistakes. The failure to bring a case against Amazon is an indication that the government's approach to antitrust hasn't kept pace with the ways technology companies have changed the marketplace, Khan wrote. Prosecutors have for decades identified anticompetitive behavior by whether it harmed consumers in the form of higher prices or degraded services. Neither of those factors played a role in the Amazon-Quidsi case. Indeed, instead of raising prices, Bezos, prioritizing growth over profit, drained Quidsi's lifeblood by *lowering* prices—in effect, discounting them to death—a practice Khan called "predatory pricing."

Khan observed that large companies such as Amazon use their dominance in one market to benefit them in others. Amazon, for instance, enjoys an unfair advantage when it comes to delivery costs. Amazon was such a big customer of UPS, for example, that the delivery company granted it deep discounts. To make up for lost revenue, UPS charged other customers more. Economists call the sloshing prices the waterbed effect.

Khan is part of a group of legal reformers pushing to change the criteria the government uses to decide which antitrust cases to pursue. The movement has been nicknamed "hipster antitrust," which makes fun of them unfairly, I think. They've also been called neo-Brandeisians, after former Supreme Court justice Louis Brandeis. He was the one who said, "We can have democracy in this country, or we can have great wealth concentrated in the hands of a few, but we can't have both." Khan's view of Amazon runs counter to conventional wisdom. Its power over retail and delivery may enable the company to behave in ways that are "potentially anti-competitive but not understood as such under current antitrust doctrine," she wrote. But the tide may be turning. In 2021, President Joe Biden picked Khan to lead the Federal Trade Commission, the government's main antitrust watchdog.

Khan and the other neo-Brandeisians are dynamiting whatever's left of the myth that the biggest tech firms only have the good of humankind in mind. That's a fairy tale that was more fashionable when the internet was new and Silicon Valley was buoyed by utopian visions that were uttered but not

honored—in other words, before the accumulation of histori-
cally vast wealth. Today, it's important to see the landscape the
way it is: tech companies are more powerful than the regulators who make the rules they're obligated to follow. We need to
do what's right for consumers. As Apple CEO Tim Cook said,
"Tech should serve humanity, not the other way around." That
means fair competition.

When it comes to policing antitrust violations, consumers
must rely on government attorneys who've been reluctant in the
past to hold Big Tech accountable. That has to change, as do
the outdated rules to address the vast concentration of power
in the digital marketplace. There are a host of ways consumers
can help level a tilted playing field. First, though, let's look at
some other obstacles that we're pushing against.

DIGITAL FINGERPRINTING

The Big Four are notoriously tight-lipped about how their data-
gathering systems work and exactly what they do with the information they collect. What we've been able to figure out comes
mostly from patent filings and brochures from advertising
agencies touting how they can slice and dice audience data to
successfully target the right ads to the right people. Consumer
Reports' Digital Lab took a close look at big companies' data
practices and found that they're vague about their intentions,
often reserving broad rights to use data for "research," "product
improvement," or "advertising."

Not all the data collected by platforms is easily traced to
an individual user, but large internet platforms have, over time,
designed their systems to make the linkage easier. Google, for
instance, has merged various properties, such as search and

email, so it's able to tie data to the identities of Gmail or Android users.

It's not shocking that websites collect a lot of data when users fill out forms. More of a surprise is their tracking of mouse movements or the text entered into forms before users submit them. You may have noticed in the last couple of years more websites informing you about their use of cookies, which are tracking devices that follow users across cyberspace. That's because the European Union's General Data Protection Regulation, or GDPR, came into effect in 2018, requiring websites to give notifications prompting consumers to choose whether to reject nonessential cookies. Because the internet connects the world, people around the globe see these prompts—and they're annoying, hard to navigate, and a burden for those who want to say "no." Some claim that companies designed the prompts for the purpose of creating an inconvenience so people would just click through or complain about the new regulation. As TechCrunch's Natasha Lomas put it, "Make no mistake: This is ignoring the law by design. Sites are choosing to try to wear people down so they can keep grabbing their data by only offering the most cynically asymmetrical 'choice' possible." And even though some big fines have been handed out to larger companies, Lomas notes that overall enforcement of the cookie-consent regulation is lackluster. The European Union needs to step it up or, even better, take the burden away from consumers and simply ban these tracking devices.

Companies are always inventing new ways to keep their eyes on us. They have techniques other than cookies to track users, such as digital fingerprinting—a technique that identifies people based on browser and device settings. Not all tracking devices have shadowy intent. Consumer Reports gives visitors to its website the ability to control the use of their data, but we do use cookies to check to see if people have come to our website before, determine whether they're CR members, and ask whether they'd be interested in joining. We minimize what third parties have access to, but like any nonprofit advocacy organization, these methods are a way to broaden our network and draw new people into the consumer movement. We're limited to the tools available to us. At the same time, we're working hard to develop methods to dismantle potentially harmful online interactions and model a new way forward. We appointed our own chief privacy officer to guide our work precisely because privacy has to be by design, and we're striving to do this better.

As an acknowledgment to privacy advocates, Google announced in 2020 that it was phasing out, over the next few years, the use of cookies on its Chrome browser. While some hailed this as a victory for internet privacy, critics cautioned that Google would use the phase-in period to come up with a new way to track users that didn't use cookies. In fact, Google did just that, announcing Federated Learning of Cohorts, or FLoC, which tracks Chrome users by sorting them into groups based on their interests and demographics. As *Consumer Reports'* Thomas Germain wrote, privacy advocates "argue that the move eliminates one privacy problem by introducing another. Google will continue tracking consumers, albeit in a slightly more anonymous way. And the change seems likely to consolidate more data in Google's hands, hamstringing competitors."

In 2022, Google killed FLoC and replaced it with another option, called Topics. It relies on a user's browsing history to make educated guesses of the topics they'd be interested in and then shares those with publishers of targeted ads. Users can delete topics they don't want shared. While some critics considered Topics a small improvement, they pointed out that the internet giant is still tracking users and continuing the controversial practice of selling targeted ads. "It's just not feasible for someone to track and control their Topics on a week-by-week basis," said Justin Brookman, Consumer Reports' director of consumer privacy. "Who would do that?"

There are other secretive methods to obtain personal data. Hardware manufacturers can preinstall software to report information about our buying behavior. They may also be able to configure phones to transmit your location. Each phone has an internet protocol identifier, and Facebook, for example, can track users' rough location based on the IP address—even if a user has opted out of data collection.

A host of companies can gain access to detailed information about users' movements over the course of the day. Precise location information has become a thriving black market. In one example, telecommunication companies such as AT&T, T-Mobile, and Sprint sold information for years to an aggregator that then sold it to an estimated 250 bounty hunters who make their living tracking down people who skip bail. One bounty hunter used the service more than eighteen thousand times in just over a year, according to records obtained by the investigative reporting site Motherboard. Suspicious lovers, too, could pay a little extra on their smartphone bill and track the movements of their significant others.

Once an app is granted permission to access geolocation, there are few limitations on what it can do with the data. Both Apple and Android phones offer the option for customers to disconnect location history from identity, but that's not the default setting.

A number of services and apps can't be used without location services active, and not just GPS driving directions. Today, it's hard to even meet someone without sharing your location data. Dating apps like Hinge and Tinder can only connect you with individuals around you if you share where you are, and by default many consumers leave their location services on continuously. You just have to keep your fingers crossed that companies are responsible with the data.

Grindr, an online dating application for the LGBTQ+ community, came under fire in July 2021 when *The Pillar*, an online newsletter, was able to obtain data about a Grindr user, combine it with additional location data and other information, and connect it to Monsignor Jeffrey Burrill, general secretary of the US Conference of Catholic Bishops. The newsletter publicly shared both Monsignor Burrill's use of the dating app and his visits to multiple gay bars. This led to his resignation from the bishops' group.

Privacy advocates sounded the alarm. Grindr claimed that it was impossible for someone to use its data to do this, but *The Pillar* suggested that's exactly what happened. "A mobile device correlated to Burrill emitted app data signals from the location-based hookup app Grindr," the newsletter noted. "The data was obtained from a data vendor and authenticated by an independent data consulting firm contracted by *The Pillar*."

As the *Washington Post* put it, this could be the first example of "phone data being de-anonymized and reported publicly." It raises the question: If *The Pillar* can do it, who can't?

FROM THE PERSONAL TO THE POLITICAL

Of course, your location data is just one piece of your private life that companies collect. Often, that collection is framed as a way to get something faster, do something fun, or even learn something about yourself.

You might be familiar with the Myers-Briggs test, the 172-question exam that attempts to slice up the population into "personality types" such as extroverted or introverted. It was meant to be used by employers to gauge a worker's fitness for a managerial job. Since World War II, the test has been copied by others, including Facebook's myPersonality app in 2007.

In the five years that the myPersonality app was live, about four million Facebook users volunteered to participate in psychological research by filling out a personality questionnaire. The creators of the app, academics at the Psychometrics Centre at England's University of Cambridge, vowed that the information they gathered would be used only for research. The problem was that third parties didn't always keep the data secure.

Enter myPersonality's stepchild, Cambridge Analytica, which built on its predecessor's work but far surpassed it in shamelessness. Even its name was misleading. There was no connection to the University of Cambridge other than piggybacking on the school's legitimacy. Cambridge Analytica had a unique way of obtaining data from millions of people. It didn't just extract information directly from them without their consent; it also vacuumed up data from peoples' contact lists. That was how it got the goods on most of the world. Although the company didn't trumpet some of its achievements, such as a successful suppress-the-vote campaign in the Caribbean, it still boasted that it had amassed five thousand data points on each of eighty-seven million Facebook users. That was enough data for Cambridge Analytica to sort people into personality types, so the company could predict not only *how* people would vote, but *why*. That information is pure gold if you're looking to get people to change their minds or to choose your preferred candidate. It was nothing less than the deepest and widest collection of people's intimate data ever put together in one place, analyzed for persuasion purposes down to the individual.

This was a new thing for American democracy, because Cambridge Analytica deployed the data to help candidates who were running for office, including Senator Ted Cruz in his primary race for president and Donald Trump when he was a candidate in the general presidential election.

Because Cambridge Analytica could put together what it called "psychographic profiles" of every US voter, it wasn't targeting ads to specific *types* of people, as its predecessors did. It was targeting ads to specific people. Before Cambridge Analytica, political data experts had been able to come up with categories for different kinds of voters based on information that either was given to them by the voters themselves in questionnaires or interviews, or they acquired through tidbits available on easily obtainable public searches—information such as gender, age, zip code, real estate ownership, and occupation. That's how nicknames for people who represented certain voting behavior, like "soccer moms," were conjured. It was a notoriously inexact science. In fact, the process seems quaint, like using stone tools, compared with the nuclear age introduced by Cambridge Analytica. Facebook data made predictions much more precise. Forget soccer moms. Cambridge Analytica could zero in on the single voter in a certain subdivision for whom gun rights were the number one issue, then target—*micro*target, the company called it—that person with Facebook ads touting a candidate's pro-gun views or playing up another candidate's gun-control positions.

Cambridge Analytica's chief executive officer, Alexander Nix, told *Bloomberg*'s Sasha Issenberg that "behavioral micro-targeting" was the company's "secret sauce." The company had created a new paradigm for the advertising industry, Nix said, taking it from "mad men of old to math men of today." A former employee later said that the data firm owned the "psychological profile of an entire country."

It was all made possible by stealing people's personal data.

When the disreputable origins of Cambridge Analytica's success came to light, Facebook, at least in the US, largely escaped the hammer. Cambridge Analytica, however, was annihilated. After investigations by the UK Parliament and the US Congress revealed its unsavory advertising strategies, Cambridge Analytica became radioactive and sought bankruptcy protection in 2018.

But this doesn't mean that the use of our personal data, or the sharing of that data, is gone from politics. While Cambridge Analytica's practices became a big news story, it was hardly the first company to use our data to win elections. During the 2012 presidential race, for example, Barack Obama's campaign also created a Facebook app that it used to collect data about those who signed up—and their friends—to help target voters across the country. In this case, at least the people who signed up knew they were giving data to a political campaign. Not so for their friends.

Today, political campaigns continue to collect our information through online sites. They follow the modern practice of handling people's data by continuously sharing it with others in a cycle that ensures our personal details may be in the hands of countless candidates and causes we've never heard of.

So many people have access to our personal information because data has become the currency of the marketplace. It's possible to choose strict privacy controls and still have your data pinging around the internet, from one entity we know nothing about to another. More and more technology is collecting this data.

And every day, we help them, playing an important role in our own surveillance. Most of the time we don't even think about it.

Until the moment we do.

THE SPY IN MY LIVING ROOM

Danielle's Oregon home was wired. Amazon Echo, summoned by her voice and the voice of her husband, turned lights on and off, regulated the temperature, played the music they selected, and managed the security system. Danielle and her husband would joke that the devices were secretly spying on them.

One evening in 2018, Danielle's husband got a call from an employee. He told them to unplug everything. Something fishy was going on.

The employee, 175 miles away in Seattle, asked if Danielle and her husband had been discussing hardwood floors. They had. The voice-controlled Amazon Echo had recorded their conversation and sent it to what appeared to be a random contact in their email address book—the employee.

"I felt invaded," Danielle told a local TV station. "I said, 'I'm never plugging that device in again, because I can't trust it.'"

What happened to Danielle and her husband might sound like the opening scene of a movie in which evil robots take over, but there was an explanation. Digital assistants like Amazon Echo and Google Home have what's called "wake words" that trigger the devices to start paying attention. For the Echo, it's "Alexa." For Google Home, it's "Okay, Google." Apple, of course, has "Siri." In response to a frantic phone call from Danielle, who didn't want her full name to be used, Amazon pieced together the chain of events that led to a private conversation in Portland being recorded and sent to a man in Seattle.

Apparently, Echo perked up due to a word in the conversation that *sounded* like "Alexa." Then it heard, erroneously, one of the voices say, "Send message." Alexa asked, "To whom?" and interpreted what it heard next as the name of the employee in Seattle. When Echo double-checked, it heard an affirmative. Danielle and her husband evidently weren't paying attention to Alexa because they were talking to each other and not to the digital assistant, so the device must have taken its cues from whatever snippets it pulled from their conversation. Amazon said at the time that these kinds of incidents occurred infrequently. "As unlikely as this string of events is," a spokesperson said, "we are evaluating options to make this case even less likely."

David Choffnes, a Northeastern University computer science professor, set out to see how easy it might be to get a smart speaker to go rogue. He and an associate, in consultation with Consumer Reports, put four Amazon Echo devices through a test. They played three audiobooks and nine episodes of the talky TV dramedy *Gilmore Girls* to see whether the speakers would respond to the chatter.

The team recorded sixty-three false positives in twenty-one hours. Some of the triggers sounded like the devices' official wake word. According to Choffnes, Alexa was activated by sort-of soundalikes such as "I need medical assistance"; "It's actually"; and "I like (plus a word that begins with 's')."

For Google Home, trigger phrases mistaken for "Okay, Google" were "goofball" and, especially problematic for dog owners and watchers of dog videos, "good girl."

"Google and Amazon executives want you to think that Google Home and Amazon Echo are there to help you out at the sound of your voice," said John M. Simpson, the privacy and technology project director for the California-based advocacy group Consumer Watchdog. "In fact, they're all about snooping on you and your family in your home and gathering as much information on your activities as possible. Instead of charging you for these surveillance devices, Google and Amazon should be paying you to take one into your home."

One in four Americans owns a smart speaker, a product that came on the market just a few years ago. But the rapid growth of sales may start to slow as consumers get hip to the devices' tricks. In 2021, one-third of American adults said worries over the devices recording what they say was a top reason for not buying one. That's a figure that has more than doubled since 2018.

The simplest way to control what your smart speaker hears is not to invite one into your living room. But if you're one of the sixty-six million Americans who has, mute it when you're not using it. It won't respond to voice commands until you turn it back on.

TVs, too, are silently spying on us. Newer smart TVs increasingly have the ability to send viewer data to the manufacturer or a third party. A *Consumer Reports* investigation in 2018 showed that several major manufacturers were using a variety of technologies to distinguish what content was being displayed on TV screens. The TVs used "automated content recognition" to send screenshots to a service provider, who compared them against a library of images to match up against known programming. The companies are so interested in your data that it helps keep the cost of TVs down.

In 2017, the Federal Trade Commission sued smart TV manufacturer Vizio, alleging that Vizio collected and shared viewing behavior without consumer permissions. Those permissions, even when you can find them, aren't always easy to understand. Other devices, such as the Amazon Fire TV Stick, have the capacity to collect viewing behavior. It's tougher to monitor viewers who watch through the web or through stand-alone applications.

Smartphones have wake words too. Operating systems have been found to collect and transmit conversations they were never intended to. Carriers can typically see whom you're calling or texting, and mobile apps can request permission to access your phone's contact list.

Those contacts have been essential to Facebook's growth. The social network scours them to populate its People You May Know function. PYMK, which pops up every time a user logs in, reminds Facebook members of people they might not have heard from in a while and encourages them to widen their personal network by "friending" them. Expanding PYMK could be a reason that Facebook acquired Instagram and WhatsApp—the more contact lists, the better. Facebook denies using information from WhatsApp for People You May Know, but as reporter Kashmir Hill pointed out, WhatsApp's privacy policy shows that Facebook has given itself the right to do so.

Facebook's PYMK algorithms try to match users with friends and friends of friends, which sounds innocent, but, as we'll discuss further in Chapter Four, the algorithms have no idea what it's like to be human. PYMK suggested that a psychiatrist's patients friend one another; people who met at an Alcoholics Anonymous meeting were no longer anonymous once they were matched by PYMK; and PYMK suggested that one Facebook user "friend" their rapist. According to Kashmir Hill, Facebook discovered early on that there were some people who could never be friends, and the PYMK team adopted an unofficial golden rule: "Don't suggest the mistress to the wife." The team didn't say anything about suggesting a wife to a wife. A Washington State man was busted for bigamy after the social network suggested that his two wives become Facebook friends.

Unwanted connections can also be made through photos posted on social media. Details about when, where, and how a photo was taken are captured automatically by smartphones and digital cameras and stored in what is known as exchangeable image file format, or Exif. Information on everything from exposure settings to altitude may be included. The Exif data travels with the photo—from the camera to your hard drive to a website. So when you text a photo or post it, you're sending that information out into the world. When you store your photos in Google Photos or Apple Photos, the Exif data is preserved. This is the same data that allows you to quickly find an old photo or locate an album of the family's trip to Niagara Falls. So you may be reluctant to disable it completely. Both Google and Apple have features that allow you to share photos without that information attached. One expert suggests texting or posting a screenshot of the photo instead of the uploaded photo itself. The screenshot won't have your data freeloading on a trip around the internet.

The Amazon Ring has also been embroiled in controversies. By far the world's most popular doorbell camera, Ring offers what seems like a miracle: around-the-clock video and audio from outside your door transmitted to your smartphone. It's hard to believe the product was turned down by all five investors on the TV show *Shark Tank*. Billionaire Richard Branson invested in it after a guest to his private island spoke remotely with a delivery person at his door back home.

But there's a dark side to the miraculous technology. *The Guardian* newspaper called Ring "the largest civilian surveillance network the U.S. has ever seen." About two thousand police departments have signed deals that allow them to access security video from the doorbells, 1.4 million of which were sold in the US in 2020. And they can do it without a warrant.

Ring video has been instrumental in nabbing "porch pirates" who commit petty crimes like delivery-package theft and vandalism. But it allows a single resident to decide whether to share recordings of their neighborhood with police. Doorbells are different from the surveillance cameras that businesses have been using for years. When we mow our lawn or walk the dog, we presume a measure of privacy that we don't expect while we're shopping in a brick-and-mortar store.

In response to complaints from civil liberties groups about possible abuse, Ring has made tweaks to its format. Following an incident, instead of police asking Ring users directly for relevant footage, law enforcement requests are now posted publicly on Amazon's Neighbors app, a kind of neighborhood-watch network with ten million monthly users. Ring owners who reside within half a mile of the incident are notified that law

enforcement would like them to share their videos. They can ignore the request or click a link to provide the video. If users opt
to ignore, law enforcement agencies have no way of knowing
whether they saw the request. If users choose to share footage,
the Ring app directs them to select video clips that might be
useful and shares users' home and email addresses with police. Ring users can opt out of receiving requests from police
altogether.

Law enforcement can ask Ring users to provide as much
as twelve hours of video. In a crowded city, that could mean
footage from hundreds of cameras for hundreds of hours. The
worry is that police would identify and pursue people whose
presence they deem unusual, such as a person of color in a
white neighborhood, or spy on a legal political demonstration.
The Electronic Frontier Foundation reported that Los Angeles
police requested Ring footage of a Black Lives Matter protest
in 2020.

This kind of monitoring is different from the tracking that
follows us when we use an app or visit a website. The two are
similar in that they remind me of the surveillance that chased
my parents out of Cuba in 1961. I empathize with the feeling
of safety promised by a Ring doorbell and appreciate the convenience enjoyed with the help of a digital assistant like Alexa.
Still, the parallels with Cuba concern me. I'm worried about
how easily a dream technology in the wrong hands can turn into
the oppressive surveillance and control apparatus of an autocratic leader. We can't trust Amazon, or any of the Big Four, to
do the right thing for us when we're counting on them. What incentives do they have beyond more profit, more influence, more
power over the marketplace? Who gets to decide how much of
ourselves we share with people who may not have our best in-

terests at heart? Who gets to turn off the doorbell cameras and block the digital assistants from transmitting what we do and say? What may seem paranoid to an American raised on the presumption of privacy and the rule of law might be a more plausible future to someone who experienced the breakdown of those cherished rights under Castro or any other autocratic regime.

What can we do?

WHEN HACKERS ATTACK

Millions of Americans have received a particular email or letter via snail mail. The notice tells them that their personal information—the kinds of things they wouldn't say out loud in a public place, such as their Social Security number or credit card numbers or home address—has been stolen by hackers and released to the world for anyone to do whatever they want with. The news is usually accompanied by what's meant to be reassurance, written in a lawyerly bureaucratese that's so vague it only worsens the sinking feeling that a yearslong, soul-draining battle against identity theft has just begun.

One of the first memorable data breaches was also one of the biggest. In December 2016, Yahoo announced that hackers had accessed the data of more than a billion of its subscribers— and that they'd done it in 2013. Less than a year later, Yahoo disclosed that the number was actually three billion users. At the time, Yahoo was negotiating the sale of itself to Verizon, and the data breach lowered the price that Verizon eventually paid. An investigation found that although the attackers unlocked account information—such as security questions and answers—plain-text passwords, payment-card details, and bank data weren't stolen.

Since 2013, the fifteen biggest data heists have netted information on billions of users and have included invasions of Alibaba, LinkedIn, Sina Weibo, Facebook, and Marriott. The Equifax breach in 2017 potentially exposed the information of 143 million Americans, which doesn't even land it in the top fifteen of the century's biggest hacks, but it resulted in a $575 million settlement with the Federal Trade Commission. A more recent breach at T-Mobile affected the stolen files of almost eight million regular monthly customers and more than forty million records that belonged to prospective customers who had applied for credit.

Such breaches are not an unavoidable reality of modern society. Companies can and should do more to minimize the potential risk, and potential damage, of these hackings. *Consumer Reports* interviewed a number of data and information-security experts and came up with these five steps we should take:

1. **Limit the collection of data.** This would minimize the impact of a breach. Right now, companies view data as a continuous source of content they can profit from— potentially. Alan Dayley, a technology analyst and research vice president at the business advisory firm Gartner, told *Consumer Reports* that over 70 percent of data stays "dark," unused by the companies that collect it. Much of this pool of personal information doesn't help businesses, but it does create a nice target for hackers.

2. **Improve security practices.** Many companies should be taking more security steps, including separating different kinds of data into different computer systems and limiting how many employees have the ability to log into sensitive

systems. These are basic precautions that experts believe too many companies don't follow.

3. **Take the protection of all data seriously.** Businesses are often too casual with data that isn't financial in nature. Nonfinancial information can still help hackers scam consumers and succeed with identity theft. Companies need to prioritize the protection of all data, and state and federal leaders should require it by updating legal safeguards of personally identifiable information.

4. **Notify the public of breaches expeditiously.** It often takes months or years before consumers hear about a company's data breach. Sometimes this is due to negligence, but sometimes companies just hold on to the information. That's why Consumer Reports has called for a national data breach notification law. This has to be a priority. The sooner people know that their data has been accessed, the more quickly they can lock down accounts and change passwords.

5. **Penalize companies for laxity.** Breaches have gone largely unpunished, especially when the impact on consumers is taken into account. Take, for example, the successful hack of Equifax, which affected around 143 million people. The settlement, which required the company to pay at least $575 million, was a historic amount, but given how many people were harmed, it's still a pittance for individuals who had their Social Security numbers, addresses, driver's license numbers, and credit card numbers stolen, just for starters. Europe has increased the punishment for allowing such breaches, with companies

potentially losing up to 4 percent of their total annual revenues for severe violations. The US already holds health providers accountable for the mishandling of medical data, including the threat of jail time. Why wouldn't failing to protect consumers' other personal information incur the same level of punishment?

These are actions that companies and government leaders could enact today to help protect every American. But people need to know how to protect themselves now, which is why Consumer Reports offers the CR Security Planner. It's a free, easy-to-use guide that not only provides personalized and expert advice to help protect you from breaches, but also includes other general online safety topics, like keeping social media accounts from being hacked, locking down smartphones and home-security cameras, and reducing intrusive tracking by websites.

It can also help you decide whether a virtual private network (VPN) is right for you. A commercial VPN can help secure your privacy by creating an encrypted connection between your device and a remote service. With the rise of encryption at most websites, VPNs offer less protection than they used to, and even people who recommend VPNs have a ton of caveats—for example, there are many problematic VPN options that people fall for; you may only need a VPN in certain circumstances like traveling; you may have to take additional complicated steps for otherwise simple internet usage, et cetera.

You can find the CR Security Planner at securityplanner .consumerreports.org. For more specific tips on how you can protect yourself if you fall victim to a breach, turn to the individual-action section at the end of this chapter.

DIGITAL STANDARD

Hacking, tracking, TVs that snoop, digital assistants that send your Portland conversation to a random friend in Seattle, and giant companies that can do whatever they want with consumers' personal information without consent are indications of an electronic world gone wild. People have needed a list of what consumers and regulators have a right to expect from the digital industry, but companies have never taken it upon themselves, like good corporate citizens, to establish a code of conduct, which seems as though it should have been a natural undertaking at some point during the online revolution. So Consumer Reports' Digital Lab decided to fill the gap, creating the Digital Standard, a simple list of main principles for internet participants:

- **Privacy.** Consumer information that's collected by any product or service should be safeguarded and kept private.
- **Security.** Electronics and software-based products must implement security best practices to reduce the risks from attackers, malware, and other threats.
- **Ownership.** When consumers buy products, they should be able to alter, fix, or resell them. (I talk more about the "right to repair" later in this chapter.)
- **Governance.** Products should be designed to help protect freedom of expression, address accessibility, and combat harassment.

This list sounds simple, but implementation is tough. There's little incentive, especially if these principles are in competition with the bottom line. So, unsurprisingly, most companies have not risen to the challenge of honoring them.

Weirder things, however, have happened. Surprisingly, one of the boldest moves to advance online privacy came from an unlikely source whose motives weren't so simple.

APPLE'S GAMBIT

Not long ago I might have said it would be too optimistic to expect industry Goliaths such as Google and Facebook to change their ways without new laws or lawsuits to twist their arms. But after years of press attention and a shift in public opinion, in late 2020 one of the Big Four broke ranks. Sure, the move was self-serving and may have brought up as many troubling issues as it seemed to solve. It appeared, however, to be a turning point: Apple announced it would be tossing sand into the digital-surveillance machinery.

Apple said it would launch an operating-system update, iOS 14.5, that would require iPhone mobile applications to ask for consumer approval before they could gather personal data from multiple apps. For the first time, users would be given the option of keeping developers out of their private business by clicking an opt-in/opt-out prompt. Apple called it App Tracking Transparency.

The announcement made a splash. One-third of the US population owns an iPhone, so it was suddenly possible that advertisers would have to quit internet-stalking some 116 million American mobile customers. Without insight into the personal preferences of so many users, a big chunk of the ads we see could no longer be targeted. Advertisers would be going back in time, to a world where they'd have to estimate based on inexact data what people would respond to. Their enticements would be aimed at a wider universe of consumers, theoretically making their ads less effective. Of course, this was how advertising had worked for all of history before about 2003, but it wasn't the way Big Tech had amassed their princely fortunes. For Apple, however, it was a win-win: the iOS 14.5 upgrade was an ingenious way to respond to growing indignation at our powerlessness—guaranteeing the kind of positive public reaction that can buy favorable treatment from lawmakers, guarantee return business, and lift the stock price—while at the same time trolling its competitors.

Facebook freaked out. Zuckerberg and his company were already entangled in a yearslong feud with Tim Cook–led Apple, and the social network took Apple's move as a direct attack. Perhaps it was. Certainly it posed a threat. Advertising made up more than 97 percent of Facebook's $86 billion in 2020 revenue. Zuckerberg and his lieutenants fought back with every weapon in their public relations arsenal. Facebook took out full-page ads in prominent newspapers like the *Wall Street Journal*, contending that Apple's opt-in prompt would hurt small businesses weakened by loss of demand during the COVID-19 pandemic. It cautioned users that opting out of the all-seeing eye would threaten Facebook's ability to provide its services free of charge. It issued detailed alternatives to its advertisers "to support your efforts to preserve user privacy and help you run effective campaigns." It warned that consumer choice would damage the $350-billion-and-growing online-advertising industry, which was true: it would siphon business away from one of the industry's biggest players. If Apple's gambit were to have the intended effect, Facebook could no longer demonstrate to advertisers that targeting individuals based on personal data led directly to sales of specific products, a metric the social network relied on to charge advertisers enough to become the sixth-largest company in the world.

The proliferation of targeted ads is often the reason given for Zuckerberg's success. Some studies have said that consumers are nearly three times as likely to click on an ad that's targeted to them as they are on one that's not. Other studies say that targeting certain factors, such as gender, is less effective than targeting others, and still other studies show that ads don't work at all if consumers are aware that advertisers are pandering to them. The statistics are consistent about one thing: publishers, who run the ads on their websites, earn next to nothing of the proceeds while Facebook skims off the top, middle, and most of the bottom.

Facebook's public relations campaign against Apple was a failure. iPhone users overwhelmingly rejected tracking. In the first month after the April 2021 unveiling of iOS 14.5, 96 percent of Americans opted out, meaning that only 4 percent of Apple's US app customers consented to be followed around the internet by iPhone mobile apps.

"This sort of tracking is something no sane person would agree to," wrote John Gruber of tech blog *Daring Fireball*. "Just because there is now a multibillion-dollar industry based on the abject betrayal of our privacy doesn't mean the sociopaths who built it have any right whatsoever to continue getting away with it." Gruber concluded, "No action Apple can take against the tracking industry is too strong."

Before we celebrate Apple's actions too much, let's consider this: in the upgrade, Apple's homegrown apps didn't have to show a prompt for the same affirmative click that was required of apps created by outsiders, and all app developers needed to sign in with Apple, making sure the phone maker could keep tabs on competitors. There was also the not-so-small issue of apps simply ignoring the directive not to share personal data. Privacy-software maker Lockdown found that some apps kept communicating behind the scenes with third-party data companies called trackers. They can receive a flood of information from your iPhone, potentially revealing how you use apps and even your location, and sell that data to brokers. One more thing. If there were a pixel of doubt about the influence such a large company might wield in the marketplace, iOS 14.5 made it clear that when Apple fiddled a tune, the entire digital world danced.

I discussed this issue with Ben Moskowitz, director of Consumer Reports' Digital Lab, and he explained how this was a glass-half-full development. "I'm glad that Apple is turning up the heat on surveillance advertisers," Ben said. "But it scares me that Apple has that much power."

TECHNOLOGY IN THE PUBLIC INTEREST

The fine print in Apple's action and the response by other technology giants shows we can't rely only on companies to save us. We have one goal: our data should belong to us, and it should be ours by default. No need to check or uncheck dozens of boxes every day. So how do we get an online world that works for consumers and not against us?

What we have is technology that makes a few companies insanely rich by taking our data or by burdening us with the duty to always be saying, "No, don't do that." What we need is technology in the public interest—a new status quo where the purpose of the technology is the general welfare of society.

Of course, there's no single fix that will get us there, but tech visionaries have been working on possible remedies. One idea is that of a data trust or data cooperative, which would pool users' personal information to create bargaining leverage for consumers. Imagine how this might work. By signing up for a data cooperative, you'd have the option to decide what kinds of data you want to share with companies and what kinds you don't. With enough people joining in, this might enable a form of collective bargaining not unlike what happens when workers create a labor union. Think of hundreds, thousands, or even millions of internet users deciding how their data could be used and how this would level the playing field with tech companies that depend on that data.

You'd also have the option to donate your data for public interest research that could be used to improve the lives of consumers in countless ways that might otherwise be impossible because the data was locked up in black boxes. By pooling their data, consumers might figure out where in the country utility costs are the highest, or who's overpaying for things like car insurance or health care. The cooperative could push for lower rates and better services.

In their 2018 book, *Radical Markets*, Eric Posner and Glen Weyl wrote, "Empowering users not just to be aware of their data but also to be able to claim the benefits of it will require allowing trusted agents to access data in appropriate formats." That's why, in 2021, Consumer Reports started experimenting with a service called Permission Slip. It's a mobile app that lets consumers set their own permissions for what companies can do with their data, and with CR as the authorized agent, Permission Slip will contact companies and facilitate data-related requests on your behalf based on your preferences. The app started out exclusive to California, which passed a significant law enabling this type of agent, but the goal is that its success will encourage similar action in other states and empower us to expand Permission Slip to people across the country.

Another possible solution, charging money for tech companies to gather user data, might deter them from constantly collecting it. But I agree with consumer activists who say our privacy shouldn't have a price tag. Certainly, there are buyers. But privacy is a right. Would you sell your right to vote?

To help right-size the Big Four, we need governments to pursue a more aggressive antitrust agenda that fits the new digital marketplace. There are signs that the myths prosecutors and lawmakers hold dear about the Big Four—that what's good for them is what's good for America—are fading. We gave away the store because we believed in the public relations pitch of what the internet could be, not what it became. The online business model works only by exploiting us. The Big Four are living in a consequence-free zone. That needs to end. Consumers need government to hold the companies accountable. Let's see what Facebook looks like without Instagram and WhatsApp. Google could split its phone business from its web search, and Amazon could spin off cloud storage, just for starters.

While government at the state level can sue companies for anticompetitive practices, only the federal government can provide the nationwide support consumers need. But it needs more technical capacity and expertise to keep up with giant tech companies. That's why Congress should have its own Office of Technology Assessment, like it did in the 1990s, and the Federal Trade Commission should have a Bureau of Technology to focus on this growing area of our economy. We need more boldness from government at all levels to put consumers first.

To make competition stronger, some advocates have also suggested what they call interoperability. That means making different technologies work with each other, including the ability for consumers to carry their data seamlessly between internet services. If you wanted to use your contacts and other information from Facebook with another social network, ideally it would simply take a click to migrate your timeline, your photos, and your personal data to the new platform. Each of the Big Four is now walled off from the world, castles with impenetrable moats, nobles tending to their various fiefdoms.

Mandating interoperability would be one of three initiatives that, according to author and internet-rights activist Cory Doctorow, could help tame the Big Four. Another of his initiatives is making it possible for people to reverse engineer a company's products. Allowing independent engineers to look under the hoods of the Big Four would usher in a new era of openness: competitive compatibility, or "comcom" as Doctorow calls it.

Part of this is the idea of "right to repair," which would be another advancement for consumers. Right now, there are often barriers for, say, an independent car repair shop to try to fix a Ford engine by tinkering with Ford's proprietary software. Often a vehicle owner will have to go to Ford to get it fixed. Same for other systems. These kinds of mini monopolies are unfair and expensive. Most Americans agree. A 2020 survey found that 86 percent supported right-to-repair regulations.

The clamor for the right to repair reached the White House, and in July 2021 President Joe Biden issued an executive order encouraging people like farmers and cell phone users to be allowed to fix things on their own, without the requirement that manufacturers be the only ones to tinker with the products. It was a step in the right direction.

Doctorow's third initiative is a privacy law that would forbid sharing user data without consent, "because with interoperability, you start to open up new data flows from these big data-hungry silos like Facebook and Google, or even your cars." So we need to make sure that our data is secure and that we can have better control over whom it's being shared with.

In the meantime, companies can make high privacy the default mode. Why shouldn't the factory settings be pro-consumer instead of an assault on people's privacy, security, and data control?

Some states have led the way with comprehensive privacy legislation. The California Consumer Privacy Act, for example, allows consumers to demand to know what personal information a business is collecting about them and how it's used, ask businesses to delete most personal information collected from them, and opt out of the sale of their data. Businesses aren't allowed to generally discriminate against consumers for exercising these rights, such as denying you services, charging you different prices, or providing different quality of goods. Protections like these are an important step and should be part of the rights extended nationally under a federal digital-privacy law.

Finally, let's get rid of ads that encourage the misuse of our privacy. One option is to follow the lead of a coalition of antitrust, consumer rights, and privacy organizations—including US-based groups such as Ranking Digital Rights, Public Citizen, U.S. PIRG, and the Center for Digital Democracy—that are calling for a ban on surveillance advertising, which they define as "the practice of extensively tracking and profiling individuals and groups, and then microtargeting ads at them based on their behavioral history, relationships, and identity." Banning surveillance advertising would end companies' need to secretly collect people's personal details. Platforms could still make money from advertising. The ad industry flourished for one hundred years before tech companies started identifying individuals' preferences online and selling them to advertisers, who use them in ways that can be invasive and problematic.

The technology isn't necessarily malicious. It's the way it's handled that can be exploitative. Netflix knows from surveying your preferences what movie to recommend that you watch next, and delivery services can save you time by asking you the equivalent of "The usual?" Consumer Reports uses this technology too. As a member-driven nonprofit organization, we employ analytics to learn the interests of our users. We do so to remain competitive in the publishing industry as we advocate for consumers to have control over their own data. What must change is the unfettered way many companies exploit the technology.

Of course, a ban on surveillance advertising would put a big hurt on the Big Four. They grew so rich from targeted ads that they have more money than they know what to do with. In September 2021, Alphabet, Google's parent company, was sitting on $142 billion in cash, cash equivalents, and marketable securities, a towering pile. Apple had $91 billion, even after buying back stock and raising dividend payments to shareholders. At the same time, Amazon had $79 billion, and Meta, Facebook's parent, $58 billion. We don't have to let them abuse our data to pile profits on top of profits.

Then there's a proposal from Paul Romer, a Nobel Prize–winning economist and once the darling of Silicon Valley for his advocacy of a hands-off approach by government when it came to tech companies. Romer changed his mind about supporting policies that allowed companies to get as big as they are after observing the "collapse of competition" that followed.

Romer is pushing for a tax on digital ads with the goal of pushing tech companies toward subscription models instead of selling people's personal information. In February 2021, Maryland became the first state to approve such a tax. Romer now sees government intervention as the only way to save America from the monopolistic power of these tech leaders that influence critical components of our everyday lives. As he told the *New York Times*, "I really do think the much bigger issue we're facing is the preservation of democracy." That got my attention.

But it's not just about the personal data that ads use. Romer wants us to disrupt a model that incentivizes and spreads misinformation that takes advantage of vulnerable people.

Secretive data-gathering by the biggest tech companies, and the targeted advertising it enables, hasn't only pandered to our preferences when it comes to buying things. It has also built bubbles around us, making us comfortable in our prejudices. By controlling what we see online based on what will make us ripe for manipulation, the tech giants have driven us off the information superhighway and onto an unpaved back road that leads to a dead end. The relentless peddling of false narratives has broken up families, alienated longtime friends, and led to some of the most mystifying and horrific events in the country's recent history, as we'll see in the next chapter.

WHAT CAN I DO NOW?
Reduce Collection of Your Private Data

Your social media platforms and phones are collecting personal information about you in so many ways. The good news is that many of these features can be turned off—even if the platforms and devices don't make it easy for you to do so. Whether you

take advantage of the iPhone's feature to limit how apps track
you or change your Facebook or Google settings, spending the
time to turn off these collection features goes a long way to
protecting your privacy. These settings are always changing, so
if you have trouble finding them, turn to privacy groups (like
Consumer Reports' Security Planner) for the latest instructions
on how to boost your data security and privacy.

Use Search Engines and Browsers That Collect Less Data on You

Alternative search engines and browsers like DuckDuckGo and
Firefox often track a lot less information than other systems.
If you deal with sensitive information, turning off as many
data-tracking aspects as possible might be your preferred path.

Keep Companies (and Others) from Tracking Your Location

Why would we want Twitter, Apple, or anyone else knowing
every location we visit every day? Let's put a stop to these technological stalkers by limiting their location-data permissions.
From hitting "refuse" when Google asks for your location to
changing your phone settings to ensure that your apps only
know your location when you're using them, there are many
ways you can limit sharing this private information for all your
technology.

Learn How to Respond to a Data Breach

With our data being distributed to so many companies and
groups, the risk that a hacking attempt will release our personal
information has grown over the years. So what do you do when

you know there's been a breach? Here are some steps that Consumer Reports' experts have put together:

- **Find out specifically what was breached.** Companies will sometimes let you know about the details, but you can also use the website Have I Been Pwned? (haveibeenpwned.com) to search across multiple data breaches.
- **Change passwords.** If your password was compromised, you need to change it *everywhere* it's used. One of the easiest ways to do this is through a password manager. There are a number to choose from, and Consumer Reports reviews them on our website.
- **Use an authentication app.** If your name and phone number were released, hackers could use them to get into your accounts. Start using multifactor authentication (MFA) for your financial, social, and other sites. Some MFA methods are better than others. If you use text messages, switch to an authentication app like Google Authenticator or Authy. You can also use a hardware security key like YubiKey.
- **Remove your home address.** If your address was part of the breach, review where it's been posted, and report it. Several popular sites and search engines, including Twitter, Facebook, Reddit, Google, Bing, and others, have reporting systems to help you get them removed.
- **Freeze your credit.** When Social Security numbers or financial information is part of the breach, contact each of the three major credit-reporting companies (Equifax, Experian, and TransUnion) with a request to freeze your credit. This will make it hard for hackers to open accounts in your name. Just be aware that if you want to

apply for a credit card, rent an apartment, or conduct other financial business, you'll have to temporarily lift the freeze in many cases.

- **Delete accounts you don't use.** More accounts mean more opportunities for breaches. Get rid of those you don't already use.

MORE INFORMATION

For more references, details on these solutions, updates on these issues, and ways to get engaged in taking action, go to BuyerAware.CR.org, or use the QR code below.

CHAPTER TWO

THE MISINFORMATION MARKETPLACE

MARK AGUIRRE HAD BEEN KEEPING AN EYE ON THE AIR conditioning repairman for days.

The former Houston police captain and his team of freelance investigators were convinced the technician was hiding 750,000 fraudulent mail-in ballots for the 2020 presidential election. They believed he was getting "Hispanic children" to sign the ballots "because the children's fingerprints would not appear in any databases," according to an arrest affidavit. Aguirre told police the election fraud had been financed by Facebook's Mark Zuckerberg.

At five thirty in the morning on October 19, 2020, the air conditioning man started his workday. He hadn't been driving his truck for long before Aguirre's SUV rear-ended him. Police said that when the repairman got out to see what happened,

Aguirre pointed a gun at him and told him to lie facedown on the ground. By the time the first police cruiser arrived, Aguirre had his knee on the technician's back and was holding the gun on him. Aguirre told the cop, "I hope you're a patriot." The repairman said he thought he was being robbed. He said he feared for his life.

No ballots were found in the technician's truck, just tools and air conditioner parts. No ballots were found in his home, or in a shed in his yard. Police said Aguirre's claims of election fraud were baseless. Aguirre was charged with aggravated assault with a deadly weapon, a felony punishable by up to twenty years in prison.

That didn't stop Aguirre from getting paid for his "detective" work. The next day, police said Aguirre received $211,400 from an organization called the Liberty Center for God and Country, run by a YouTube wellness-product pitchman named Steven Hotze. Aguirre had already been advanced roughly $50,000 by Hotze's group. There was a Facebook connection. On November 6, three days after the election, the Liberty Center posted this message on its Facebook page: "The Communist Democrats created massive election fraud across the country. Trump and the Patriots will expose this. The U.S. Supreme Court will decide in Trump's favor. Then the civil war will begin in earnest. Get prepared. Patriots will defeat the Communists." Months later, the post remained on the group's timeline.

The whole operation, from beginning to end, was senseless. It was *proved* to be senseless. Nothing Aguirre did, or his rationale for doing it, had any relationship with reason. But if there's one thing we've learned over the last few years, conspiracy obsessives aren't looking for truth. They're looking for validation. And when their fictitious claims are debunked, they don't see the light. They see a cover-up. Whether it's the belief in a stolen election, COVID-19 vaccines killing people, a sex-trafficking ring run out of a Washington pizzeria, 9/11 being an inside job, or the Earth being flat, they find their validation on social media.

Of course, the conspiracies are driven by the same forces that drive the most problematic advertising: someone willing to deceive people, and an often vulnerable population all too ready to be deceived. Whether they're selling bogus election conspiracies or fake diet pills, today's online con artists get to use the same personal data we discussed in the last chapter to hone their deception and lock in on the best targets for their lies—the ones who will not only believe them, but preach them.

Tricking people into caring is the oldest con there is. That's because it can be so successful. It's also a technique that adapts well to different situations. And its most insidious impact is creating a vacuum of trust. That's why shams, deceptions, and deals too good to be true have always sprouted across the world.

MAGIC BEANS

We've all heard the fairy tale. Lacking money to feed her family, Jack's mother sends the young man to sell the family's only valuable possession, their cow. On the way to market, Jack falls prey to a flimflam man, who persuades him to trade the cow for "magic" beans.

How misguided could Jack be? This part of the tale is obviously cautionary, a lesson to avoid scam artists hawking phony remedies for profit. If the story ended here, I would endorse the message.

But the tale continues. The beans yield a magic beanstalk. Jack climbs it and discovers a giant's castle, where he finds treasures like the goose that lays golden eggs. When the giant chases him, Jack chops down the stalk, and the giant plunges to his death. Jack and his family never have to worry about money again.

If only.

Trust, once earned, is a glorious thing. But millions of children have been told this story about a naive underdog trusting a fast-talking salesperson. That the huckster's claim of magic turns out to be true is where the story does its damage.

Maybe "Jack and the Beanstalk" planted a magic bean in our minds, giving us the idea that scammers might, in the end, be trustworthy. That we can believe that magic beans will sprout a miraculous beanstalk leading us to a goose who lays golden eggs. The con artist and the gullible rube are regular characters in narratives old and new for a good reason. People have always played those roles.

In his 2016 book, *The Attention Merchants*, author Tim Wu, now a White House adviser on technology and competition, describes a particularly vivid reenactment of this dynamic from the 1893 Chicago World's Fair: the sales pitch of Clark Stanley, the first snake oil salesman. Far from the Ferris wheel and the main concourses, Wu wrote, Stanley stood in front of a crowd wearing a colorful cowboy costume. Behind him a booth crawled with rattlesnakes. While his audience watched, he plucked one of the snakes, asphyxiated it with ether, and plunged it into a pot of boiling water. Soon, "fatty remnants of the snake rose to the top, which Clark skimmed and, on the spot, mixed into an elixir." Stanley told his gullible rubes that the tonic was good for rheumatism, neuralgia, sciatica, lumbago, toothaches, sprains, swellings, and—the most important word in the list—et cetera. Other patent-medicine peddlers bragged that their potions could cure death. Yet another admitted that the medicine didn't matter because it was all about the marketing. They all sold well.

With the rise of shady dealers, however, came those trying to shed light on them.

By 1905, as Wu tells it, *Collier's Weekly* reporters were investigating the wild claims promoted by makers of the magical tonics. One elixir, called Liquozone, claimed to cure a long list of ailments, just as Stanley's Snake Oil had. The journalists discovered that it actually didn't. "Coming in a more trusting age, when such revelations had greater power to shock," Wu wrote, the *Collier's* exposé caused "an astonishing outcry."

Magic beans were getting harder to foist on unsuspecting consumers, but not impossible. The merchants of misinformation continued to adapt.

In her 1925 book, *Through Many Windows*, Helen Woodward, the first woman advertising-account executive in the US, offered some advice to those who came after her in the business. "If you are advertising any product," she wrote, "never see the factory in which it is made. Don't know too much about it. Don't watch the people at work. . . . When you know the truth about anything, the real inner truth—it is very hard to write the surface stuff which sells it."

That's one thing that hasn't changed much in the last hundred years: Advertisers are not in the business to promote the "real inner truth." They're in it to sell products. As Stuart Chase and Frederick Schlink put it in their 1927 best seller, *Your Money's Worth*, "when the technique of advertising is arrayed on the side of the private balance sheet, may the Lord have mercy on the consumer's soul, for there is no mercy in the world of dollars and cents." In other words, don't depend on businesses to play fair. If the consumer "is ever to find adequate protection," they wrote, "he must reach out and take it for himself."

Chase and Schlink warned readers about the deceptive practices of advertisers and the manufacturers who lied about the quality of their goods. Chase, an author, and Schlink, an engineer, both believed in scientific testing to prevent businesses from getting away with dubious practices. Consumers had few formal protections. This was a time of freedom for manufacturers, and they churned out household products that contained radioactive materials and hair dyes that resulted in mass poisonings. Medicines killed people. The rules that existed weren't enforced. This meant that businesses could get away with all sorts of outlandish claims: Soda pop is good for babies! Doctors want you to smoke Lucky Strikes!

Your Money's Worth attracted consumers who were looking for answers to the same core question we ask today: Who can I trust? For the authors, it was clear there was a large audience of people concerned about their role in the marketplace and where they might be getting ripped off. Readers yearned for a source of information that put their interests first, a voice they could rely on to give them practical advice on what to buy. That was how Consumers' Research, the first nonprofit consumer-testing organization, was born in 1929. By 1932, the number of subscribers to its newsletter had grown from 565 to more than 42,000.

The group was a "technical organization," it wrote in the first issue of what could be considered the precursor to *Consumer Reports* magazine. The main effort of its staff was to "conduct research and tests on consumer goods and to provide consumers with information which will permit them to buy their food, their clothing, their household supplies and other products most intelligently." They were engineers and scientists who were fix-ated on product performance and quality. They believed in sci-ence. They were suspicious of advertising's ability to persuade people with emotion. They had no use for sentiment or pitches that evoked fear, anger, insecurity, nostalgia, romance, or what-ever feeling could persuade a consumer to buy a product.

Linking science-based reviews with an explicitly justice-oriented mission defined a new model of advocacy—and the basis for the birth of Consumer Reports in 1936. For eighty-five years, we have used reputable testing, data-driven reviews, and public-service journalism as tools to keep the advertising indus-try honest. The "test and protest" model, a term coined by Con-sumer Reports board member Norm Silber, shames bad actors, serves as a catalyst for marketplace change, holds government regulators' feet to the fire, and incentivizes a race to the top for companies that make consumers a priority.

THE NEW WORLD OF MISINFORMATION

Although we've made abundant progress over the years, we're in a new world with more ways to target and mislead con-sumers. Regrettably, separating truth from deception has only grown more and more complex for consumers. Today we have to ask some tough questions: With advances in data harvesting that far outstrip government rulemaking, "news" that caters so precisely to our prejudices, and pervasive, increasingly insid-ious attempts to persuade us to buy things, how do we find sound advice on important subjects? What's real and what's a sales pitch masquerading as a rigorously tested fact? How do we stand for truth and scientific inquiry when we don't have a common understanding of the facts?

The question that remains at the core: Who's trustworthy? The onslaught of nonsense can be overwhelming. Whereas millions used to count on local newspapers for reliable information, the lines between news, opinion, and entertainment have blurred. Many Americans see commentators like Sean Hannity and Rachel Maddow as news anchors, not thought shapers. We all know that many people get their news from comedy shows like *The Daily Show* and *Saturday Night Live*. Fox News attorneys successfully defended a lawsuit against host Tucker Carlson and his influential evening show by claiming that he offered entertainment, and no "reasonable viewer" would take his opinions seriously. Yet millions do. Millions of Americans recite fiction as settled fact and cast doubt on truth.

There's the problem of "native ads," which can look like legitimate news stories but are sponsored by an advertiser, such as a pharmaceutical company touting its own products. They can top your list of search results or appear as exchanges between real people on social media—if you miss clues such as the ever-shrinking word "Ad" in the corner of your Google search or a barely legible "Promoted" crouching beneath a tweet.

There's clickbait, such as the attractive, provocatively clad person in the photo with the headline "See What 80s TV Stars Look Like Today—You Won't Believe #8." Click on it in a weak moment and be bombarded with pop-up ads that drown the screen.

And there are political "news stories" that don't seem like ads right away. At least on TV and radio, you have the voice of the political candidate telling you that they "approve this message." No such guidance online.

The system is fertile ground for manipulation. Charlatans skulk everywhere. Even the reviews from fellow consumers, which are supposed to help guide us, can often be treacherous if trusted.

ONLINE REVIEWS

In the 1990s, when Amazon was still just a gleam in Jeff Bezos's eye, he said that offering user-generated reviews on an online shopping platform would be one of the most powerful benefits of internet commerce. Bezos considered user reviews an important element in his early vision for Amazon, calling them "egalitarian and credible."

Since internet commerce has become a daily part of many Americans' lives, online reviews have changed. Many of them have become tools of business. The landscape of Jeff Bezos's egalitarian dream is now peppered with reviewers peddling magic beans. In many sophisticated ways, brands have gamed the reviewing system. They hijack reviews by making a positive evaluation for another, completely different product appear to be a thumbs-up for their product. They can switch a new product into an old listing, allowing the recommendations for the old product to carry over. *Consumer Reports* reporter Jake Swearingen looked into these underhanded practices in 2019 and ended up reporting many of them to Amazon. Although Amazon dealt with the deceptive reviews that Jake reported, the company wouldn't discuss how the abuses had occurred. Chris McCabe, a former Amazon investigator of seller accounts who's now a seller consultant, told Jake, "We've helped numerous sellers escalate their cases of hijacked or sabotaged listings because otherwise they find action by Amazon teams hard to come by. Typically sellers say they get no reply at all, or a generic reply saying that the team will look into it."

Another scam, trading five-star reviews for free goods, is illegal, but fraudsters have found ways to do it. In 2019, Buzz-Feed profiled one paid reviewer, a twentysomething woman who reviewed over seven hundred items worth more than $15,000 on Amazon in one year. She bought the products with her own Amazon credit card, then was reimbursed by the manufacturers, an unconvincing ruse to appear to follow the letter of the law. The only thing asked of her was to give all the products five-star reviews regardless of their quality. She had so much business she used a spreadsheet to keep track of her accounts.

In 2019, Amazon said it spent $400 million to protect consumers from review abuse, prevented more than thirteen million fake-review attempts, and punished five million sellers for manipulating reviews. While we encourage Amazon to take action against fake reviews, the company isn't acting fast enough to keep people from seeing them and being influenced by them. The UK's Competition and Markets Authority opened an investigation in 2021 into whether Google and Amazon were doing enough to "protect shoppers from fake reviews."

It irks me to talk about the spread of this kind of fraud, because trustworthy product reviews are foundational to the trust that generations of Americans place in Consumer Reports. As Colston Warne, one of the organization's founders, wrote, "The central faith of the consumer movement is that free choice lies at the very core of democracy in an economic system. But free choice depends upon a fair exchange of knowledge." Times have changed, but consumers' need for accurate, unbiased knowledge has not.

Consumer Reports is different. We can speak freely about products without fear of losing revenue because we don't accept advertising. We don't take samples or freebies. We buy the products we review at full retail price, from a $10 mop to a $100,000 sports car. Principles define our mission. We believe that consumer power can make the marketplace fair, competitive, and just.

In 2021, we spent over $27 million to test, rate, and review more than eighty-five-hundred products and services. Those tests are designed and administered by experts under rigorous scientific protocols, and we also tap consumers to test for usability. All of it is paid for by donations and membership subscriptions. Our members are not simply contributing to a shopping experience; they're part of a community that believes the marketplace should be accountable to them.

Consumer Reports will always deliver independent, non-biased information. But what do you do if the information you find online isn't trustworthy? What do you do in a free-review culture that on the one hand provides us all with the agency to contribute information about our experiences, but on the other hand tries to outsmart us by feathering in fake reviews and taking part in tactics that are both deceptive and biased?

When Consumer Reports tests products, we apply rigor and expertise. But in a world where reviews have become ads for an online marketplace in which consumer advice needs to be present at the point of sale, how do we show up where consumers are and make a dent in the misinformation and commercialization of those reviews?

To help fight fake reviews, we introduced CR Recommended, a program that showcases our objective recommendations wherever you shop online. Our research highlighted the fact that consumers rely heavily on "seals of approval" at the point of sale. We saw a way to be there for all consumers, not just those who could afford to pay for a CR membership, and to provide guidance on important items, like infant car seats and air purifiers, during the pandemic. Once a product receives a recommendation from us, manufacturers can display the CR Recommended mark online or in stores. (Full disclosure:

Companies pay a fee to display the mark and must agree to our strict usage guidelines. These fees help defray our operating costs, including monitoring the mark to assure proper use. But companies only pay after we've reviewed and recommended their product, not before.) The mark gives consumers easy access to objective, reliable recommendations they can feel confident about because they're backed by our organization's second-to-none standards.

CR Recommended needs to expand to fill the trust void, but it will never be available for every product out there. So what steps can consumers take to protect themselves?

The first is to be skeptical. There's no shortage of baseless opinions, and it's hard to know whether a reviewer has even used a product. Despite recent crackdowns on paid reviews, vendors still solicit fake testimonials. Half of Americans who read online reviews report having purchased a product based on a web review and only later finding out that the performance or quality of the product didn't match the evaluation. Many people are taken in by so-called influencers on platforms like Instagram, YouTube, and TikTok. Influencers who amass millions of social media followers are attractive to brands, and companies often pay them to promote their products. Even Consumer Reports has hired influencers to talk about our work, ensuring that it was clear they were compensated. Many influencers make their recommendations not based on value or quality but because they're being compensated, and some of them don't disclose that they're getting paid, making their endorsements look like personal preferences instead of financial transactions. Lack of disclosure is against the law, though the law is rarely enforced. Others, who aren't paid by sellers, entice followers with promises of product giveaways, then use the attention to market themselves to companies. So while not every online review is a scam, don't take what you see at face value. You may quickly regret it.

Second, dig into the site to determine if it's free of conflicts of interest. For example, in 2014, *Consumer Reports* noted how OpenTable, the restaurant-reservation site, admitted that one goal of its user-review system was to benefit "our restaurant partners." The partners are tens of thousands of restaurants that pay tens of millions in fees for the service—and then get to nominate "featured reviews," which are the ones customers will most likely see. You can bet they didn't pick any negative reviews for that first impression. In the UK, Consumer Reports investigators found that TripAdvisor, the popular online travel counselor, had hundreds of suspicious reviews posted on its site. Controls were so lax that a prankster's garden shed became "officially" the best restaurant in London. One way to figure out whether reviews are fake is to look at what percentage of them give three or four stars out of five. Investigators found that few scam artists bother with anything but five stars, so a high number of three- and four-star reviews could indicate a degree of honesty.

You should also look for sites that include verified standards for its merchants. For example, eBay's Top Rated Seller program applies to those that "deliver exceptional customer service," including a "defect rate less than or equal to 0.5%," a "late shipment rate less than or equal to 3%," and other requirements that protect consumers. This makes it easier to find sellers that are more trustworthy.

Finally, treat user reviews as anecdotal insights, and look for tips that only product owners would know, such as whether a brand's clothing sizes run big or small, or how easily a car's alignment goes out of whack. Online reviews can be very help-ful, but if you're not sure, look for additional support from or-ganizations that provide objective evaluations, like Consumers' Checkbook, the Better Business Bureau, and Consumer Reports. A number of organizations exist to help people stay vigilant about their purchases. I've included some on our resource website (BuyerAware.CR.org).

While the burden for verifying that a product's quality matches its glowing reviews shouldn't rest on consumers, we all need to be on guard. Be careful. Online, you never know who could be in on the scam.

MISINFORMATION STRIKES BACK

Snake oil peddlers and online-review scams are everywhere, and they're just the warm-up act. We're witnessing the growth of misinformation in our society on a larger scale than ever before. This has become especially apparent in the last few years.

I began this chapter with a story of how the prevalence of false information can lead to tragic and absurd acts. Of course, that was a single story in the larger, misguided effort to nullify a fair presidential election. Add to that a pandemic with people spreading the bogus narrative that COVID-19 was either ex-aggerated or pure fiction, and that vaccines developed to stop it were dangerous. These scams have had widespread conse-quences. Stop the Steal, the baseless conspiracy theory that the 2020 election was rigged, became a violent assault on the US Capitol and our democracy. The injection of partisan politics into a public health issue has lengthened the pandemic and caused needless deaths. We've all heard heartbreaking stories about people who denied COVID—then died of COVID. The results of each conspiracy were all the more terrible because they were avoidable.

Like most Americans, I was horrified by both misinformation campaigns. I had a personal stake in each. I'd spent countless hours in the Capitol building early in my career as a member of Senator Bill Bradley's staff. It was a dream job, working for my home-state senator, and I can still feel the pride and awe I experienced every morning when I got to the top of the escalator at the Union Station Metro stop and began my walk toward the Capitol. The sight of its majestic dome took my breath away. To me, the Capitol is the most inspiring building in the world, truly a sacred place for the promise of democracy. On January 6, 2021, rioters smashed windows to force their way inside. They used the marble hallways as their latrine. They hunted members of Congress. They called for the hanging of Vice President Mike Pence. They paraded a Confederate flag. They looted offices. They beat Capitol police with flagpoles and fire extinguishers. Members of Congress barely escaped harm. A woman was shot and killed. Two law enforcement officers lost their lives as a result of the insurrection. It was needless, baseless, and a terrifying example of the violence that a steady diet of misinformation can trigger.

The propaganda campaign surrounding COVID-19 and the vaccine also shook me on a deep level. Both my parents are in their nineties, and their vulnerability to the deadly virus was a constant concern to me. The buzzing of the pandemic deniers, who took to the airwaves in Spanish as well as English, was an infuriating distraction throughout that time, as were the pitches of the many carnival barkers who took advantage of people's fear and confusion by peddling counterfeit cures such as a malaria drug called hydroxychloroquine, the horse-deworming agent ivermectin, Lysol, and even bleach. When the vaccines were ready for distribution, I was relieved. I saw them as bringing on the beginning of the end of the lockdowns, the economic downslide, the nasty disputes over wearing protective masks, and the threat to the lives of my mother and father and millions of others. But the steady drumbeat of vaccine misinformation, discouraging people from getting the shots, thumped on.

How much of the blame for these fiascos should be assigned to the social media platforms that amplified misinformation by providing microphones that moved this fringe content to the center of the national conversation?

In the case of a vast, imaginary conspiracy to fix the 2020 vote, Aguirre and his fellow "patriots" relied on Facebook, the world's biggest social media platform, for support. In the first week of October, a month before the election, an advertisement claiming that "hundreds of piles" of Republican ballots were being dumped as part of "a massive underground mail-in ballot fraud coordinated by Democrats" ran on Facebook as many as forty thousand times at a cost of less than $200. Facebook removed the ad after receiving an alert from a watchdog group called the Election Integrity Partnership, but the preposterous story lingered on the social network.

Facebook executives were also aware early in the pandemic that unfounded claims about the coronavirus were being shared on the site. On March 25, 2020, a little over a week after the national lockdown began, Nick Clegg, the former UK politician who became Facebook's vice president of global affairs and communications, told NPR that misinformation wouldn't be tolerated on the social network. "So, if people say drinking bleach is going to help you vaccinate yourself against coronavirus, that's dangerous," Clegg said. "It leads to real-world harm. We will not allow that to happen. We won't even allow folks to say social distancing makes no difference in dealing with this pandemic."

It was what most people wanted to hear. But was it just spin? Was Facebook serious about sacrificing clicks to champion the truth? *Consumer Reports* decided to find out.

DAILY DOSES OF BLEACH

Kaveh Waddell, one of our investigative reporters, tested Clegg's claims by conducting an experiment to see how well Facebook screened advertising content. He created a Facebook page for a phony organization called the Self Preservation Society and submitted a series of seven advertisements to Facebook, each of which were intentionally misleading about COVID-19.

"People under thirty are 'safe' and should go to school, work, or parties," asserted one ad. Another announced, "Coronavirus is a HOAX. We're being manipulated with fear. Don't give in to the propaganda—just live your life as you always have." Kaveh also took on Clegg directly: "'Social distancing' doesn't make any difference AT ALL. It won't slow the pandemic, so get back out there while you still can!" There was even an ad that informed readers they could "stay healthy with SMALL daily doses" of bleach.

Each of the ads passed Facebook's initial review, an automated process. The social network's algorithm missed several warning signs that might have been caught by a human screener, including the fact that Kaveh's sham Self Preservation Society had only been established a few days before it began submitting ads, offered no profile information, and had an image of the coronavirus as its profile picture. The ads reached a prepublication queue before Kaveh, not Facebook, withdrew them.

Facebook says it looks over paid ads before publication. The ads are bound by the company's advertising policies, which cover more than two dozen categories, from misinformation to tobacco and vaping products to copyright infringement. The company has also published specific rules governing coronavirus propaganda. They include bans on "claims that are designed to discourage treatment or taking appropriate precautions," and "false cures . . . like drinking bleach." Posts to individuals' Facebook accounts, which can be published immediately, don't undergo any fact-checking.

"While we've removed millions of ads and commerce listings for violating our policies related to COVID-19, we're always working to improve our enforcement systems to prevent harmful misinformation related to this emergency from spreading on our services," Facebook said in a statement to *Consumer Reports* in reaction to Kaveh's experiment.

In 2021, however, the social network shut down a New York University study of the website's political advertising and disabled the personal accounts of the researchers. The project, called the NYU Ad Observatory, asked people to download a browser extension that collected data on what political ads the users saw on Facebook and how those ads were targeted. Facebook said the data collection violated company policy meant to protect users from data theft. The researchers said the Facebook claim was a pretext because they were uncovering unflattering information about the platform. "If this episode demonstrates anything," said one of the researchers, "it's that Facebook should not have veto power over who is allowed to study them."

It's true that Facebook deals with a fire hose of misinformation, but it's an information source for half of all American adults, so how well the platform polices itself can become a matter of grave importance to the country, even of national security. Advertisers' methods can sometimes look like the tools of propagandists. And they're too easily deployed on the social network.

Paid ads aren't the only problem. They're not even the most serious. Individual posts, by real human accounts or fake accounts posing as individuals, can cause the worst disruption. Whether by passing misinformation within a circle of followers or creating like-minded groups, sometimes dedicated to conspiracies, that pull more people into an echo chamber of misinformation, individual accounts do a lot of the work of driving lies across the internet.

As I noted before, the misleading Facebook ad about ballots being stolen was taken down, but the message lived on through posts and conversations by individual social media users. That's just one example.

In 2013, many Twitter users spread false allegations about supposed suspects in the Boston Marathon bombing. While this was done out of a desire to bring justice, it only served to implicate innocent people, who were targeted by others with online attacks.

In 2018, just days after the heart-wrenching school shooting in Parkland, Florida, a top-trending YouTube video wrongly suggested that one of the survivors of the tragedy was an actor.

And in 2016, our country learned how fake accounts, in a coordinated effort by a foreign government to undermine our elections, can spread misinformation. That year, according to Facebook, roughly 126 million people—the equivalent of one in three Americans—were exposed to eighty thousand posts containing Russian propaganda spread by regular accounts, not ads. Such efforts haven't stopped. A 2021 Facebook report said the company had discovered disinformation campaigns in over fifty countries since 2017, with Russia being the top source. At the same time, the number of individuals sharing posts from these campaigns and other misinformation has only increased. According to one study of Facebook, likes, comments, and shares of articles from news outlets that regularly publish lies and other misleading content essentially tripled from the third quarter of 2016 to the third quarter of 2020.

Whether people are exposed to paid ads, posts from individuals, or even messages from the social media companies themselves, we know that these platforms have a real impact. Small differences in Facebook feeds, for example, can influence people to go to the polls. A 2012 study involving sixty-one million Facebook users showed a 2 percent shift in voting, based on the positive feedback their Facebook friends received for casting ballots. The research team estimated that the experiment resulted in 340,000 additional votes that election year. It's a short step from getting people to cast ballots to pushing them to vote a certain way or to not vote at all.

What's most terrifying to me is Facebook's ability to sway people's *emotions*. According to a 2014 study, researchers observed and measured the moods of nearly seven hundred thousand Facebook users whose feeds had been manipulated without their knowledge to elicit different emotional states. Facebook did this by adjusting its algorithm so that some users' timelines displayed positive content while others were fed a steady diet of gloom. After a week, the researchers concluded from the content of the users' posts that "emotional states can be transferred to others . . . leading people to experience the same emotions without their awareness."

Clandestine experiments on Facebook users are common. In fact, every user will be involved in an experiment at some point, a Facebook product manager confessed to Shoshana Zuboff, as reported in her book *The Age of Surveillance Capitalism*. The seriousness of the experiments varies. "Whether that is seeing different-sized ad copy, or different marketing messages, or different call-to-action buttons, or having their feeds generated by different ranking algorithms," the product manager said, "the fundamental purpose of most people at Facebook working on data is to influence and alter people's moods and behavior . . . to make you like stories more, to click on more ads, to spend more time on the site." That's the goal at just about every tech platform and every advertising agency, but few others have such a vast laboratory at hand to discover so quickly what works best. This kind of power to control emotions begs for strong ethical limits and incentives that go beyond profit.

What's even worse, Facebook's Instagram has a horribly corrosive effect on the self-esteem of teenage girls. Thanks to whistleblower Frances Haugen, a former Facebook executive, and the thousands of documents of Facebook's internal communications she took with her when she left the company, we know that the company's own research shows that, among other factors, a constant parade of influencers showing off their toned physiques on Instagram makes body-image issues worse for one in three teen girls. Among teenagers who reported suicidal thoughts, 6 percent of American users traced the desire to kill themselves to Instagram.

In public, Facebook never mentioned its own shocking findings, and has, in fact, claimed the opposite. "The research that we've seen is that using social apps to connect with other people can have positive mental-health benefits," Zuckerberg told a congressional hearing in March 2021. Instagram, which is four times more popular with young people than Facebook, was well on its way to launching a special version for children younger than thirteen, the minimum age to join the established network. Only under pressure did Instagram abandon the plan.

Other revelations from Haugen—such as Facebook's successfully taking action against only 2 to 3 percent of hate speech on its platform, and 0.6 percent of incitements to violence—tossed fuel on the fire long stoked by Facebook's critics. Zuckerberg's response to the whistleblower's revelations, meant to mollify, seemed defensive and emotionless. It only intensified calls for a range of controls to rein in Facebook, including forcing the company to make its data available to the public, creating a government agency with oversight power over tech companies, and breaking Facebook into smaller businesses that would be better managed.

CORRECTING THE RECORD

To their credit, other social media companies have tried different approaches to address the problem of misinformation, such as banning political ads and removing disputed content. Twitter created what it called "friction" or "virality circuit breakers" to disrupt the misinformation process. If a user was set to retweet a news story they hadn't clicked on, a prompt asked if they wanted to read the article before passing it along.

Twitter also tagged some tweets with a disclaimer: "This claim has been disputed."

The companies need to do more.

The best immediate solution would be a larger investment from companies in enforcement, even if it's only for the policies they already have. When it comes to paid advertisements, the standard can't be focused on removal once misinformation is already shared. Had Kaveh Waddell gone forward with his sham Self Preservation Society ads, it's likely that Facebook would have eventually caught them and taken them down, but only after they had been posted. Even if Facebook were quick about it, millions of pairs of eyes could have seen the ads while they were on the site. To paraphrase Jonathan Swift, lies take flight while the truth comes limping after. The damage would already have been done.

Unfortunately, much of the reviewing these platforms perform on questionable content has been automated to save money. Clearly that isn't working. Companies need to invest in a process that involves more human moderators who, while empowered by advanced technology, can make the nuanced decisions that a robot reviewer can't.

Companies should also make sure their systems aren't actively sharing misinformation. Whether it's Facebook suggesting that you join problematic groups or YouTube recommending videos filled with misinformation, these companies need to do a better job of cracking down on themselves. Again, this would mean spending money to refine their algorithms and to hire more human eyes to ensure that their platforms aren't making our misinformation crisis even worse.

It won't be cheap and it won't generate revenue, but more online media companies, social and otherwise, should meet an ethical duty to take further action, because many users believe that by just showing up on the platforms, ads can be trusted. In fact, the companies have invested a lot of time talking about their review process specifically to reinforce the sense of safety. Why wouldn't consumers believe that the ads have been vetted?

We should expect these companies to sufficiently address the problems they've created. Longtime tech critic Kara Swisher was right when she said about Facebook, "Why build a platform that requires an arbiter of truth if you don't want to be one?" Technology companies have reshaped society, and with that success comes responsibility.

It's easy to *expect* corporations to do the right thing. The real question is how we get them to *do* the right thing. Public shaming is one of the few tactics we can deploy right now to push these companies to change. Thankfully, consumers' outrage is starting to reach Washington, DC. We're seeing bipartisan efforts to help tip the scales and encourage action.

Probably the biggest impact would come from changing a provision in a US law known as Section 230 of the Communications Decency Act. Established back in 1996, when the internet was younger and smaller, and Friendster and MySpace hadn't even been born yet, this provision was created to protect internet companies from liability they could incur due to content posted by customers using their platforms. Today, the internet is everywhere, and a few technology Goliaths have amassed enough power to control and influence major parts of our society.

Policy changes to incentivize internet platforms to police their users' content could be the stone and sling we need. By updating the law, we can tilt the scales and create the motivations that companies currently lack, in part because harmful content is so often good for business. Platforms need incentives to put consumer well-being ahead of the bottom line.

Congress has identified Section 230 as a possible lever to get the tech companies to move. In 2021, more than twenty bills came up for consideration that would amend Section 230 in a variety of ways. Perhaps the best means to encourage action against misinformation is to make companies more liable for that content. When legal action becomes a greater reality, suddenly a company's financial incentive shifts toward moderating and enforcing its own rules.

A bipartisan bill introduced by Senators Brian Schatz, a Hawaii Democrat, and John Thune, a Republican from South Dakota, would help put some of the onus on internet companies to minimize misinformation. Any law, however, would need to be a balancing act. This is a nuanced issue that requires tiptoeing between thoughtful moderation and broad censorship, between recognizing harmful misinformation and cracking down on political speech.

Just look at Facebook's decision to kick President Donald Trump off the platform when his posts praised violence and appeared to provoke an attempted coup. After making that decision, Facebook somewhat muddled its message, delegating the question of whether Trump could be reinstated to an appointed oversight board. "Facebook's Supreme Court," as it was derisively called, ended up suspending the former president from Facebook and Instagram for two years and gave him a path to return to the social networks, presumably if he behaved himself in the interim.

Few people were satisfied with Facebook's handling of the situation. Some supporters of the former president accused Facebook of overstepping its authority and silencing a key right-wing voice. The American Civil Liberties Union questioned whether banishments were a good idea. Republicans in Congress called for a reappraisal of Section 230. Some Trump opponents said they would prefer congressional regulation of the tech giants over ad hoc banishments. Former Danish prime minister Helle Thorning-Schmidt, co-chair of Facebook's oversight board, took issue with the social network itself. She admonished Facebook for inventing penalties as it went along, and for being "a bit lazy" by not setting specific guidelines to deal with the kinds of provocations Trump had committed.

While Zuckerberg faced blowback for Facebook's indecisiveness, over at Twitter, which had profited from Trump's avid involvement for years, CEO Jack Dorsey banished the former president from the platform for life, closing the door, if not discussion of the subject, for good. The ban did what Twitter intended. Immediately, posts on the platform concerning fictitious election fraud dropped 73 percent. The decision was expected to hurt the company's bottom line, but the opposite happened. Twitter's revenue spiked 28 percent in the first three months after Trump's exile.

Still, the controversy continues. Trump has sued the tech companies, claiming censorship, and debate on the topic will likely continue.

Just because the solutions are complicated, however, doesn't mean we shouldn't pursue them. The stakes are too high. The online spread of misinformation continues to shape our country and muddy the definition of what's true. For one thing, social media platforms should increase their efforts to discover and delete bots, which set up the fake accounts that have helped spread misinformation and foreign-government propaganda campaigns. That would still leave the problem of what to do about real people who spread lies. Stubbornness is a major obstacle. Research has shown that fixing people's internet posts for accuracy is likely to backfire. People don't like to be corrected. It makes them feel defensive, causing them to double down with an even more biased slant and to serve up extra helpings of "language toxicity" in subsequent postings.

Some news organizations have tried to head off inaccurate posts before they happen. During the 2020 election, *The Guardian* put up online banners identifying its older articles. That way readers could distinguish between relevant news and old news, which internet instigators often use to incite fresh outrage.

We have to look to larger solutions to address misinformation on a societal level. We live in a world where facts are less widely accepted every day. Social media, talk radio, cable TV, and other forums for news and discussion have become more fragmented, like high school cliques: you choose your group, cut yourself off from the others, and live in your own reality.

NEWS OF THE WORLD

Tech companies can't be the only solution. We need a societal shift that's bigger than even the Big Four.

The last twenty years have been particularly dismal for local news. In 2018, newspaper circulation fell to its lowest level since 1940. As readers moved online to get the information that newspapers provided, and as they sold their personal items on eBay or Craigslist when they once had used newspaper classified ads, local news sources took a big hit. Between 2008 and 2018, newspaper-advertising revenue dropped 62 percent, while employment at newspapers fell 47 percent. This is bad news for beating back misinformation, because there's evidence that local news sources can help combat political polarization. One study measured the impact of a local newspaper's experiment: the paper removed national political stories from its front page and left only local stories. The research showed that polarization "slowed down," a reversal of a particularly durable trend accomplished simply by changing one page of the newspaper every day.

It's no secret that local media has been in decline for a long time. The economy of the twenty-first century makes it particularly difficult to support this important part of our democracy. "The market is simply not providing local newspapers the resources they need to deliver the civic benefits they're capable of," said one author of the polarization study, Louisiana State University assistant professor Joshua Darr.

Still, projects such as the Local Media Association's Lab for Journalism Funding give us reasons for optimism. They're planting seeds in small towns around the country that may one day grow into a forest. The lab provides a funding model that includes a mix of philanthropy, advertising, and sponsorships so local outlets can bring needed attention to problems afflicting an underserved constituency.

One newspaper involved with the Local Media Association, the *Record-Journal* of Meriden and Wallingford, Connecticut, created the Latino Communities Reporting Lab during the pandemic. Its first step was listening to Latino residents to see what they thought local journalists should cover and in what format. "A big part of it was, How do we better serve our local audiences?" said Liz White Notarangelo, the fifth-generation publisher of the 154-year-old paper.

The area's Latino community was awash in misinformation about COVID-19, and Latinos lagged the white population in vaccinations. In collaboration with local organizations, the

Record-Journal in April 2021 launched a three-month vaccine-reporting project with features such as "Ask the Expert," Facebook Live videos, and news stories on vaccines, all of it available in Spanish and English. An amazing 82 percent of the people who clicked on the website were new visitors. Within three months, the area's Latino vaccination rate had become roughly even with that of white people.

"It's always been about how to transform and evolve," said White Notarangelo. "Trusted local journalism is the foundation of a community that's thriving. When it's gone, you miss it."

Government, too, can help make it easier for local news outlets to survive. Some bipartisan solutions have been proposed, like the Journalism Competition and Preservation Act, sponsored by Senators John Kennedy, a Louisiana Republican, and Amy Klobuchar, a Minnesota Democrat. It would help publishers collectively negotiate fair advertising terms with large tech platforms. Other suggestions involve more direct government help, like giving Americans tax breaks for subscribing to local newspapers, creating a payroll-tax credit to support the creation of nonprofit news organizations, providing direct government grants to help small media outlets hire reporters, and renewing the country's financial support of public media.

Today, we have a crisis when it comes to accepting provable facts. We can't be afraid of bold actions to reconnect our society with the truth.

THE NET'S HUCKSTER HOUSEGUESTS

When I was young, we took road trips to the Jersey shore and to Florida in our Ford Fairlane station wagon, which, memorably, lacked air conditioning. I used to be fascinated by the billboards along the road. The eye-catching imagery. The clever phrases. The products that seemed like must-haves. I would stare at the advertisements and the alluring messages as we drove by. Then my attention would move to something else.

The internet, however, is not something you can just drive by. The internet ushers you in the door, makes you feel comfortable, and says, "Stay a while." And you do. Because so many of your favorite things—and more and more of the things you need to get through life—are found online. So you clutch your phone, almost afraid to let it go, and check your social media feeds as if you're expecting life-altering news at any moment. These platforms are designed to get you hooked. When they do, they keep you hooked.

The internet itself is not the problem. In fact, it does a fantastic job of advancing, complementing, and improving modern life. As Sir Tim Berners-Lee, inventor of the World Wide Web, said, "Anyone who has lost track of time when using a computer knows the propensity to dream, the urge to make dreams come true, and the tendency to miss lunch." The problem is the other houseguests that the internet invites to stay: the ads that surround you at all times, the deceptive links that look like expert information but are just cons, the conspiracy theorists, bots, and messages that, if you aren't careful, inundate you with misinformation and misleading advice. You're not in a car driving by. You're trapped in a room, and they're luring you, waiting for you to slip up, waiting for your click.

I've seen this happen in my own family. My father has been a *Consumer Reports* reader for a long time, but even so, he almost fell victim to an internet health scam.

He doesn't get around as easily as he used to, and many of his friends are gone, so he satisfies his active curiosity by clicking and scrolling. The internet can be empowering. We can get answers to health-related questions, access expert commentary, take an active role in our own treatments, and even keep up with the grandkids, which my father loves to do.

Type 2 diabetes runs in the family, and my father was diagnosed with it nearly fifty years ago. He'd kept it under control all that time—until internet hucksters targeted him. *We'll show you a better way to manage your diabetes,* the come-ons read. *Send us your money, and we'll let you in on secrets the medical establishment doesn't want you to know.* Many of the enticements masqueraded as independent research known only to a few maverick insiders brave enough to take on the status quo, but they were really just efforts to take his money.

I didn't know about it until one day I saw him break out in a sweat and get dizzy, a sign of a blood sugar imbalance. It scared me. He told me he'd followed the online advice to stop taking his medication. I scrolled through his iPad and saw how aggressive the sales pitches had gotten. *What your doctor isn't telling you! Independent research blows the cover off Big Pharma! Stop taking your medications!* He was vulnerable, and he had believed them. Thankfully, I got him to his doctor, who persuaded him that his meds were what had been keeping his blood sugar levels steady and healthy.

Older people have been scam targets for time immemorial, and the internet has given criminals one more avenue to ply their trade. The FBI says elder fraud is a $3-billion-a-year business. Older people are trusting and polite, they usually have money socked away, and many of them don't know how to report a con or are too embarrassed to contact law enforcement. They're not as savvy about the internet as folks who grew up with it as part of their lives.

But let's not kid ourselves. They're not the only ones who fall for the fraud and misinformation that infect the internet. We're all at risk, even if we haven't planted any magic beans. While the fairy tale never tells us if Jack in his old age was ever cheated out of his golden goose eggs, it's a guarantee that the frauds and con artists gave it a try.

WHAT CAN I DO NOW?

Be Skeptical of Online Misinformation

When it comes to any news or information source, the best practice is to doubt its authenticity, at least at first. Take a moment to look up the source. Note its agenda and where its revenue comes from. It's also critical to teach this skill to children, as believing everything they see and read can be harmful to their health and safety. Caution costs only a few minutes, while the alternative could cost you so much more.

Ads are getting harder to spot. Here are a few tips to help everyone in the family tell whether what they're reading online is trying to sell them something:

- Look for the small label—though how it appears is inconsistent. Sometimes it's only the small word "Ad" in the corner or "Promoted" on the edge of a social media post.
- Just because it looks like news doesn't mean it is. Watch out for articles labeled "sponsored content"—they're paid for by advertisers and not objective news.
- Disregard the news content in anything that pops up. It's almost always an ad.

Take Steps to Avoid Fraudulent Online Product Reviews

Consumer Reports' team suggests that the best and most basic step to protect yourself from scammers is to read more than a few reviews before buying anything. Never rely on the number of reviews or the average score. Look for the same positive language repeated in multiple reviews, and watch for descriptions of products that don't relate to what you think you'd be buying. Those are signs of possible fraud. Even if the overall scores are good, if the more recent reviews seem negative, it's a common red flag that the product quality might have dropped or the vendor might have switched in a different product to take advantage of past positive reviews. James Thomson, former business head of Amazon Services, told *Consumer Reports*, "My recommendation to all customers is to look at not only good reviews, but also the bad reviews. How recently were they posted? Do you see reviews for completely different products?"

If you think you've found a product on Amazon with hijacked reviews, report it, either through the link appearing under every review to report abuses, or by including the tag @Amazon in a tweet with a screenshot and using the hashtag #StopReviewHijacking.

Online user reviews have an important place in helping consumers. But like anything else, they should be read with a high degree of skepticism.

Speak Out Against the Spread of Misinformation

We should all speak out against misinformation within our circle of friends, acquaintances, and social media followers. According to Leticia Bode, a Georgetown University professor who's studied the effect of misinformation corrections on social media, "It's important to call out misinformation you see on social media because it provides a counter narrative." Instead of taking on the entire internet, focus on your friends and family first. Make sure you come prepared with your own research from expert sources, and show a diplomatic attitude. Accusatory tones won't help persuade people.

Support Local News

As noted in this chapter, local media has been hit hard in recent decades, but it serves an important role in our goal of undermining disinformation and ensuring a better informed public. We encourage everyone to support their local sources of news so more communities don't lose these important pillars of our society.

MORE INFORMATION

For more references, details on these solutions, updates on these issues, and ways to get engaged in taking action, go to BuyerAware.CR.org, or use the QR code below.

CHAPTER THREE

FINANCIAL FAIRNESS

THE MARKETPLACE IS WHERE WE GO TO REALIZE OUR AMBI-
tions. It's where we find the help we need in the form of
loans. Borrowed money is the only way to fulfill so many of our
goals—a car, a home, an education, starting a business, helping
a loved one. Few of us would be able to succeed without taking
on debt.

Then there are times when borrowing is done in desperation. We're between jobs and a payment is due, or a storm
destroys our roof. One of the kids totals the car and gets hurt
in the accident. There's a fire or a dreadful diagnosis. In order
to keep our lives going, in order to take care of what we need to
take care of, we have to find a way.

We borrow, we repay, we borrow again. Debt shapes our
lives. We're lucky that, in the US, we have a functioning credit

market where there's money available to borrow. If we choose to go down that road, it's open to us.

The market, however, is frequently tilted against certain borrowers. There are barriers and dark corners and unsavory lenders who make it more difficult than it should be. We live in a time when markets may be as fair as they've ever been, thanks to consumer vigilance and government oversight, but to become a homeowner or a college graduate or an entrepreneur, we must still climb onto the debt treadmill. If we're not able to keep pace, we wake up in the middle of the night with the monthly bills we can't afford to pay interrupting our sleep. Our dreams can haunt us.

Even if we've kept within our means, made sacrifices, done all the right things to dutifully pay our bills on time, we can still step in financial potholes. Most of us know what it's like to struggle with fine print, blink incredulously at bills that are bigger than we expected, and rage at wasted hours on the customer service carousel. We've all heard the sad stories or, when we're short of money, found ourselves living them. The sailor in California who paid $7,000 interest on a $1,900 loan, the Virginia widow who was turned down for a car loan because of a mysterious error on her credit report, the single mom in Tennessee who could afford the house but couldn't afford the mortgage, the thirty-five-year-old who still owes $42,000 on his student loan, the Chicago man who signed a contract without knowing he'd given away his legal rights.

Senator Elizabeth Warren, when she was a Harvard law professor and writing books about how the middle class was being squeezed, coined the term "tricks and traps" to describe business models that rely on deceiving customers to make profits. When asked for an example, she explained that credit card contracts in the 1980s used to be about a page and a half long. They described interest rates and the consequences for late payments, and that was about all. More recently, the contracts had grown to about thirty-one pages long.

"So, tricks and traps?" she said. "It's that other twenty-nine and a half pages."

The contracts are so impossible to read that not even a contract-law professor such as herself can understand them, she said. And when the terms are basically "'we'll charge anything we want any time we want for any reason or no reason at all,' what's the point of reading it?"

The financial world has expanded in complexity, thanks to deregulation, no regulation at all, and the internet. Some charlatans prey on the desperation of consumers. State legislators have allowed payday lenders, who charge triple-digit annual interest rates on small loans, to proliferate to the point where there are more of their storefronts in the US than McDonald's restaurants. Payday shops are getting increased competition from bad alternatives like car-title loans, which accept your vehicle as collateral, and probate-advance companies, which provide the money up front that mourners expect to receive from a recently deceased loved one's estate. Victimized consumers include folks from every corner—no one is too broke or too miserable to be a target. It's tough but not impossible to fight back. Checking your credit score, for example, can take time and effort, but its errors can be corrected. A higher credit score may make you eligible for better interest rates than payday lenders offer. Often, firms that promise to help you overcome debt are only interested in getting you indebted to *them*. Be wary. If you do fall prey, there are more resources than ever to truly help you escape destructive cycles.

It's so easy to feel overwhelmed by the power of the complexity experts, the rip-off artists, the hidden-fee chargers, the equity strippers, the nickel-and-dimers, the predatory lenders, the graveside hucksters, the tricks-and-traps devisers, and just about anyone promising to keep your best interests in mind who breaks that promise as quickly as they can. But don't be discouraged. Consumers are a sleeping giant. We outnumber them. We're a force to be reckoned with. Even the federal government, which is notoriously slow to help consumers and even slower to respond to a changing marketplace, has offered a hand. The Consumer Financial Protection Bureau, which Consumer Reports advocated for, was created in 2010 and in its first nine and a half years returned $13 billion to aggrieved fraud victims, offered protection to whistleblowers, and provided Americans a place to lodge complaints with the hope that the weight of the US government could be brought to bear on the side of consumers.

Scammers have always been around, and they feasted during the COVID-19 pandemic. Reports of losses due to financial fraud jumped nearly 50 percent from 2019 to 2020. Illegal activity is just one part of the problem. Legal transactions can be devastating to consumers too. In this chapter, we'll examine a rogue's gallery of law-abiding lenders, many of which charge ridiculously high interest rates, chip away at consumers with hidden fees, and force disgruntled customers to settle disputes in an alternative legal system of their own invention. We'll talk about how to check on your credit scores and how to avoid the worst student loan traps, and we'll discuss trust, without which a fair and efficient marketplace would be impossible.

THOU SHALT NOT

Usury—charging interest on loans—has been deplored through-out history by moral leaders and in religious texts from all over the world. Plato and Aristotle were thumbs-down on it. Gau-tama Buddha included usury in a list of villainies that also in-cluded deceit, treachery, and soothsaying. In his last sermon, the prophet Muhammad preached that Allah had forbidden charging interest. To this day, doing so is taboo in the Islamic world. In the Torah, the first five books of Jewish scripture, charging interest within the Jewish community, especially to the needy, is condemned multiple times. And for hundreds of years, Christian leaders and philosophers like St. Thomas Aqui-nas echoed that moral sentiment, condemning the charging of interest to anyone.

This prohibition has relaxed over the years. The meaning of the word "usury" has even changed from merely charging inter-est, which has become widely acceptable in the US, to charging *excessive* interest.

Excessive-interest loans are the business model of payday lenders, who got that name because their products originated as advances on workers' paychecks. Think of them as subprime personal loans. As you might remember from the 2000s, sub-prime mortgage companies took advantage of lower-income and minority home buyers by charging higher rates and by hard-selling mortgages with adjustable interest rates that ballooned in cost after two years. Similarly, today's payday lenders profit from the despondency of people who have nowhere else to turn in an emergency. In Mississippi, the poorest state in the country, payday lenders can charge up to about 20 percent interest on a two-week loan. That's equivalent to an annual percentage rate (APR) of 521 percent, and it means that a $100 loan, if stretched out over the course of a full year, would cost $621 to pay back. Mississippi is also the state with the largest percentage of Black residents, a correlation I'll explore further in Chapter Four.

Mississippi, of course, is hardly the only state that allows payday lenders to ring up inflated profits. California allows APRs up to 460 percent. In Wisconsin, it's 516 percent, in Alabama 456 percent, and in Utah 652 percent. Twelve million Americans, with an average annual income of $30,000, use payday loans every year. Borrowing at payday-loan interest rates is like getting stuck in a debt whirlpool. Unless you can grab hold of something solid, there's nowhere to go but underwater. Eighty percent of payday loans are taken out within two weeks of a previous payday loan, meaning the original money didn't turn out to be the solution the borrower was looking for. One in four payday loans is rolled over rather than repaid on time. The numbers grow even more grim when you look at just how expensive the loans can become. For lenders, excessive interest makes even the smallest loans worthwhile. In 2021, while thirty-year mortgages cost in the historically low 3 percent range and credit card balances averaged APRs of 16 percent, the typical payday loan's APR, when all fees to the lenders were added up, was 396 percent. According to the website Balancing Everything, the average payday loan user spends $520 in fees to borrow $375, but in the worst case, the borrower could pay as much as $1,415 to borrow $375.

Even these outrageous rates aren't high enough for some lenders. AMG Services, run by former race car driver Scott Tucker, charged an APR as high as 700 percent from 1997 to 2013, according to the Federal Trade Commission. In 2018, the FTC said it was returning $505 million to a million former borrowers who had been victimized by AMG and seven related companies.

During the pandemic, with joblessness spiking to historic levels and countless numbers of businesses closing their doors due to lockdowns, we lived as if we were two Americas. Payday-lending companies reported doing better than they ever had, while the Federal Reserve encouraged the country's corporations to borrow at the lowest rates they'd ever seen, which they did in record amounts.

The subprime personal loans have so eroded ordinary Americans' ability to escape debt that the concern has reached the Pentagon. In 2017, 44 percent of active-duty members of the military said they'd used a payday loan at least once. For military personnel, pushing their shaky finances closer to the cliff wasn't the only problem. The Defense Department was worried that high levels of debt could endanger service members' security clearances, distracting them from their duties and making them vulnerable to bribes. In its guidelines for personnel to appeal being rejected for a security clearance, the Naval Criminal Investigative Service, or NCIS, advises service members on the best ways for them to prove to the brass that they've resolved their debts. According to the guidelines, they need documents showing that the debt has been discharged; simply writing "I paid that loan off" on the appeal application isn't enough.

Congress has acted, to a point. Federal lawmakers left payday loans alone, but they made it illegal to extend another quick financial fix to active-service military: car-title loans. Unlike with payday loans, which are unsecured—meaning there's no collateral for the lender to seize if the loan isn't repaid—borrowers agree to surrender their cars if they fall too far behind in their payments. That doesn't mean title loans are any cheaper than the payday variety. Most of them carry APRs of more than 300 percent, and one in nine loans defaults.

These financial products attract borrowers at their most anxious, and the cascade effects can lead to bankruptcy.

For more than a dozen states and the District of Columbia, the practice of charging such outrageous rates is beyond the pale. They've either banned the excessive-cost loans altogether or set caps on the annual interest that lenders can charge, usually at a still-pretty-steep 36 percent. However, in many state capitals and in the halls of Congress, lenders hold sway. Their justification is that they extend loans to people no one else will lend to, and the high rates are warranted because of the risk they take. The payday-lending industry also possesses a bit of political savvy. In the 2020 election, payday companies contributed nearly $2.7 million to candidates. In the 2018 election, it was over $2.9 million.

More than one-third of that 2020 money came from a single payday lender: Tampa-based Amscot Financial, founded more than thirty years ago by an immigrant from Scotland named Ian MacKechnie. MacKechnie says Amscot had a run-in with regulators in the late 1990s and ever since has been diligent about sticking to the rules. "Any good business supports good, well-intentioned, fair regulations," he told a local business publication. "We don't want bad operators in our industry." Though Amscot is active in the communities where it has storefronts, sponsoring Miami's annual Calle Ocho street festival and joining law enforcement in regular bike-helmet giveaways, the company has a less than sterling reputation with customers—at least those who post online reviews. In one forum, Amscot received thirty-five evaluations, each of them giving the company the lowest rating of one star out of five. "I wouldn't recommend Amscot to the devil," said a reviewer.

Payday lenders also enjoy the financial support of some of Wall Street's deepest pockets and most influential players. Shareholders in one company include BlackRock, the world's biggest asset manager; Renaissance Technologies, the hugely successful hedge fund where Robert Mercer, a primary backer of Cambridge Analytica, made his billions; and mutual funds run by 401(k) stalwarts Vanguard and BlackRock's iShares. Mariner Finance is owned by the private equity firm Warburg Pincus, whose president is Timothy Geithner, secretary of the treasury under President Barack Obama. Mariner caps its interest rates at 36 percent annually, but the firm seems to be trying to make up the difference elsewhere. A list of the fees Mariner charges (shown later in the chapter) would be comical if it didn't add up to real money for cash-strapped borrowers.

The Consumer Financial Protection Bureau is an excellent resource for borrowers who think they might be getting ripped off. The regulations the agency is required to enforce have changed over the years; some lawmakers complain that the rules are so strict they'll discourage lending, while others say thoughtful regulation is essential to maintaining fairness. Through it all, the CFPB website (www.consumerfinance.gov) provides advice and an outlet for airing grievances, and it sometimes follows up with companies on consumer complaints.

Although a handful of influential economists have implemented the discredited theory that money sprinkled on banks and other wealthy institutions will eventually trickle down to the rest of society, others have advocated for policies that help narrow the gap between rich and poor. For instance, the federal minimum wage in 2021 was $7.25 an hour. If it had kept up with rising worker productivity over the years, economists estimate that in 2021 it would have been $24 an hour. Since the

2008 financial crisis, which became the biggest wealth transfer from poor to rich in memory, the Federal Reserve has kept what's called its benchmark annual interest rate at near zero. That's the base rate to calculate what banks and creditworthy corporations pay on their debts. It doesn't take a lot of financial smarts to see the difference between just over 0 percent and 664 percent, the top annual interest rate for payday loans in Texas. The Center for Responsible Lending estimates that, combined, payday and car-title loans drain nearly $8 billion in fees from the poor and desperate and send the money to the wealthier each year. Without regulation—or a sense of ethics—investors can get incredibly wealthy. But because they do it at the expense of their neighbors, there ought to be a ceiling on how much they can charge. It's only fair. That's why Congress should pass the Veterans and Consumer Fair Credit Act, a bipartisan bill that establishes a nationwide usury limit of 36 percent annual interest. One of the biggest traps of payday loans is their short payback periods. As Syed Ejaz, policy analyst at Consumer Reports, noted in a letter to Congress, this bill would mean many lenders "would have to restructure their loans to have longer terms, making them more affordable and manageable for borrowers."

Government can only do so much. We also need investors in industries such as payday lending to make their money work on behalf of the vast majority of Americans and to consider the well-being of the country and their neighbors. Let's ensure that gains come without milking the last pennies from the neediest among us, and, in doing so, weakening our country. As we'll discuss later, some signs indicate that sentiment among certain investors and the country's top business leaders is headed in that direction.

In the meantime, let's go over what other shady practices we're up against.

"HEARSE CHASERS"

In a world of financial products to fit every lifestyle, Americans can do everything from borrowing against their tax refunds to arranging loans based on future litigation results. Some schemes are more worrisome than others, such as probate advance. That's when a lender fronts money to a grieving person in the expectation of getting repaid a higher amount when the dearly departed's estate is dispersed, a process that can take years. Lenders scour death notices for prospects. A California woman recalled receiving a letter shortly after the untimely death of her daughter, offering cash in exchange for a future payout from the proceeds of her daughter's estate. She was appalled. "These people are like hearse chasers," she told the local newspaper.

Probate-advance companies don't charge interest, but they do profit, sometimes outrageously, by taking a big chunk of people's inheritance. In transactions such as payday loans, borrowers are usually stressed due to their financial situation. In the case of probate-advance customers, add emotional upheaval to the mix. Mental health professionals advise mourners to avoid making business decisions soon after the death of a loved one. It's a difficult time. That's when the probate-advance people get to work.

"We're proud of the service we provide and the highly ethical way we conduct our business at IFC," Doug Lloyd, chairman and chief executive officer of Inheritance Funding Company, told my colleague, *Consumer Reports* reporter Ryan Felton. Lloyd said that, given the risks companies like his take on, "It's easy to understand why banks and other financial institutions are not in this business."

There's also what Wall Street calls reputational risk. It's possible that banks and other financial institutions stay away from making these deals to avoid looking bad. In a stunning 2021 *Consumer Reports* article, Ryan showed how exploitative the loans can be. First of all, the industry declines to characterize them as loans and calls them advances instead. If they were making loans, their businesses would be subject to usury laws and to lending requirements about disclosing the arrangement's true cost.

Industry leaders say it's impossible to calculate annual percentage rates because payoff dates are unknown. Up front, that's true. Some estates clear probate quickly, others don't. But using data from completed transactions, Consumer Reports was able to clear the fog and show the surprising profitability of the deals. A handful of cases dragged on for several years, lowering effective annual percentage rates to 5.5 percent. Others, however, ranged as high as 490 percent. The average APR in the cases that Consumer Reports reviewed was 86.9 percent. That may not be as soul crushing as a payday loan, but it's a lot more expensive than, say, a cash advance from a credit card.

According to the Consumer Reports analysis of nearly 240 transactions involving about one hundred beneficiaries in eight states, the bereaved received cash advances of $2.53 million. In return, they agreed to give up $4.51 million to the companies, a difference of 78 percent. On average, consumers relinquished 45 percent of their inheritance. Calculating for APR, as a loan would be, one in four of the transactions hit triple digits.

Like payday lenders, probate-advance companies say their earnings are justified because of the risk. Previously unknown debts can emerge in the probate process, narrowing the slice of the pie that goes to heirs, and the slow progress of clearing probate—in an extreme and unique case, Marilyn Monroe's last will and testament took forty years—means a long time may pass before they're repaid, if ever. But in an analysis of hundreds of cases in one California county, David Horton, a law professor at the University of California–Davis, found that the companies recouped their entire investment 97.5 percent of the time.

By saying it advances money rather than lending it, the industry has so far succeeded in skirting oversight, leaving what the California woman called "hearse chasers" to profit off the grief of families that are bereaved, and often broke.

"This is a problem of policy," Horton said. It needs a solution. For individuals, it's important to educate yourself about your other options. In the long run, you're likely to lose out by taking these deals. As Ryan Felton put it, "The companies claim that a borrower holds no liability if they take an advance, but given the substantial amount that consumers relinquish on average, it would seem useful to try to seek out other alternatives, if possible."

We also need policy solutions. It seems logical that government regulations should be amended so these companies can't call what they do advancing money rather than lending. Other states should follow California's example by requiring these businesses to file their contracts in court. The state's law not only creates more transparency, which hopefully narrows chances for abuse; it also allows judges to weigh in on whether a particular probate-advance agreement is "unconscionable" and should be voided. While it seems people should try to avoid these agreements in general, government needs to ensure that the most abusive contracts are brought to light and ended.

HOUSE OF GAMES

In David Mamet's 1987 movie, *House of Games*, a con artist played by Joe Mantegna describes how he succeeds in deceiving people. He says that grifters such as himself start their scams by demonstrating trust in their victims. They might tell them an incriminating secret or ask them to watch the grifter's car and hand them the keys. Showing confidence in the target makes the target more comfortable trusting the scammer, and therefore more likely to fall victim to the con artist's game.

When we talk about scams, we're talking about trust. It's too flip to say we should never trust anyone, that the best defense against getting ripped off is to decline to enter into any contract. That would cut us off from the world and hamper our own ambitions. Sometimes we do need a loan or insurance or any number of financial products that can improve our lives if executed correctly. We may do everything we can to lessen the downside, but at some point when we're shopping in the marketplace, we need to trust.

It doesn't always work out, as I know from personal experience. In 1998, my father bought a home-health-care insurance policy. He was a healthy seventy-two years old at the time, but having witnessed firsthand how dementia had ravaged my mother's side of the family, he wanted to know the two of them would be taken care of without burdening their children. He trusted a salesman. He bought a policy and faithfully paid the monthly premiums.

Some twenty years later, the day arrived when my father needed to claim the policy's benefits. I didn't know about the policy until he showed it to me, but I was relieved to see it, given my parents' limited options and their desire to continue to live at home. He asked for my help in filing the claim. I began by doing an internet search of the insurance company, which was unfamiliar to me.

My heart sank. It was a scam, and a legal one—what we at Consumer Reports call junk insurance. My father had been paying premiums for two decades but would probably never see a dime in claims. The hoops he and my mother would have to jump through to receive a payment made it nearly impossible for anyone to collect on the policy, let alone a couple in their nineties. The insurance company had made it clear that if my parents did file, there was no guarantee they would receive their benefit.

How could I tell my father what I'd learned? He'd trusted the person who sold him the policy. It never occurred to him that the insurance company would betray that trust. In the end, my parents didn't receive any money from the policy.

Their story is too common. Similar cases can be found on every consumer-complaint message board on the internet. But there are ways to avoid these scams. Resist pressure—some are often pushy to get you to agree quickly—get a second opinion, and check their license online with your state insurance department. For those employed, your job might offer long-term coverage, so take advantage of that if you can.

There are plenty of other health-related scams to steer clear of. One that made the rounds offered a family health plan for three dollars a day that wasn't actually insurance but a kind of discount coupon. Good luck finding a medical provider who would honor it. Another grift came in the form of a robocall claiming to be from a local branch of the Health Insurance Marketplace, tied to Obamacare. It scared consumers with the threat of a fine if they didn't sign up for government-mandated health insurance, and told them they could avoid punishment only if they would "press 1," when they'd be asked to supply personal data such as income and Social Security number. Needless to say, it was better to just hang up.

Denials of claims for insufficient reasons happen all the time. It's almost as if companies want to gauge how much fight consumers have, how far we're willing to go to defend ourselves. If it's a big enough dollar figure, maybe people will fight back. If it's just a smattering of dollars here and there, we probably don't even notice. If we do catch on, perhaps we think the amount isn't worth the trouble to bring in the cavalry.

That's what they're betting on.

NICKEL AND DIMED

It's hard to find anyone who's avoided an unexpected fee tucked away in the fine print of a monthly bill or hidden in the middle of a list of legitimate-looking charges. Consumer Reports conducted a survey in 2019 that showed 85 percent of Americans have experienced the unpleasant jolt of realizing they're paying a bogus fee, and 96 percent of them found it annoying.

Nickel and diming customers is by no means exclusive to the finance industry. The two main add-on fees from airlines—reservation-change fees and baggage fees—accounted for a combined $7.6 billion in revenue in 2018, an increase from $6.8 billion in 2015. The hotel industry raked in a record $2.9 billion in fees and surcharges in 2018, and online ticket sellers are notorious for layering on extra expenses for every ticket purchased just when you've got out the credit card and are ready to pay.

The explosion in extra fees is partly an outgrowth of the rise of online shopping websites such as Expedia and Hotels.com. The sites allow consumers to compare prices from multiple sellers and choose the best options. That kind of competition has helped lower prices for many goods and services, but it has a consequence. One way to appear to offer the best prices, and get the clicks, is to start low and add fees later. Original prices, before fees, get picked up by shopping-portal engines, giving certain companies the edge before they add charges later.

Of course, as long as fees are disclosed somewhere in the shopping process, consumers can, theoretically, calculate their true costs. The reality is that add-on fees can be difficult to spot, requiring consumers to click through multiple web pages or scour fine print to find the information—a gradual-reveal strategy that economists call drip pricing.

Drip pricing works for companies. "Once people have spent time searching a price, they're less likely to start over when they see the fees," says Vicki Morwitz, a marketing professor at the New York University Stern School of Business. "They often mistakenly assume competitors will have the same fees."

A 2018 study using data from StubHub, a secondary market for event tickets, showed that to be true. StubHub ran a pricing experiment in which one group of shoppers was shown the full ticket price up front, including fees, and a second group saw those charges only at the end, when they were just about to make a purchase. People who saw the fees at the back end spent almost 21 percent more than those who received the all-inclusive prices at the start.

Companies have studied drip pricing and perfected its practice. They see that consumers who spend time finding a satisfactory product or service often are loath to start the search again even if they encounter charges at the end of the process. You may recall that I mentioned Mariner Finance, the lender backed by former treasury secretary Timothy Geithner's private-equity firm, Warburg Pincus, and how it charges "only" as much as 36 percent in interest and seems to be using fees to pile up the profit. Mariner appears to be one of those companies that bank on consumers deciding that since they've already sunk time and effort into applying for a loan, tacking on a few fees at the back end won't scuttle the deal.

Here's a menu of charges the company posted online in 2017—the costs of borrowing money from Mariner:

Recording/Satisfaction Fee: $23 to $151
Legal Fee: Actual Cost Incurred
Repossession Fee: Actual Cost Incurred
Late Fee: 5% of the Unpaid Installment
Bad Check Fee: $15
Check by Phone Fee: $6
Internet Payment Fee: $2
Loan by Mail Commitment Fee: $10
Refinancing Fee: $150
Non-Filing Insurance: $25

It's important to note that Mariner hasn't been accused of any wrongdoing, nor are its practices that much different from its competitors'. The firm provides more useful information online than a lot of high-interest lenders, whose websites' main function, it seems, is to funnel your attention to the button that says, "Click to Apply."

That said, if you're borrowing from Mariner, you're already short on cash, so the fee to "record" the loan has to sting. Mariner is betting that borrowers aren't going to back out of a deal to borrow thousands of dollars because that extra fee is tossed in—they'll just pay it.

As for the repossession fee, it's adding insult to injury for a delinquent borrower to have to pay for the repo people to break into her car and drive it away. And having consumers pay Mariner's legal fees seems unfair. Evidently, the $60 billion firm, with offices in Europe, South America, China, India, Southeast Asia, and on Lexington Avenue in New York City, wants to charge customers, who are already in dire straits, for suing them.

The list also includes additional charges for paying monthly installments by phone or internet. This is legal, and many other entities, such as utilities, also do it. But unless you're using the US Postal Service or traveling to Lexington Avenue and handing them cash, Mariner has determined that it's reasonable to charge you extra to pay them.

All these fees chip away at a consumer's bank account and their mental health. But it's Mariner's refinancing fee that's the killer. Forget for the moment that paying a company $150 to bring them more of your business could be a pretty good definition of an unhealthy financial relationship. The fee incentivizes Mariner to keep consumers in a never-ending spiral of borrowing. The longer Mariner can maintain the relationship, the more money you pay them.

To be sure, the $2 internet payment fee won't bring down anyone's financial empire, and when compared with the scams some multibillion-dollar companies run, the numbers are a speck—what Wall Street calls budget dust, or not big enough to even be a rounding error. With that $2, however, Mariner is spitting in the face of its customers. How petty for a $60 billion company to drain that last drop of cash from the bottom of the well. Borrowers obviously could use the $2 more than Mariner needs it. For consumers living on the margins, $2 a month over time can mean paying for a winter's worth of heat. It's also sitting there on the bill as a nagging reminder of the unfairness of the situation they've gotten themselves into. Mariner can charge just about whatever it wants, and it chooses to charge $2 for you to pay online. This is a trap. Do you want to dynamite the entire process over a $151 recording fee and have to start the rigamarole all over again with another lender who may or may not charge you even more? If you're ever late with a payment, or stop paying altogether, that's when Mariner's fees really start kicking in. Going to court to make sure those charges are paid is, after all, a process that borrowers appear obligated to pay for. Nickel and diming is an antiquated expression. It's a practice that can cost a consumer hundreds and, in some cases, thousands of dollars.

When the charge is only $2 a month, consumers are likely to grumble and pay it. There's one add-on, however, so universally despised that the grumbling can swell into a rumbling: the overdraft fee. Whenever a bank customer withdraws more than they have in their account, the banks typically charge $35, even if the amount overdrawn is less than a dollar (or, to be fair, more than $35). During the 2020 pandemic, Senators Cory Booker and Sherrod Brown tried to temporarily ban overdraft charges due to the financial hardships many Americans were going through. The legislation went nowhere. Banks ended up taking $8.8 billion in overdraft fees that pandemic year. JPMorgan Chase led the way with $1.5 billion, followed by Wells Fargo ($1.3 billion) and Bank of America ($1.1 billion). At a congressional hearing, Senator Elizabeth Warren asked Chase's chief executive officer Jamie Dimon if he would refund the fees. Dimon simply said no. The CEOs of the other banks, also in attendance, had no response.

There's an ironic punch line to the overdraft saga. In April 2020, as the pandemic raged, the Federal Reserve, the nation's bank for banks, waived overdraft fees for financial institutions such as Chase, Wells Fargo, and Bank of America. The banks got the same consideration from the Federal Reserve they weren't willing to extend to their own customers.

The good news is that in many cases it's possible to fight back against fees and win. Three out of ten people in Consumer Reports' survey who said they'd experienced a hidden charge in the past two years reported that they questioned it, and almost two-thirds of those who did said they were successful in getting the charge refunded or taken off the bill.

In 2019, Duke Energy scaled back a proposed 238 percent hike to the company's fixed fee—the amount customers have to pay regardless of how much energy they use—because customers, along with Consumer Reports and other groups, complained to South Carolina's utility commission. Speaking out seems to have also worked to stem rising cable TV fees, which along with phone and internet fees were the most commonly reported extra charges in the Consumer Reports survey. Cable companies add what amounts to a 24 percent surcharge on top of the advertised price, according to the survey, generating nearly $450 per year per customer from the fees. Based on the total number of US cable subscribers, cable companies could be making an estimated $28 billion a year from charging extra fees. Predictably, customers aren't happy about paying for services they don't use, and they don't like mysterious charges blindsiding them on their bills. That's why Consumer Reports began a campaign with consumers called What the Fee?! Through the program, 140,000 cable TV subscribers around the country signed a petition demanding that cable providers eliminate add-on fees and advertise only the service's total price. Lawmakers listened. In 2019, they passed the Television Viewer Protection Act, which

Consumer Reports supported. Its requirements went into effect at the end of 2020. They include:

- making cable and satellite TV companies disclose the full monthly price of your bill when you sign up (no hiding fees)
- allowing new customers to cancel at no penalty within twenty-four hours of getting that full disclosure
- banning companies from charging people for equipment they don't use

This victory is proof that consumers can fight back against predatory fees that companies like to hide. It's an achievement we can continue to build on in other areas of the growing hidden-fee marketplace.

COMPANIES EMBRACING ETHICS

A realization has sprouted among financial investors that slavish devotion only to short-term profits isn't the best path for America's future. They've created investment pools called ESG funds for their focus on environmental, social, and corporate governance issues that invest only in shares of companies that strive to do good, both in the world and in the way they do business. The funds are proving increasingly popular, with record investments in 2021 and the expectation that their numbers could climb to $1 trillion in investments by 2030. There's also evidence that ESG funds make more money than conventional ones. Investors realize that we need satisfied consumers and diverse workforces living in thriving communities, and that businesses milking as much spare change as they can from their customers is a dead end. The marketplace needs to rebalance in favor of consumers. That's synonymous with working toward a better world.

Given Wall Street's growing interest in ESG investing, it was still a pleasant surprise to hear similar ideas come from the Business Roundtable, a member organization of the biggest US companies and their chief executive officers. For decades, the group had been vocal proponents of a much narrower measure of success. They placed rising stock prices above all other considerations, with the planet, the communities where they did business, the welfare of their workers, and the contentment of their customers mattering only to the extent that they could help push shares higher. Putting shareholders first made decisions simple. Anything that caused a bump in price was good, and anything that caused a dip was bad. This opened the door for irresponsible, short-term thinking. Corporate boards tied executive compensation to the stock price too, muting the importance of worthy goals such as sustained growth, inclusivity, and world citizenship. If being a better company, or better people, couldn't boost the stock price, there was no reason to do it. Tricks and traps became an accepted way to do business.

The world, however, intervened. Forest fires and destructive storms devastated communities as the climate crisis worsened, waves of refugees forced from their homes by murderous weather and political violence crowded past international borders, and the #MeToo and Black Lives Matter movements began to change minds about how our society treats women and racial minorities. The business community's MeFirst model seemed out of touch and even less defensible than it had ever been. In August 2019, the Business Roundtable announced it had gotten the news. The group released a statement, called the

Purpose of a Corporation, signed by 181 CEOs who said they were committed to "lead[ing] their companies for the benefit of all stakeholders—customers, employees, suppliers, communities, and shareholders." It was a stunner, a powerful repudiation of years and years of greed and selfishness, and a path for companies to become, and remain, forces for economic, social, and environmental progress.

"Americans deserve an economy that allows each person to succeed through hard work and creativity and to lead a life of meaning and dignity," the CEOs wrote. "We believe the free-market system is the best means of generating good jobs, a strong and sustainable economy, innovation, a healthy environment, and economic opportunity for all."

The business leaders promised to deliver value to consumers, invest in their employees, deal fairly and ethically with suppliers, support their communities, and generate long-term value for shareholders. The last part is significant because it implicitly acknowledged that making decisions with an eye on the stock price—and, incidentally, how it affected their own compensation—wasn't always the wise or moral thing to do, and that taking a longer view was financially sustainable.

"Each of our stakeholders is essential," the CEOs continued. "We commit to deliver value to all of them, for the future success of our companies, our communities, and our country."

Embedded in the manifesto is the idea of the fiduciary, that people and companies ought to accept the bigger responsibility of being caretakers, with ambitions wider than simply making a buck. Profits remain an essential goal, but they shouldn't be the only goal. We all need to treat others as human beings, not as pawns that can be forgotten after a deal goes through, or marks for tricks and traps.

The term "fiduciary" comes from the financial world. Some investment managers have a fiduciary responsibility to their clients and are required by law to make decisions with their best interests in mind. Others are legally permitted to nudge their customers toward products that wouldn't necessarily be good for them but that pay higher fees to the money managers for selling them.

Serving your customers' interests should be the norm in any industry. Let's follow the lead of these new business models and have more companies and individuals feel a caretaker responsibility toward people. We should all be fiduciaries now.

FORCED INTO ARBITRATION

A good way to start toward that goal would be to provide consumers with access to the American legal system when they have disputes with corporations.

One tactic many companies use is forced arbitration, instead of the courts, to settle problems, even serious ones, in the marketplace. By simply buying certain products, millions of consumers unknowingly promise companies that, if there's ever a legal conflict, they agree to submit to a closed-door conflict-resolution process that includes only themselves, a company representative, and a paid arbitrator. This isn't good for consumers. In arbitration, appeals are prohibitively difficult, and basic principles of the American legal system, such as the influencing factor of precedent in deciding cases and the exchange of evidence called discovery, don't apply. These and other factors are why arbitration in general gives consumers far less of a chance of winning than if they were to take their complaint to court. Just 6 percent of consumers who represent themselves in arbitration win. It's yet another tactic to reduce consumer power.

Mandatory arbitration was established on a national level in 1925 as an efficient way for businesses to resolve conflicts with other businesses. The practice spread to cover some financial products, but since the 1980s it has really caught on with all kinds of companies that want to avoid litigation with consumers. In 2019, eighty-one of the hundred largest US businesses used arbitration in place of the court system. So instead of a judge and possibly a jury deciding whether a business did something wrong and should take steps to correct it, companies can keep the proceedings hush-hush and make the complaints go away without fixing anything.

That's what happened with financial giant Wells Fargo, which between 2009 and 2016 opened some 3.5 million bogus bank and credit card accounts in the names of real customers. Beginning in 2013, customers tried to sue Wells Fargo, but because of arbitration clauses buried in the fine print of their agreements, they were forced into confidential settlements. As a result, the bank's practices remained hidden until the media exposed them. That led to a government investigation and, ultimately, a huge financial settlement for consumers who were harmed.

Wells Fargo was finally brought to some measure of accountability, but the national media and Congress shouldn't have to get involved in order for people to have a chance. The vast majority of cases won't be nearly as big as the Wells Fargo affair and won't get that type of attention. That doesn't mean people don't deserve a fairer pathway toward justice.

Most have no idea they've agreed to arbitration. We're tricked into it. Consumers don't have to sign anything, or even click "I agree" on a website, to be bound to it. The clause can appear on product packaging or be hidden deep in warranties, user manuals, or even a website's terms of use. "You don't think of a washing machine as coming with a contract," Lauren Saunders, associate director of the nonprofit National Consumer Law Center, told *Consumer Reports.*

Multiple courts have ruled that even contracts a customer didn't see or didn't have any choice but to sign are enforceable. The law has evolved, says Brian Fitzpatrick, a law professor at Vanderbilt University and a former clerk to Supreme Court justice Antonin Scalia. "The sky's the limit in how many arbitration clauses corporations are going to be able to ensnare consumers in," he told *Consumer Reports.*

The widespread use of arbitration makes it far less likely that consumers can file class action lawsuits, in which a large group of plaintiffs pools resources, legal representation, and evidence to take a company to court. Class actions deter misconduct, Fitzpatrick says, and that's reason enough to keep them.

In a case concerning front-loading washing machines, owners complained of mold buildup, foul smells, and ruined laundry. It turned out that the rubber gaskets around the machines' doors trapped moisture, among other problems. By 2017, companies such as Bosch, Electrolux, LG, and others settled class action suits, with some of them, such as Whirlpool, agreeing to compensate owners with cash or rebates on new machines. Now, Whirlpool, for one, imposes mandatory arbitration provisions on consumers.

In some cases, arbitration can be a good option for consumers, provided they understand the trade-offs and can deliberately choose arbitration over the court system after a dispute arises. Arbitration is even being used as a tool to fight back against its own overuse. Some Amazon users may have noticed in the summer of 2021 that the company shifted its policy away from arbitration. Not out of the goodness of its heart, but because consumers started using the abusive system to protest. In the last few years, as reported by the *Wall Street Journal*, some law firms have "used online marketing and other tools to sign up consumers and employees en masse to file arbitration claims. . . . The filings can overwhelm arbitration providers and the targeted companies, which are accustomed to paying the fees for small numbers of claims but not tens of thousands all at once." That's what happened to Amazon, when over seventy-five thousand arbitration demands came in from Echo users, leaving the company with "a bill for tens of millions of dollars in filing fees." When consumers started gaming the system designed to be stacked against them, Amazon folded, allowing customers to now file actual lawsuits in court.

Amazon isn't the only target. When DoorDash was hit by arbitration filings from over five thousand of its drivers, the company had the gall to ask a federal court to let it break its own terms so it didn't have to pay the arbitration-filing fees. The district judge said in response, "In irony upon irony, Door-Dash now wishes to resort to a class-wide lawsuit, the very device it denied to the workers. . . . This hypocrisy will not be blessed."

Amazon is the only company so far to actually leave arbitration behind, which isn't surprising. The Amazon customers' method of consumer protest isn't an easy or cheap one to pull off, and other companies are already reworking terms to make it even more difficult to do.

We can't rely on companies to end the practice of forced arbitration, so we need to fight for the policy action that will ban it. That's why Consumer Reports supports passing the Forced

Arbitration Injustice Repeal Act. This wouldn't "ban" arbitration, but it would stop arbitration from being imposed as a precondition for obtaining a product or for obtaining or continuing service or employment. Consumers, workers, or small businesses could freely choose arbitration if they determine it to be fair and a better option for them than the courts. This proposed legislation is about ending a shield that helps corporations shirk real legal accountability when they do harm.

THE STICKIEST DEBT

Here's a statistic that ought to be taught in high schools as a warning: forty-five million Americans, or roughly 14 percent of the country, have outstanding student loans. Barring a sweeping cancellation of the debt, the $1.7 trillion owed will probably climb between the time I write this and the time you read this. Measured in dollars, student loans rocketed past credit card debt and car loans to become the second-tallest pile of debt in the US, eclipsed only by mortgages.

If I had to pick one investment that changed my life it would be education. Ask any first-generation college graduate and they'll probably tell you the same thing. It starts with knowing all about jobs that don't offer paid vacation, sick days, health care, or retirement support. My father worked for a small family-run retail business, so he had none of those benefits. My mother was lucky enough to land a union job, which got us the health care we needed. Higher education was my best shot at a life that wouldn't subject me to those continuing struggles, though it wasn't a guarantee. It was the only path I had to reach my aspirations, the reason I could ever even dream of becoming an aide to my home state's US senator, a vice president of a global philanthropy, and a CEO. But to gain access to that education, I still needed teachers who took an interest in me, the internships that exposed me to professional environments my parents lacked access to, and the financial aid to make it possible.

While the average four-year university was far less costly when I attended school than it is now, paying for my college education was still a major burden for my family. That's why I attended Fairleigh Dickinson University in New Jersey, close to home. Living in a dorm sounded great, but we couldn't afford it. FDU had an innovative financial policy: if one of your siblings attended, you got your tuition half off. Three out of the four of us signed up. Even then, I had to find a job and do work-study throughout college.

When I swung for the fences and applied for a Yale graduate program, I was fortunate to be accepted, but I was even more fortunate to get the financial backing to actually attend. I was the recipient of the Graduate Professional Opportunity Program, a federal support program that no longer exists. I had to go to New Haven to start classes before even knowing if I'd been accepted for the program, and I realized I might have to almost immediately turn around and drive home. Thankfully, with the help of people advocating for me, I did receive the support. Otherwise, I never would have gotten where I am today.

US universities attract thousands of students from other countries, and a college education is still universally considered a coveted passport to a better life, especially as earnings decline for people who don't have the diploma. In fact, for first-generation Americans, it's often considered the only bridge to social mobility. But a postsecondary education is becoming increasingly harder to attain, with years of crippling debt payments to look forward to. Many of today's college students and recent graduates speak hopefully about the government canceling the loans, or a percentage of the loans, or sending them checks to make payments easier. They've told pollsters that school costs are their biggest obstacle to a happy life. Even when young people try to keep their costs down, they get sucked into the debt vortex. Students in public universities—the schools that for decades enjoyed adequate funding from legislatures, were considered affordable, and stood tall as the pride of their states—now borrow an average of $30,000 for their bachelor's degrees.

It's staggering, but just when I thought I couldn't possibly hear another statistic concerning student debt that hadn't already outraged me, I was outraged by this: the age cohort that owes the most is thirty-five- to forty-nine-year-olds, with student debt totaling $602 billion. I'm not sure what I expected—that the loans would be paid off by middle age? They aren't. Not by a long shot. Interest just piles on more debt.

But there's more: 2.3 million Americans over the age of sixty-two owe a collective $86.8 billion in student loans. These people should be thinking about retirement, but they're helping children pay off debt, or they're still paying off loans from going back to school later in life. Except in certain circumstances, student loans can't be forgiven in bankruptcy, and the government, by far the biggest lender, can garnish wages, including Social Security payments, if a borrower falls behind. There's no statute of limitations on federal loans, so the debt, unlike other money you may owe, can follow you to the grave. Student loans might be the stickiest debt there is. They're nearly impossible to shake.

Student debt is so high because higher-education costs have risen twice as fast as inflation since the mid-1980s. There are a lot of reasons for that steep increase—and for why the higher-education business model is failing. For one, state legislatures have become more and more stingy. In 1975, states were contributing 58 percent of state university budgets. From 2008 to 2018, state spending on higher education fell by 13 percent, or $6.6 billion, with forty-one states allotting less money to colleges in 2018 than they did in 2008, resulting in students shouldering more of the burden.

It's also gotten more expensive to run a college or university. Schools had to grow to accommodate more students than they had in the 1970s. Enrollment went from 8.6 million in 1970 to about 19.6 million in 2019. But it's not just more students. The number of services that higher-education institutions provide has also skyrocketed—to include health care, academic support, and counseling. Traditional services, like instruction, dormitories, and facilities, have had to expand not only because of more students attending, but also because what schools have to offer to compete with each other has grown more complex and costly.

This model seems to be broken, even driving away students. Enrollment has fallen since the 2011 peak of 21 million students, and the COVID-19 pandemic has only increased the attrition rate. That means fewer students paying for tuition, leading to even higher fees for those who do attend, which will lead to even fewer applicants. The way we fund colleges and universities in this country is making higher education less a bridge to social mobility and more a cycle of increasing financial barriers.

Despite the financial crisis within the system, when schools think about competing to attract students, their focus generally isn't on costs. In her book *Weapons of Math Destruction*, mathematician Cathy O'Neil describes how universities became locked in a rivalry to attract students thanks to, of all things, the *U.S. News & World Report*'s annual college rankings. Creators of the rankings wrote an algorithm measuring fifteen statistics—including average SAT scores, application-to-admission percentages, professor-student ratios, and class sizes—on which they rated institutions of higher learning. The annual issue that includes their list became such a smash hit that today just about every family checks it when they have a child thinking about where to apply to college. That caused administrators to work overtime to please the *U.S. News* algorithm by improving their performance in the fifteen areas upon which the algorithm judges them. The problem, as O'Neil points out, is that for decades, the rankings didn't take into consideration the cost of the institution. College presidents, to satisfy the rankings algorithm, never had to keep tuition or other costs at a reasonable level to stay competitive in the all-too-crucial rankings.

To *U.S. News & World Report*'s credit, this changed in 2021, when student indebtedness became one of the factors that went into the rankings. However, it's a mere 5 percent of the ranking factors, even less than class selectivity, and only takes into consideration students with federal loans and students who actually graduated with a bachelor's degree. As the head of an organization that also uses reviews and rankings to better inform the public, I can see the potential value of a judging system for educational institutions—but only if the rankings take into consideration the areas that are critical to a better higher-education system. We don't review products and ignore their cost to families' budgets, and similarly, the financial cost of colleges and universities should be significantly weighted.

"We cannot place the blame for this trend entirely on the U.S. News rankings," O'Neil wrote. But in a society that "embraced not only the idea that a college education is essential but the idea that a degree from a highly ranked school can catapult a student into a life of power and privilege," the rankings "created powerful incentives that have encouraged spending while turning a blind eye to skyrocketing tuitions and fees."

The students who suffer the most are the ones further down on the economic ladder. So-called for-profit colleges have catered to them, contributing to the crisis by aggressively marketing their programs, persuading students to enroll, taking their money, and then delivering poor-quality instruction. Nationwide, a small fraction of students attend for-profit schools, but they make up almost half the borrowers who wind up in default. Closures of schools like Corinthian and ITT Tech left thousands of students stranded in debt without receiving their graduation certificates. Many of those students have filed claims to get their loans canceled and are still waiting for relief years later.

Students from all backgrounds ought to inform themselves as completely as they can before taking on loans to finance their education. To this end, many high schools began offering classes in financial literacy in the wake of the 2008 global financial crisis. It's a good idea, and understanding the mysteries of annual percentage rates and debt-to-income ratios are valuable skills for anyone to have, especially those just entering the marketplace. But they don't come close to being a substitute for the elimination of the tricks that lenders use to trap borrowers in a debt spiral. To prescribe greater financial literacy as the sole remedy for getting ripped off is misguided. The lure of something valuable and necessary, such as a higher education, could make even the savviest consumer overlook a crucial phrase in the fine print.

It's wrong to blame consumers when the financial industry, with all the influence and all the money, plays games with our future while borrowers are left to climb steep mountains of debt.

Those mountains of debt have national ramifications. Many overleveraged graduates live with their parents because they simply can't afford to pay market rent with a monthly student loan payment hanging over their heads. The debt is causing them to postpone what economists call household formation. In other words, debt is delaying the start of independent life for many college graduates. Indebtedness could even be one factor contributing to the low US fertility rate as twentysomethings put off starting their own families. A 2016 Consumer Reports survey of fifteen hundred Americans with student debt pinpointed the depth of the problem. Because of student debt, 37 percent of respondents said they're waiting to save for retirement or to start down the road to other financial-planning goals, 28 percent are putting off buying a house, 12 percent are postponing marriage, and 14 percent are changing careers. Through no fault of these graduates, the pandemic has frozen even more of them in place. All of this has ripple effects, not just for the individuals but for the country's economy.

Our society pays what I would call a spiritual cost too. For those fortunate enough to attend college, those years used to be a time to explore the possibilities of different careers or to follow less-traveled paths of inquiry. They were the only period in your life when you were expected to indulge your curiosity and expand your understanding of the world for its own sake. You could study a language you might never speak, or take an anatomy class if you were an English major, or a Shakespeare class if you were an engineer. You could volunteer at a shelter or try rock climbing or write jazz-show reviews for the school paper, or get a job as a roofer or a park ranger—just because you were interested in doing it. Such an experience might steer you to a career you'd never anticipated, as it did for my niece after she spent hours volunteering as a suicide help-line counselor. She ended up becoming a therapist.

More than ever, with the specter of debt shadowing the college years, students don't have time for adventure, intellectual or otherwise. It becomes even more critical that they focus on fighting for the right internships, running themselves into the ground to graduate on time (or early to save money), and lining up job prospects so that someone will hire them before they fall behind on debt payments.

The richest country in the world should make postsecondary schooling affordable for anyone who wants to continue their education or job training after high school. Instead, America has succeeded in yoking its young people to the debt carousel at an earlier age, robbing them of the years when they might be widening their horizons and driving them toward an existence that revolves around loan payments, month after month after month. It's as though student debt has sliced a chapter out of their lives and delivered them to the hamster wheel, where they'll struggle to keep up until they're as old as their parents.

Ideas abound for how our society could deal with the problem. Debt cancellation would provide an enticing immediate relief, and perhaps a form of it is a good place to start. After all, more than half of those who default on student loans have less than $10,000 of federal undergraduate debt, and most of those who owe lower amounts are minority students. A 2020 poll found that more than 60 percent of Americans supported reducing student loan debt by $20,000 per person, and only 24 percent opposed the idea. It seems as though immediate relief of $10,000 to $20,000 would be politically acceptable to most Americans. Even the bottom of that range would eliminate $429 billion in debt and make more than one-third of all borrowers debt-free, while reducing by half the balances for another 20 percent of all borrowers.

What about longer-term solutions for future generations? Free public-college tuition is an idea that's gained popularity in recent years. President Biden favored an ambitious plan to make tuition-free community college available to all young adults before the proposal was shot down. That would have made two years of post-high-school education a financially viable option for a lot of students. Community colleges can help give young people a push in the right direction. The University of Tennessee tracked the performances of students in the state's free community college program. They found that the students had higher rates of completion and higher earnings. My oldest brother went to community college before transferring to a four-year state school, but that avenue is still too expensive for many Americans. Opening the door to free community college would go a long way to expanding people's educational opportunities and financial success.

I also see the benefit of providing free tuition for a four-year higher education, especially in a model where students can study at no or little charge but after graduation are obligated to serve the country in another way, say, teaching in an underserved area or becoming part of a civilian infrastructure-construction team. An existing program that follows a similar model, Public Service Loan Forgiveness, has been so inconsistently implemented that the Department of Education needed more than one attempt to straighten it out. Just as the name of the program suggests, student borrowers could work for ten years in a public-service job, such as in the military, and get their outstanding debt erased. But millions of borrowers work at a qualifying employer and don't even realize they're eligible, and many have been denied forgiveness. In good news, the Education Department revamped the program in 2021 to make the process clearer and easier. They also committed to reaching out to those who'd been wrongly rejected, though even this reformed effort has hit potholes.

Let's also do away with some of the draconian methods of collection. For one thing, the Internal Revenue Service ought to quit garnishing the earned income tax credit of defaulted borrowers. This benefit is aimed at households earning less than $30,000. Families are barely making ends meet in today's America. Forty percent say they don't have $400 to spare in case of a financial emergency. Let's not place yet another burden on their backs. Instead, we can rethink repayment plans that fit their abilities to pay. We should also reduce interest rates on the loans, and limit interest capitalization, to prevent ballooning balances over time. Those options would cost a lot less than blanket loan cancellation.

Many borrowers report exploitation at the hands of debt servicers, the companies responsible for collecting the monthly loan payments. In recent years, servicers have been the target of state investigations for abusive practices and mismanagement that have frustrated borrowers' ability to manage their loans, access legal rights to flexible repayment options, and stay out of default. In 2021, California created a standard that requires loan servicers to minimize extra fees, improve record keeping, and train staff to provide borrowers with accurate information about their repayment options. It bans what it calls "abusive" student loan practices that take advantage of borrowers' confusion over the repayment process, and establishes a student loan advocate to review borrower complaints, gather data, and issue reports to the state legislature. The Consumer Financial Protection Bureau is crafting federal regulations for student loan servicing, and the agency's work is important to setting fair standards for the entire country.

Let's not forget to remind lawmakers of their obligation to appropriately fund state higher education. Thirteen states reduced higher-education funding in fiscal year 2021. This needs to reverse course, because when states cut money to higher education, public colleges and universities usually pass costs on to students.

We're at a crossroads in higher education, and while it might not directly affect everyone in the country, the number of people burdened by student debt and the cost of higher education is only increasing. What's more, the financial burden on such a large number of Americans hurts our entire economy. Solutions that minimize debt, keep borrowers out of default and in good credit standing, and protect students from abuse are victories for everyone.

CREDIT MYSTERIES

Credit scores were designed to reduce our financial lives to a single number in order to make decisions easier for lenders. They were never meant to be checked by employers before they hire, landlords before they rent, or insurance companies before they write policies. But some bosses, landlords, and insurers do it anyway, and a weak credit record can hurt your chances of landing a job, renting an apartment, or buying affordable insurance.

Americans are legally entitled to access credit reports for free once per year, but they don't have a similar right to their credit scores, except under limited circumstances. That's why it's such a blow to so many consumers to find errors in their credit reports—when they're able to see them. Of the six thousand people who responded to a Consumer Reports survey that asked about their credit, one-third said they caught at least one mistake. Most of the errors related to their personal information, such as the spelling of their name or a wrong address. That's one reason why 10 percent of the respondents found it difficult to get a look at their own credit histories. The credit companies had their information filed under a mistakenly spelled name. "I answered the questions correctly, but because it didn't match the wrong information they had on file, they wouldn't allow me to access my credit report," said Lori Vann-Guthrie, who took part in the survey.

Credit-report mistakes can cost real money. *Consumer Reports* reporter Lisa L. Gill spoke to Victoria Ross after her husband of forty years died of a heart attack. Ross had to somehow set aside her grief to focus on financial issues, such as selling the family home and downsizing into a condo. When she thought everything was settled, she applied for a car loan. But an error in the credit reports from TransUnion, one of three reporting companies, stopped her. It mistakenly showed that a PayPal credit card she'd paid off still had a balance due of $1,200. The other two credit companies, Equifax and Experian, correctly reported the account as paid off and closed, she said.

TransUnion's mistake meant she didn't qualify for a low interest rate at the car dealership. "Instead, they gave me a 12% rate, which would have increased my monthly payment by more than $100," Ross said. "I'm on a fixed income, so every dollar counts."

Ross filed multiple disputes with TransUnion, to no avail. It was only after Consumer Reports intervened that TransUnion corrected the error. It's too bad all disputes can't be solved like that, and because they can't, credit-score companies can generally be as stubborn as they want. "We're really at their mercy," Ross said.

That Ross, or any other consumer, would have to pay to get an additional glimpse of their credit report only adds more indignity to the process. "They not only put the burden of monitoring reports on customers' shoulders, but then they charge them for accessing their own information," says Ed Mierzwinski, senior director of the federal consumer program at U.S. PIRG and a former member of Consumer Reports' board of directors.

The credit-reporting system is full of quirks. Paying rent on time often won't help your score, but paying a mortgage on time will. It doesn't matter whether late payments stem from your own irresponsibility or from things out of your control, such as an illness. A slipup means you could be punished for years. Beyond its idiosyncrasies, the credit-reporting business is broken. Errors pop up too often. A lack of transparency ensures that many of them go uncorrected, and it's often impossible for a consumer to directly dispute their score. The system rewards people who have debt and makes it hard for those who don't have bill-payment histories to establish credit, limiting options for many potential borrowers. And the companies are simply too powerful. A system this flawed can't be allowed to wield so much influence on important questions such as whether a consumer can land a job or find a place to live.

Phone apps, developed to help make the credit-tracking process easier for consumers, have been a disappointment. A 2021 *Consumer Reports* investigation found that the apps often don't do what they say they'll do. The scores they make available aren't always the ones that lenders use, they charge for services that are free elsewhere, and they promote options that aren't always fair deals for consumers.

Consumer Reports examined five popular apps that give consumers access to their scores: Credit Karma, Credit Sesame, Experian Credit Report & FICO Score, myFICO, and TransUnion: Score & Report. MyFICO was the only one that showed users the credit scores that lenders typically use to make lending decisions. But it's not free. The lowest rate charged by myFICO for access to so-called industry scores was $19.95 per month, which adds up to more than $200 annually. The other four apps charge for credit reports that consumers are entitled to see free of charge once each year at AnnualCreditReport.com.

All five apps collect a significant amount of private information and appear to share the data with other parties. The companies use the data in the usual way—to develop detailed user profiles for marketing purposes. Because the data is shared, it can be vulnerable to hacking or otherwise fall into the wrong hands.

Four of the apps—Credit Karma, Credit Sesame, Experian Credit Report & FICO Score, and TransUnion: Score & Report—give "advice" or "recommendations" for raising credit scores or saving money but say in the fine print that those solutions may not be in the consumers' best interests. Taking the advice may, however, be in the best interests of the apps, as the companies make money when users sign up, and they stand to earn the most from the deals listed most prominently on the apps.

Instead of harvesting users' personal data and profiting from "helping" consumers, the credit-app services ought to provide free access to the credit scores that lenders use and to direct users to access their free credit reports through AnnualCreditReport.com.

On these matters, we're left looking to public policy for remedies, beginning with raising accuracy standards to minimize errors and properly investigate disputes. The Consumer Financial Protection Bureau and the Federal Trade Commission, which have oversight responsibilities, should flex their authority to penalize companies for any violations.

Consumer Reports supports two pieces of federal legislation that would make credit reporting work better for consumers. The Comprehensive Credit Act would allow consumers free access to credit scores that lenders use, and the Protecting Your Credit Score Act would establish a secure portal where consumers could obtain their own credit reports and scores free of charge an unlimited number of times. Allowing free access to credit scores only once a year serves the interests not of consumers but of the credit-reporting companies. Their business models shouldn't rely on a lack of transparency perpetuated solely for their private gain.

It's also important to limit the role of credit reports in consumers' lives. Credit reports should be used for the purpose for which they were developed—to reasonably assess whether someone will be able to repay a loan. They shouldn't be used for any other decisions about a consumer, such as insurance pricing or suitability for a job or apartment.

These solutions would go a long way to easing the burdens on consumers, as credit scores, which are so important to being treated fairly in the marketplace, still remain a mystery to many. But they're only solutions for *most* people, not all. About twenty-six million American adults lack any credit history and have no scores at all. For them, borrowing at a decent rate from a reputable lender is nearly impossible.

It's to those millions of Americans who are blocked from participating in our economic system that we turn our attention in the next chapter.

WHAT CAN I DO NOW?

Avoid Payday Loans and Their Sky-High Interest

The best way to prevent being trapped by the absurd interest rates of payday loans is to avoid them completely and find alternatives to your needs. Consumer Reports has a few suggestions:

- Look for interest-free loans—from friends or family who might be able to help you, or from local nonprofits that offer emergency credit. Even some employers offer advances.
- If you do have to borrow at interest, investigating lower-rate options must be a priority. Some credit unions offer lower-interest payday alternative loans (PALs) or quick loans. Even credit cards or traditional banks have "installment loans" which, while charging fairly high interest rates, are generally better options than payday rates.
- Start building an emergency fund now, setting aside ten to fifty dollars when you can, so you're ready for the challenging situations that push people toward payday loans.
- Selling possessions (at yard sales or on sites like eBay or Craigslist) could be a first step if you need quick cash. While doing this may understandably be emotionally dif-

ficult, the debt you could pile up from high-interest loans will take a much larger toll on your life in the long run.

Prevent Hidden Fees from Hurting You

It's hard to find an industry that doesn't have a fee hidden among the details—and they can really add up. The first step is to recognize fees, which means reviewing charges again before clicking "buy" or looking over statements periodically to make sure new fees haven't been added that you're automatically paying.

You can also join Consumer Reports' efforts to fight back. Initiatives like What the Fee?! push back against hidden fees in travel and entertainment, and it's with the support of consumers like you that similar efforts helped us secure a federal law stopping sneaky fees from cable TV providers. Visit action .consumerreports.org/whatthefee to read about our current efforts against hidden fees.

Keep Up with Student Loan Payments

Nearly two-thirds of college students graduate with student loans. If you're one of them, know that picking the right repayment plan is critical. The lowest monthly payment might not be what's best for you.

Some borrowers qualify for federal loan forgiveness. For the majority of borrowers, who will have to repay their loans, here's a quick look at CR's advice on that process:

- To pay the least amount in the long run, you'll want to pay more than the minimum monthly payment. Use FinAid.org to help you calculate how much you can save by paying a bit more each month. Just be mindful of balancing that with your expenses and building some savings.

- Make sure your loan servicer uses the extra payments to pay down the principal and not the interest on your highest-rate loan. This will help reduce your overall payment. The Consumer Financial Protection Bureau website even has a sample letter you can use. Double-check to ensure that the loan servicer is actually directing that payment where you want it to go.

- If you can't afford the standard payment on federal loans, a number of income-based plans are available. You can find them all listed at StudentAid.gov, on the page labeled "Apply for an Income-Driven Repayment Plan" (from the website's home page, click on "Manage Loans").

- Students and parents with private loans have the fewest options. Rates on private loans change, meaning you could end up owing even more interest over time. Avoid refinancing your federal loans into private ones, as you'll lose important protections, such as the ability to defer or stretch out payments.

Check Your Credit Report

As of the writing of this book, you can obtain free yearly reports from the three credit companies (Equifax, Experian, and TransUnion) by going to AnnualCreditReport.com. You'll have to answer a number of security questions, and if you fail to answer correctly you might have to go through the process of requesting your reports in writing.

Some credit cards now offer to provide you with your FICO credit score—one of the scores most commonly used by financial services—for free as a member. If so, you can likely find it by logging into your credit card account online. Here are some of the credit cards that, as of 2021, offer this service free of charge: American Express, Bank of America, Barclays, Chase, Citi, Capital One, Discover, U.S. Bank, USAA, and Wells Fargo.

MORE INFORMATION

For more references, details on these solutions, updates on these issues, and ways to get engaged in taking action, go to BuyerAware.CR.org, or use the QR code below.

CHAPTER FOUR

BIAS IN, BIAS OUT

AFTER WE LEFT CUBA, MY FAMILY EVENTUALLY MOVED OUT of our three-story walk-up apartment and found a home in the Weequahic section of Newark's tree-lined South Ward, not far from a sprawling park. We were pioneers, of a sort—the first Latinos in what had been a largely Jewish neighborhood that was changing rapidly. Weequahic High School, one of the highest-performing in the state, was just around the corner, and so was Beth Israel Hospital, founded in 1901 because unwritten rules prohibited Jewish doctors from practicing medicine elsewhere. It was the 1960s, and all across the country countless white families were leaving America's cities for the suburbs and being replaced by middle-class Black families and a new wave of immigrants. As a child, I didn't understand the larger economic forces or, certainly, the racial dynamics, but I could see how my community was changing. Seemingly overnight, more and more of the kids I played hopscotch and double Dutch with were Black or Latina. My family had been part of that change.

The new neighborhood quickly became home. I remember the pleasure of walking to the comic book store with some change in my pocket to buy the latest edition of *Wonder Woman*. I liked that she was a female superhero, and that she had dark hair, like mine. Some years later, the first issue of *Ms.* magazine would feature Wonder Woman on its cover, touting her as a presidential candidate in the 1972 election. I liked that too.

I wasn't aware of many Latina icons during my childhood— no one like what Supreme Court justice Sonia Sotomayor, Gloria Estefan, and Selena Gomez represent for women who've grown up since. But I did have a Latina I looked up to: my mom.

When I think back on the evolving roles of women in my lifetime, my point of reference is always my mother. It seemed as if she did everything. I never knew my mother not to work. She had factory jobs and eventually was promoted to supervisor. She'd wake up before dawn, and before she caught the bus she would make our lunches, which she left for us in little brown paper bags. My grandmothers, both of whom lived with us, shared laundry and dinner prep, but one of them died while I was in high school, and dementia caught up with the other. So on top of her full-time job, my mother added those tasks. When I got sick with a kidney infection and had to stay at Beth Israel, my mother spent so much time with me at the hospital she was fired from her job. I didn't know that had happened until years later, when she casually mentioned it. She never brought it up again.

Coming to the US from another country, especially in the early years, must have been bewildering for my parents. Imagine what they were thinking when they fled Cuba to seek political stability and a better life, only to have the American president assassinated not long after they arrived. And then, in July 1967, Newark's Central Ward erupted in flames. Two white police officers had brutally beaten a Black cab driver named John Smith, then charged him with assault. That injustice was the final combustible straw triggering four days of tragedy. Twenty-six people died and hundreds were injured. The governor called in the National Guard. The next year, the Kerner Commission's report on the violence in Newark and other cities said that "white racism—not black anger—turned the key that unlocked urban American turmoil." It identified a series of factors that fanned the fires, including "bad policing, a flawed justice system, unscrupulous consumer-credit practices, poor or inadequate housing, high unemployment, voter suppression, and other culturally embedded forms of racial discrimination." More than fifty years later, America still grapples with the same issues. Living in a volatile Newark in the 1960s was my introduction.

DRAWING RED LINES BETWEEN US

Our moving to a home in Weequahic wasn't an accident, though my parents had no way to tell what long-established undercurrents of law and custom had steered them there. As recent immigrants and members of an ethnic minority, we had little freedom over where we could settle, though the techniques used by homeowners and real estate agents were hidden from my mother and father. White Newark did everything it could to keep out people of color and, when that became impossible, to confine us to certain neighborhoods. There was blockbusting, a practice in which real estate agents stirred white sellers into a panic with tales about their home values dropping because Black and Latino families were moving into the area. The homeowners would put their houses on the market, and those same Realtors would buy them up on the cheap. The professionals would then turn around and sell the homes to minorities for big profits.

There was also redlining, a practice started in the 1930s and named after actual red lines drawn on maps around certain neighborhoods by the US Federal Housing Administration. The red line separated white neighborhoods, where the FHA helped home buyers by guaranteeing mortgages, from nonwhite communities, where borrowers were labeled "high risk" based on nothing more than ethnicity, race, or birth country. The government didn't extend the same helping hand in redlined neighborhoods that it did in white communities. That forced stigmatized home buyers into exploitative loans that often ended in default and financial ruin. Because of the restrictions, the value of the homes in redlined neighborhoods didn't grow, like they did in white neighborhoods. In fact, they usually fell. My parents had no idea that the home they'd scraped money together to purchase would start losing value the minute they moved in. Since owning a home is the best way to create the kind of wealth that can be passed down to children and grandchildren, government policies robbed generations of minorities of the prosperity taken for granted by white families. The process of building wealth, and the biggest purchases of many consumers' lives, was twisted and battered by the moral rot of racial and ethnic bias that still exists today.

Midcentury, the marketplace enforced the government's discriminatory policies. As author Ta-Nehisi Coates wrote, "The American real estate industry believed segregation to be a moral principle." In the 1950s, a Realtor group's code of ethics warned that a member "should never be instrumental in introducing into a neighborhood . . . any race or nationality, or any individuals whose presence will clearly be detrimental to property values." Coates cites a 1943 brochure specifying that such undesirables might include prostitutes, bootleggers, gangsters, and "a colored man of means who was giving his children a college education and thought they were entitled to live among whites."

Redlining was outlawed by the Fair Housing Act of 1968, but violations are hard to prove, and the practice of steering minority home buyers to minority neighborhoods, or making it tougher for them to buy and keep homes, never ended. It's just gotten more insidious.

In the 2000s, for example, subprime mortgages were shopped to mostly lower-income minority borrowers to feed a Wall Street moneymaking machine. Subprime mortgages attracted home buyers by offering interest rates that were enticingly low for the first two years. After that, however, rates ballooned. Mortgage lenders promised borrowers that the ever-increasing value of their homes would make it simple for them to refinance their loans before the higher payments kicked in, and during the yearslong housing bubble that sounded like a plausible sales pitch. But the bubble burst in 2008, sending home values plummeting. Homeowners were stuck with houses that were worth less than what they owed on their mortgages—and with mortgages that demanded interest rates too expensive to repay. News stories highlighted with incredulity how single moms with modest salaries could have afforded to buy real estate, but few of them mentioned the billions of dollars the biggest banks pocketed in the scheme. American households lost one-quarter of their wealth during the recession of 2007 to 2009, and ten million homes went into foreclosure. Meanwhile, the banks got government help and thrived.

Discrimination in the housing marketplace lurks everywhere. In 2020, a Black woman in Jacksonville, Florida, named Abena Horton put her house up for sale, expecting to get around $450,000. Horton was surprised when the appraiser valued it at $330,000. Suspecting bias, Horton decided to get another opinion. Before the second appraiser arrived, she put away photos of her family and books by Black authors and took her son shopping, leaving her white husband to show the house. The new appraisal came in at $465,000. After describing on Facebook what had happened, Horton was flooded with messages from other homeowners with similar experiences.

Anecdotes like Horton's are supported by statistics showing that race remains a preoccupation in real estate. In majority-Black neighborhoods, homes are valued about 23 percent less than equivalent homes in majority-white communities. The cumulative loss for Black homeowners: $156 billion. Landlords and real estate agents don't treat minority home hunters as well as they treat white people, according to an internal government study. For instance, Latinos are given 12.5 percent fewer options for housing units than whites and are shown 7.5 percent fewer housing units than whites. Latino renters are also more likely than their white counterparts to be told there aren't any homes or apartments available. Latinos, along with Black renters, are informed of the availability of one fewer unit for every five in-person visits, a form of discrimination that's almost impossible to detect. A 2017 Harvard University poll found that one in three Latinos reported being discriminated against when looking for housing.

In 2020, the homeownership rate for Black families stood at about 44 percent and for Latino families at about 47.5 percent, compared with 74 percent for white families. That's a big reason why the wealth gap between minority and white households only widens.

The erosion of property value has a cascading effect on a neighborhood. The level of wealth in an area can determine the kinds of stores that move in (a community bank versus a payday lender, say, or a health food store versus a liquor store), whether affluent people will consider buying homes there, and what kinds of services the town can provide. Many public school budgets, including those in my home state of New Jersey, are based on property taxes. Neighborhoods that are hurting economically too often produce underperforming schools, perpetuating a cycle of poverty and indebtedness that's passed from generation to generation.

In definitions of "civil rights"—a citizen's entitlement to participate in the life of society and the state without discrimination or repression—I'm always struck by the absence of any reference to economic rights. Every American's right to a fair marketplace is foundational to civil rights and to the health of our democracy. In America, money means so much, and denying certain members of our society the economic power to function as free and equal members is not only morally wrong; it stifles competition and hinders the smooth functioning of markets. It's not a zero-sum game. Extending equal economic freedom and opportunity to Americans who've been shut out of the process will help us all prosper. We may not think of it this way, but consumer rights are civil rights.

As our economic system has increasingly moved to the digital world, with algorithms and artificial intelligence undertaking tasks that until recently only people could do, technology was supposed to render discrimination obsolete. Algorithms weren't like salespeople who figured the Black man who came into the store had to be a potential shoplifter. We could, in real life, live in segregated neighborhoods, but the Amazon shopping cart wouldn't care what consumers looked like or what accents they spoke with. Numbers don't have feelings or prejudices, the explanation goes, so innovations such as the use of mathematical formulas to decide who's eligible for products such as a mortgage or urgent medical care or less expensive auto insurance would take flawed human judgment out of the equation.

It turns out, however, that algorithms do discriminate. The old computer coders' quip about "garbage in, garbage out" can be updated to "bias in, bias out." Technology has proved in many cases to preserve, rather than kill, the unfairness that's been a disgraceful part of the American marketplace for far too long.

A part of Consumer Reports' job that we hold dear is to keep shining light on the newest technologies and expose how they might be perpetuating old biases, which are able to replicate only in darkness.

CREDIT DESERTS

As I mentioned in Chapter Three, the ability to borrow money at a reasonable interest rate is an essential prerequisite of wealth accumulation in America. Of course, it pays to be smart about it. Like too much rain, too much borrowing just makes things worse. Without it, though, nothing grows.

The problem for twenty-six million American adults is the lack of any borrowing history, and hence no way for credit scores to be calculated. Without a credit score it's impossible to borrow from a reputable source. And without a reputable source to borrow from, the only places to go are payday lenders, whose reputation is so corrosive that some towns and counties—though not enough of them—have gone through the arduous process of restricting them.

Credit scores were introduced in the 1950s with the intention of objectively measuring creditworthiness based on a consumer's historical ability to pay back borrowed money. Two companies, FICO and VantageScore, create the scoring models for the three major credit-reporting firms—Experian, TransUnion, and Equifax—that track your past financial behavior. The higher your score, the more likely you'll receive a lower interest rate for a credit card, mortgage, or car loan.

Credit scores reward people who already have a credit history, but it's hard for those who don't have a credit history to establish one, a circular problem that haunts Black Americans more than any other group. If only these consumers could qualify for a credit card and repay the balance every month, they could start creating a credit history. But who'll take a chance on issuing a credit card to someone who can offer zero evidence they'll repay the money? It's a Catch-22. Thirty-two percent of African Americans versus 18 percent of whites didn't have enough information in their credit reports to generate a score in 2019. "For most lenders, everything begins and ends with that score," said Syed Ejaz, a Consumer Reports financial-policy analyst.

The result: 46 percent of Native Americans, 41 percent of Blacks, and 31.5 percent of Latinos have subprime credit scores, meaning they borrow at higher rates. For white borrowers, the number is 18 percent.

That might explain why payday lenders in California have 50 percent more storefronts in predominantly Black and Latino communities than in mostly white neighborhoods. Or why they target minority internet users with online advertising. Or why African Americans make up 12 percent of the US population but 32 percent of payday borrowers. Or why Latinos make up 11 percent of Americans but 15 percent of payday borrowers. Payday companies also do well with women, who comprise 60 percent of their borrowers, and people between eighteen and twenty-four years old, people just starting their financial lives, who are the majority of their customers.

The statistics are alarming, but they can't describe the heartache and desperation of a woman who has few alternatives to stay above water besides a payday loan. Kimberly Richardson, a Black woman living in Tennessee, got caught in a payday lender's debt whirlpool in 2020, and it wouldn't let her go until she was ruined. The journey started late that year when a COVID-19 outbreak at the factory where she worked resulted in Richardson's hours being cut, she told Bloomberg. To tide her over, she took out a $1,500 loan from CashNetUSA, which is a subsidiary of Enova International, a public company based in Chicago whose shares are traded on the New York Stock Exchange. It wasn't long before Richardson was struggling to make payments as interest accumulated at an annual rate of 276 percent.

CashNetUSA encouraged Richardson to borrow more, nudging her by email whenever she had money available on her credit line. That money seemed to be available often, thanks to CashNetUSA, which added to it as long as she kept current on biweekly minimum payments. Within six months, she'd paid CashNetUSA more than she'd borrowed. In April 2021, Richardson filed for bankruptcy, but not before having sent nearly $10,000 to CashNetUSA.

If Richardson had established that she was able to pay back even small amounts borrowed on a credit card, perhaps she could have arranged a personal loan from a less predatory firm, such as a federally regulated bank, and paid a lot less for it. Who gets to borrow and on what terms are often decisions made by predictive algorithms. Such calculations are trained to look for historical patterns of "success" to predict the future. In the credit realm, determining success usually means answering a question like "How likely is this borrower to repay a loan?" Algorithms are supposed to be objective, intelligent, and capable of incredibly complex computations. But they aren't magic. They are created by humans, are dependent on a person's history, and very often make biased assumptions based on a borrower's personal data. Sometimes the assumptions are not even based on an individual's behavior; instead, they estimate the likelihood that a borrower will repay a loan based on where they live or who their neighbors are.

There's an important distinction between algorithms that judge you based on what you've actually done and those that judge you based on what people similar to you have done. When little to no digitized information about a consumer has been collected, the credit companies are likely to use demographic shortcuts rather than actual behavior to judge you. This is called working with proxies, and it's how poor people, immigrants, and members of minority groups often get shortchanged.

Credit scores are regulated in that the credit companies can't use inputs about the color of a borrower's skin or where they were born. So tenant-screening and hiring-assistance companies rely on another measure, called an e-score. Instead of using individual credit histories—a person's proven ability to repay debt—e-scores use zip codes as proxies for race and economic class, relying on demographics rather than individual characteristics to judge people. Someone's neighborhood is a proxy. It's not a statistic that's specifically about them or their ability to repay loans; rather, it's about everyone who lives or has recently lived in the same area. It presumes that a borrower is a member of a certain racial and economic group because of where they live.

Because credit scores aren't designed to describe people in any context other than borrowing, e-scores are frequently used as substitutes by landlords to determine who they'll rent to and by employers for help in the hiring process. Since they frequently have discriminatory outputs, companies shouldn't be permitted to use proxy data in algorithms.

ALGORITHMS HAVE A RACE PROBLEM

Algorithms have wormed their way into a lot more aspects of our lives than we might realize. They're everywhere on the internet, helping advertisers, political groups, and whoever else pays for the information to predict the next thing we'll do, buy, or think. But they're enveloped in mystery, mathematical black boxes whose content is closely guarded by the companies that develop and use them. Their reliability, however, depends on accurate inputs. That's where consumers must be allowed to step in. Algorithms need to be checked and rechecked for flaws that have to be corrected.

I know people—smart people, reasonable people—who are convinced that robots will one day forcibly rule over humankind. I'm not ready to sign on to that kind of dystopian vision, but I will say this: now is the time to set rules, establish standards, and make sure that artificial intelligence serves us and not the other way around. I'm disheartened that algorithms have kicked off the brave new world of AI by carrying the baggage of their programmers' bias. But I'm glad the problems have caught the attention of academics, data scientists, businesses, and consumers so we can correct them and improve the process.

One solution to bias is to have human beings keep an eye on the algorithms, not just as they're being formulated, but as they're being implemented in real life. In a 2019 TED Talk, Sylvain Duranton, a business technologist with Boston Consulting Group who oversees hundreds of algorithm writers, said the process of including people in AI projects for business purposes, which he calls Humans + AI, is long, costly, difficult—and worthwhile. "The rewards are huge," Duranton says. "Left alone, AI can do very dumb things." And harmful things. As an example, he cites the consumer who bought a toilet seat from Amazon and was inundated by online ads. "Dear Amazon," the consumer tweeted, "I bought a toilet seat because I needed one. Necessity, not choice. I am not a toilet seat addict. No matter how temptingly you email me, I'm not going to think, 'Oh, go on then, one more toilet seat, I'll treat myself.'" When the laughter of the TED Talk audience petered out, Duranton said the same thing happened to a consumer who had bought a burial urn for his mother. For months after her death, the man received messages that began, "If you liked that . . ."

Duranton points out that no human being would have sent those ads. But the value of human interaction with AI goes beyond an idea of what it means to be human. Duranton says one clothing retailer he worked with on ways to predict consumer trends, with the purpose of making the process of buying for the coming season more efficient, performed much better using only algorithms than it did with humans. His team decided to experiment further, so they tried Humans + AI, incorporating the insights of employees who knew things about the market that the numbers used by the algorithm could never have revealed. This combination did even better than AI alone. The retailer saved $100 million in just one year, according to Duranton. "Humans have to decide what's right and wrong," he says. "Human knowledge will make the difference."

The problem, of course, is that not enough humans, or not the correct humans, are deciding what's right and wrong. The wrong inputs have been fed to the algorithms, and the algorithms have been unleashed. For example, Facebook apologized after its AI made the outrageous mistake of identifying Black men in a June 2020 *Daily Mail* video as "primates." Viewers of the video were asked by Facebook if they wanted to "keep seeing videos about Primates." No animals were shown in the video. Facebook apologized for the "unacceptable error" and disabled the AI feature that had produced the message.

A related technology, face recognition, is riddled with problems associated with incorrect inputs. This software enables machines to scan our faces and compare them to photos of other faces in a database with the aim of revealing our identities and our histories. The more benign uses of the technology include identifying and remembering customers, searching for a corporate logo on store shelves, and sorting images and videos. The more controversial use is by law enforcement to catch criminals and prevent terrorism.

The practice is overflowing with incorrect inputs. And most of them disadvantage communities of color.

A 2019 analysis of the most widely used face-recognition systems conducted by the US Department of Commerce found that Asian American and Black American faces were misidentified up to one hundred times more often than white American faces. This discovery supports a 2018 study, called Gender Shades, coauthored by Joy Buolamwini, a Massachusetts Institute of Technology researcher and the founder of the Algorithmic Justice League, and Microsoft's Timnit Gebru. It showed how three face-recognition systems—the ones sold by Microsoft, IBM, and Megvii, one of China's largest providers of the technology—were unreliable when it came to identifying darker-skinned people. Buolamwini, who is Black, further proves this point in the 2020 documentary *Coded Bias*, in which she demonstrates how a face-recognition program completely ignores her until she puts on a white mask. Only then does the software even register her presence.

In 2018, the American Civil Liberties Union of Northern California made sure this discriminatory treatment got federal attention. It conducted its own study, using photos of members of Congress, and found that the face-recognition system they used falsely matched twenty-eight members with mug shots taken by police departments. The false matches were disproportionately with people of color.

The studies were an outgrowth of years of pressure by academics and activists to rein in the rogue technology and publicize its corrosive effects. Without these protests and research studies, we may never have known about the racial discrepancies in the algorithms and seen how widespread the problem was. The protests were unfortunately augmented by real-life examples of the technology going wrong: the arrests of three Black men, based on face-recognition programs, that turned out to be bogus. The scariest part is how often this could be happening, and the fact that we might never know.

The arrest of one of the men, Robert Williams, happened on his front lawn as his wife and two young daughters watched. The episode reads more like a narrative from the old East Germany and its Stasi secret police than anything we assume could happen in the US in 2020. When the Detroit police called Williams during the day and told him to turn himself in, he thought it was a prank. But when he pulled into his driveway that evening after work, he was penned in by a police car, taken out of his SUV, handcuffed, and whisked to jail.

"As any other person would be, I was confused, scared—and yes, angry—that this was happening to me," Williams told the ACLU. "And as any other Black man would be, I had to consider what could happen if I asked too many questions or displayed my anger openly, even though I knew I had done nothing wrong."

Williams spent the next eighteen hours in an overcrowded holding cell, sleeping on the cold concrete floor, without anyone telling him why he'd been arrested. It turns out that a store had been robbed, and the store owner had provided surveillance footage to the Detroit Police Department. The Detroit police sent a blurry image from that footage to the Michigan State Police, who ran it through their face-recognition program, which incorrectly matched it with a photograph of Williams from an old driver's license.

"My daughters can't unsee me being handcuffed and put into a police car," Williams said. "They continue to suffer that trauma. Even today, when my daughters encounter the coverage about what happened to me, they are reduced to tears by their memory of those awful days. We just don't know what kind of long-term impact this might have on them. We do know that this was their first-ever encounter with the police."

Williams's conclusion is the same as mine: Congress needs to stop law enforcement from using face-recognition software until proper rules are set.

Even for the technology's more innocent uses, no guidelines exist. The industry is allowed to do whatever it wants to do, without the consent of the people whose faces are being compiled in databases. We don't even know *how*, exactly, the photos are being collected. Remember the app that uses your smartphone's camera to show what your face might look like in old age? Perhaps the game was just a way for you to give up an image of your face. Think of the many times you've gone into an office and been photographed for a security badge. Every building in New York City seems to have a camera for that purpose. When you visit a hospital or an assisted-living facility, they often take your photo. Where does it go? Who has access to it? Is someone selling it? And if so, who's buying? How about a school ID, or a day-camp photo, or any image you might post on Facebook or Instagram or TikTok or Twitter? Robert Williams was jailed because his driver's license photo tagged him as a suspect. Should we pay more attention to the accuracy of our driver's license photos? Forget looking good. A better photo might keep you out of jail. We just don't know. Why shouldn't we expect the worst?

We could blame companies such as Amazon, whose Rekognition software is the most popular with law enforcement. Amazon is a big, rich target. But wait. Shouldn't we be blaming ourselves? We're the ones who traded our expectation of privacy for the promise of stricter security. That's exactly what galls me. We had no say in that trade-off. We weren't consulted. We never gave real consent. If we were part of the process at all, it was just assumed we'd be in favor. But it turns out that any additional security we might have gained in that transaction, if we'd even wanted it, is so deeply flawed it's useless. Worse than useless— it violates the fundamental human rights of people of color.

In 2001, the visionary computer scientist Philip E. Agre published an argument against automatic face recognition in public places titled "Your Face Is Not a Bar Code." Writing while the September 11 terrorist attacks were still fresh, Agre was sensitive to the balance between safety and civil liberties, a debate that Americans seem to conduct less and less often as time goes on. One of the important points he made seems on the nose two decades later: "Face recognition will work well enough to be dangerous, and poorly enough to be dangerous as well." He meant that the two main problems with the technology are its promise of constant surveillance if it works well, and its tendency to misidentify people if it doesn't.

Agre, however, was against banning the technology altogether, even if we could. He made a distinction between the automatic scanning of faces in public places like airports, ballparks, and shopping malls, and applications that are "strongly bounded by legal due process, for example matching a mug shot of an arrested person to a database of mug shots of people who have been arrested in the past." He warned that even if face recognition were used only in the most limited of circumstances, the technology would still allow authoritarian governments such as China's "to track the public movements of everyone in the country."

In the US, we don't have that problem—yet. However, combining videos captured by Amazon's Ring doorbell cameras with Amazon's Rekognition software and making the end result available to law enforcement agencies has brought us perilously close. We can be watched, and if it isn't for nefarious reasons, that's because the watcher chooses not to do evil. Relying on the watcher to behave well and in our best interests, when the watcher has all the technology and all the know-how and all the financial incentive not to, is a perilous place to be.

That's why it was such a pleasant surprise when Amazon announced in 2020 that it was putting a one-year moratorium on law enforcement use of the Rekognition technology. (The moratorium was renewed in 2021 until further notice.) The next day, Microsoft announced that it would stop selling its face-recognition system to police departments until federal law regulates the technology. IBM had already decided to discontinue its face-recognition system.

The potential for abuse is simply too high. We can't rely on companies to make these calls. We need Congress to step in with commonsense guidelines, including a prohibition of automatic public face recognition and a limiting of law enforcement's use of the technology. Consumer Reports has crafted a model privacy bill for state and federal lawmakers to base legislation on. It prohibits companies from collecting and using face-recognition data unless such practice is in service of a particular transaction initiated by a consumer. Until such policies are implemented, we have to continue to agitate.

ALGORITHMS HAVE A RACE PROBLEM 2.0

Algorithms themselves, of course, don't harbor discriminatory attitudes about race. The bias comes from the information that's used to train the software. If images of white men dominate what's inputted, the face-recognition machine becomes more accurate at identifying white men. The US Commerce Department's study on face recognition found that algorithms developed in China tended to be better at identifying Asian faces than the American-made algorithms.

Having people work closely with algorithms might be the dream of a business technologist like Sylvain Duranton, but in other contexts humans are the bug in the AI system. Maybe you remember Tay, the AI chatbot that Microsoft introduced to Twitter in 2016. Twitter users taught Tay, which news website the Verge called "essentially a robot parrot," to spout racist and sexist garbage. In less than a day, the experimental discourse went from casual conversation to casual Nazism, and Tay was unhooked from the social media hellscape.

As you can see, artificial intelligence still has wrinkles to iron out. Until it gets to a more socially acceptable place, we're saddled with algorithmic flaws galore. Here are a few more.

In 2017, *Consumer Reports* and ProPublica discovered that drivers living in predominantly minority urban neighborhoods were charged higher auto insurance premiums on average than drivers with similar safety records in nonminority neighborhoods that had comparable levels of risk.

In 2018, the software created by Amazon to help companies identify the most promising job candidates was discovered to be biased against women. The algorithm had learned to spot "good" résumés on a diet of examples heavily skewed toward men.

Allstate, the fourth-largest auto insurer in the US, proposed big premium hikes exclusively for customers who its formulas concluded were less likely than others to jump to another insurance provider. An investigation by *Consumer Reports* and the Markup concluded that the insurance company had put together what could be called a "suckers list" of drivers deemed by an algorithm to be less likely to switch companies. Allstate used factors that had nothing to do with consumers' driving records and their risk for filing a claim. In this case, it was middle-age drivers who would have been discriminated against for no reason other than their shopping tendencies.

These examples are bad enough, but even more chilling is the use of flawed algorithms to determine medical treatment. In September 2020, my *Consumer Reports* colleague Kaveh Waddell told the story of a Black man he called Eli—not his real name—whose kidneys were so badly damaged that his doctor, Vanessa Grubbs, tested him to see if he was eligible for a transplant. Kidneys were in short supply. About 23,400 transplants took place in 2019, and more than 92,000 people were on a national waiting list.

To get a spot on the list, a patient needed to score a 20 or below on a test for what's called glomerular filtration rate, or GFR, which measures how fast kidneys can filter blood. The normal rate is 60. The test also takes into account the patient's race. For Black patients, the test lab multiplies the initial GFR score by what's called a race-adjustment coefficient. When Grubbs ordered a GFR test for Eli, she got two numbers back. The report said his GFR was estimated at 20 "if not African American," and 24 "if African American." There were no other racial categories.

If Eli had been white, his blood test result would have qualified him for a chance at a transplant. Because he is Black, however, he didn't make the cut. The use of two different numbers, one for Black patients and another for everyone else, dates to a 1999 study claiming that Black people might have different kidney function than other types of people.

Similar race adjustments, also called race corrections, crop up in all sorts of medical algorithms. This kind of information is rarely shared with patients. Some of the algorithms purport to help doctors decipher test results like Eli's. Others combine medical and demographic information to recommend a specific diagnostic test, or produce a risk score that helps determine whether a patient is a good candidate for a particular treatment. They can also help determine payouts in injury lawsuits. Black former players say a concussion settlement with the National Football League may have shortchanged them due to a controversial practice in neuropsychology called race-norming, in which Black patients' cognitive test scores are calculated differently than white patients' scores, based on bogus research that has found that African Americans perform worse on some tests of cognition than white Americans.

Needless to say, race adjustments are a hot topic of debate. Critics say the studies they're based on tend to be unreliable because they assume that Black bodies are fundamentally different from others, a premise not supported by science. Supporters of the algorithms say that although race adjustments are approximations, they can point doctors toward more effective medical treatment for their Black patients.

An August 2020 study published online in the *New England Journal of Medicine* looked at race adjustments in thirteen clinical algorithms used across specialties, including heart, lung, and kidney. The paper didn't quantify how race corrections affect health outcomes, but it raised troubling questions. In most cases, the race adjustments suggested that Black patients were less likely to be suffering from serious medical conditions than otherwise identical non-Black patients. That could make them less likely to get referred to specialists and to receive appropriately aggressive treatments, the authors wrote.

The study also showed how some race adjustments can make childbirth riskier for Black mothers. If a pregnant woman has had a cesarean section in the past, her doctor can use a risk score to help decide which kind of delivery to recommend. The "vaginal birth after C-section" risk calculator makes a vaginal delivery appear to be more dangerous for Black and Hispanic patients than for others, the study found. That could lead to medical professionals steering a pregnant woman toward a C-section, which is generally riskier than a vaginal birth. Black women are more likely to undergo C-sections than members of any other racial group in the US. The Black infant-mortality rate in 2018 was twice the rate for white babies.

Hospital emergency rooms also use calculations very much like "race corrections." If a patient arrives complaining about abdominal pain, for instance, a quick formula can help medical staff decide whether to run tests to detect kidney stones. If the patient is Black, the conventional instructions suggest that they're less likely to have kidney stones than other types of patients, reducing the odds they'll get tested. Similar race-based adjustments at emergency rooms during the early days of COVID-19 appear to have had fatal consequences.

"We've really never stopped doing these Black-white comparisons and just assuming that Black people are inherently different," Vanessa Grubbs says. In a way, Eli was lucky. Grubbs, an associate professor at the University of California–San Francisco, has long been skeptical of race-adjusted formulas. She didn't settle for Eli's initial GFR test results. "I didn't believe that just because he was Black he had higher kidney function," she says. Sure enough, when she conducted another GFR test on Eli, he scored a 20. He was eligible for the transplant waiting list.

Not every medical test or procedure involves a race-adjusted algorithm. But patients with certain chronic conditions, such as kidney disease, heart disease, hypertension, and some forms of cancer, are the most likely to encounter them, says David Jones, a Harvard Medical School professor and coauthor of the *New England Journal of Medicine* study on race adjustments. Patients have a right to ask about them, he says, just as they should feel free to inquire about any other aspect of their care.

"I'd likely ask the doctor, 'I'm just curious: Do any of the tests or practice guidelines you're using take my race or ethnicity into consideration?'" Jones suggests. If the answer is yes, Jones counsels skepticism over how the doctor is classifying your race and using it to inform the treatment they deliver.

Algorithms have penetrated the most intimate parts of our lives, with new challenges for consumers. Most of us accept that health care is a marketplace, but many of us don't question what medical professionals tell us or feel as if we're able to shop around for doctors or different medicines. I know that my parents—and this is not uncommon in Latino households—don't doubt doctors because they're seen as authority figures. But as consumers of medical care, we have to ask ourselves: How can we guard against algorithmic biases in treatment and hold the companies that use them accountable?

So far, our government hasn't pursued policies to ensure fairness in algorithms or even to require transparency in the process of how companies compile the information or what weight they may give each part of it. We haven't created avenues of recourse for consumers who might be discriminated against. We also know that industry can't be counted on to self-regulate—in many cases, companies aren't even aware that discrimination is going on until after journalists, customers, or protesters unravel it. In June 2021, for example, US senators asked Alphabet, the parent company of Google and YouTube, to undergo an independent audit to judge how its products and policies affected

racial equity—a welcome self-examination many other companies have undertaken. Two months later, Alphabet hadn't even
responded to the lawmakers. Did it reject the idea? Had the
company already conducted an audit? We don't know, because
all we heard was crickets.

Clearly, if companies simply ignore calls for voluntary au-
dits, we need new laws that compel them to bring fairness,
transparency, and accountability to the secretive world of algorithms. The good news is that consumers hold tremendous
power. By wielding our collective influence, we can press for
those laws. Many biases may still be hardwired into our society,
but that doesn't mean we have to sit on our hands as they replicate themselves in the digital economy. It's within our power—
and, indeed, it's our responsibility—to ensure that the digital
world evolves in the direction of greater equality.

DISCRIMINATION COSTS LIVES

In the medical world, treatment is hardly equal. That was true
long before COVID-19 laid bare many of the gross disparities. A
2018 report found that Latino men were 21 percent less likely
to receive optimal treatment for high-risk prostate cancer than
white men, and in a 2016 study, most of the country's medical
students said they believed that Black Americans had higher
pain thresholds than whites, leading to white Americans receiving pain medication while Black Americans were left to suffer.

Then COVID-19 came along and revealed the ways racial
and ethnic bias could worsen an already horrific situation. Many
Latinos, for example, were left on their own to deal with language barriers as they found themselves on the front lines of the
pandemic. We talk about the needless suffering of patients, and

mourn their deaths, but we don't usually discuss the feelings of guilt and frustration that linger with loved ones after the shadow of the virus has moved on. Jennifer Montesdeoca is one family member who may never get over the feeling that she could have done more. Jennifer was the English translator for her family in Philadelphia. Her mother and sixty-eight-year-old grandfather both tested positive for the coronavirus, and though her mother made it through, her grandfather died. Her family assures Jennifer that she did all she could do for her grandfather, but she doesn't believe it.

"It's real and it's very painful," Jennifer said in an interview with a local TV station. "I wish I could have done more. I was trying to translate all to my mom without crying. It was hard. I'm trying to say, 'Okay, let me cool down and let me explain it and try my best not to shut down.'"

Jennifer blamed her grandfather's death on the language barrier, which made it difficult to communicate his needs to doctors, as well as on a general failure to educate the Latino community early on in the pandemic. "I was looking at it and I was like, 'Okay, so this is happening, and we have to take these precautions,'" she said. "But in Spanish, it came late."

There was a different kind of barrier for the Black Americans who were turned away from hospitals because medical personnel didn't believe their symptoms were bad enough for them to be admitted. Here are two examples from the same region: Relatives of Deborah Gatewood, who worked for thirty-one years drawing blood at Beaumont Hospital in Farmington Hills, outside Detroit, couldn't manage to get her colleagues to believe she might have had a severe case of COVID-19. She was seen in the hospital's emergency room four times because she had trouble breathing, and she was sent away each time. She died at home.

Fifty-six-year-old Gary Fowler had COVID-19 symptoms and visited three emergency rooms at three different Detroit hospitals. He was turned away each time. He died in his bedroom chair, where he was trying to sleep upright because he couldn't breathe lying down. "No one tried to help him," his son, Keith Gambrell, told the *Detroit Free Press*. "He asked for help, and they sent him away."

Though Black Americans have been infected with COVID-19 at about the same rate as whites, and even though Deborah Gatewood and Gary Fowler couldn't get admitted to the hospital, Black Americans have been hospitalized at 2.8 times the rate as whites and have died at twice the rate. Latinos, only half of whom are covered by health insurance compared with three-quarters of white people, have fared even worse, with nearly twice the rate of cases, almost three times the hospitalization rate, and more than twice the rate of deaths than whites.

People with chronic conditions such as asthma and diabetes were more likely to catch the coronavirus and then to endure a severer bout. In Detroit, the biggest majority-Black city in the US, those chronic conditions were more prevalent than in the rest of the state of Michigan. The Centers for Disease Control and Prevention says that race and ethnicity are risk markers for underlying conditions that affect health, a list that also includes socioeconomic status, access to health care, and exposure to the novel coronavirus related to occupation, including that of health worker, first responder, delivery driver, and grocery clerk—many of whom are Black or Latino.

But there may be other factors. Due to redlining, Black residents of Detroit were forced to settle in neighborhoods that whites rejected, some of them in the shadow of industry. One overwhelmingly Black community in the southwestern part of the city is ringed by no fewer than two dozen polluters and potential polluters, including a mill run by US Steel, a Marathon Petroleum refinery, and a coal-fired power station. A link between soot and asthma attacks is well established, though a connection between pollution and COVID-19 hasn't been proved. Bad air, however, does affect the lungs of people who breathe it regularly, according to John Balmes, a pulmonologist and professor of medicine and environmental health sciences in the University of California system. And the damage from soot can be worse. "We think the immune response to the virus is weakened by air-pollution exposure," he told *Bloomberg Businessweek* magazine.

Housing segregation put these people in neighborhoods where avoiding COVID-19 was more difficult than in other communities. And as we're about to see, a consumer product with a built-in bias may have made it harder for them to survive.

BLOOD MAKES NOISE

The first wave of COVID-19, in the spring of 2020, was as frightening a time as I can remember. We were under siege. The enemy was invisible and deadly, and nobody could tell which random activity might get them infected, so people all over the world shuttered themselves in their homes to avoid it. In Los Angeles, car traffic disappeared, and so did smog, revealing the bluest skies in that megalopolis that anyone could recall. New York streets were so empty it was possible to stroll down the middle of Times Square—if you dared leave the safety of your home. People were eager to protect themselves any way they could from the pandemic, which would go on to kill millions around the world.

The virus also exposed racial bias in a consumer product called a pulse oximeter. Consumers in lockdown who were riveted to pandemic news soon learned that the medical devices, which were going for as little as twenty-five dollars, could detect a potential symptom of COVID-19. Oximeters consist of two pieces of plastic with a hinge at one end that allows it to open and close like tiny crocodile jaws. Once it's clamped on a person's fingertip, the device uses small beams of light that pass through the finger to measure the amount of oxygen in the blood. A blood-oxygen level below about 90 percent is a signal to call the doctor or visit the emergency room. Consumers flocked to buy the oximeters.

There is, however, a hitch. The accuracy of oximeters can be affected by a number of factors, such as poor circulation, skin thickness, skin temperature, tobacco use, nail polish—and skin pigmentation. Oximeters don't work as well on people who have darker skin. More pigment in the skin means the light beams used by the oximeter to measure the amount of oxygen in the blood are scattered, rendering the device less accurate. This wasn't just a problem with the types that are sold to consumers. Few medical professionals were aware of the limitations of the tool, which led, during the early stages of the pandemic, to greater numbers of darker-skinned patients getting readings that showed oxygen levels higher, or safer, than they actually were.

In December 2020, a team of University of Michigan doctors announced in a letter to the *New England Journal of Medicine* that oximeters were nearly three times as likely to miss

low oxygen levels in darker-skinned patients than in white patients. "Early in the COVID-19 pandemic, we started to recognize that these measurements seemed to be inaccurate for
Black patients," the researchers wrote. "Our study confirmed
those suspicions, for example finding that sometimes when a
pulse oximeter read 94%, the actual blood level of oxygen was
much lower." The false readings for people of color most likely
resulted in some of them being turned away at hospital emergency rooms.

There was more. The study brought up an uncomfortable
truth: the flaws of the pulse oximeter had been known for decades.
They were simply never corrected. In fact, Hewlett-Packard
years ago designed an oximeter that fit on the top of the ear
and was more accurate than the one designed for the finger.
When the personal-computing revolution broke in the 1980s,
the pioneering electronics company shifted its focus and quit
making oximeters.

That worries me, and what worries me even more is that
other kinds of products will come to market with similar flaws.
Consumer clamor can sometimes push manufacturers to change.
That means we need to speak up.

Indeed, the authors of the University of Michigan study on
oximeters said that an engineering solution to the racially biased device might already be available, and that replacing the
existing oximeters would take time because of their widespread
use, but would be worth the trouble. "Health-care providers and
patient-advocacy groups will need to demand updated technology when it becomes available," they wrote. "Recognizing this
now may lead to improvements in medical technology, better
medical care for Black patients, and greater recognition of struc-
tural racism within medicine."

The results of their research were endorsed by the US Food and Drug Administration in February 2021—but only to a limited degree. The government agency warned consumers about the inaccuracies of pulse oximeters but skipped the part about the racial bias. Nor did it mention another of the tool's shortcomings: gender discrepancies. Not only is the functioning of pulse oximeters based on lighter skin tones; the fit of the devices is nonadjustable and based on men's fingers. This causes problems for women's results. Again, we've known about this issue for years. The oximeter designed by Hewlett-Packard had an added bonus: by being fitted to the top curve of the ear, it avoided the gender disparities caused by a bad fit for many women's fingers. Despite the existence of an oximeter with a better design, the model with the gender and racial bias is the one that's widely available on the market.

DESIGNED BY MEN, FOR MEN

The design of the common pulse oximeter is only one example of a bias in favor of men that's entrenched in many parts of our society. The problems associated with male-centered design and safety testing have only recently begun getting the attention they deserve.

Women don't fit well into Kevlar vests or safety harnesses designed for law enforcement, must often use smartphones too big for their generally smaller hands, and are more likely to have to repeat themselves for voice-command systems in cars that respond better to lower-pitched voices. As NASA discovered to its embarrassment during the high-profile plans for a historic all-women space walk in 2019, there weren't enough space suits on the International Space Station to accommodate two women at the same time. The astronauts were able to success-fully complete the mission, but not until seven months later.

Offices are routinely cooled to temperatures that are too cold for women, who tend to have slower metabolisms. Deter-minations of safe exposure levels to chemicals and other dangers are often based on a hypothetical "reference man," which over-looks the potential risks to women and children. One researcher looking into why women had higher rates of cancer than men with similar amounts of childhood exposure to radiation made the shocking discovery that the body tested for exposure lim-its by the US Nuclear Regulatory Commission was based on a reference man who was between twenty-five and thirty years old, was "Caucasian," and lived a "Western European or North American" lifestyle.

Cars provide one of the most glaring and consequential ex-amples of biased design choices. It's widely known that men are more likely to be involved in vehicle crashes than women, but when accidents do happen, the resulting damage is usu-ally worse for women. Women are 73 percent more likely than men to be seriously injured in a frontal crash when wearing a seat belt and 17 percent more likely to die, even when the use of a seat belt and the individual's height, weight, and the severity of the crash are taken into account. The fact that car designs were deadlier to women has been known to research-ers since the 1980s, yet little has been done to address the problem, which stems from overreliance on a standard crash-test dummy whose body is based on a man's. It wasn't until 2003 that the National Highway Traffic Safety Administration (NHTSA) made use of a "female" dummy standard in their safety tests, but even that one was just a scaled-down version of a male dummy and didn't reflect the biomechanics of a woman's body. It didn't account for the fact that because they are shorter on average, women generally sit closer to the steering wheel when driving, or the different way women's bodies react in high-speed collisions. Furthermore, the female crash-test dummies were more frequently placed in the passenger seat during test crashes, even though half of all drivers today are women.

Since car companies are notorious for designing their safety systems with the aim of passing the tests administered by the NHTSA, the agency must improve its procedures, and it must start now. If the organization is reluctant to take the lead, Congress should intervene with legislation. Doing so will save lives.

THE PINK TAX

Design neglect that leads to potentially dangerous outcomes is bad enough, but it's just one way that women are cheated in the marketplace. Women also suffer from an unequal compensation system. The gap between what women and men earn is narrowing, but far too slowly. In 2020, women in general made eighty-two cents for every dollar men made, with Latinas making just fifty-nine cents and Black women making sixty-four cents. The gender pay divide is a shameful relic from the days, not too long ago, when a woman couldn't open a bank account or obtain a credit card without her husband's permission.

In addition to the pay discrepancy, women are often charged more for products that are similar to those sold to men. This cost difference has been nicknamed the "pink tax." The most comprehensive study of the pink tax was conducted in 2015 by New York City's Department of Consumer Affairs, and it found glaring price differences that cost women money, as the report put it, from cradle to cane. It compared a scooter for small children that was priced at $24.99 to the same model, but in pink, priced at $45.99. Pink bike helmets also cost more than blue ones. Women's clothing cost 8 percent more than men's, and prices for women's personal-care items were 13 percent higher than those intended for men, with the difference in shampoo prices a startling 48 percent. A pack of bladder-control pads for women cost the same as those for men, $11.99, but the package for women contained thirty-nine pads while the men's had fifty-two. A 1994 California Assembly Office of Research study, the latest available, found that the pink tax costs women an additional $1,351 each year for the same products and services that men purchase.

One solution is legislative. The proposed federal Pink Tax Repeal Act would prohibit the sale of substantially similar goods or services that are priced differently based on gender. It would also allow the Federal Trade Commission to enforce violations, and would empower states' attorneys general to take civil action on behalf of consumers. Until the bill is signed into law, women might avoid the pink tax by buying the less expensive alternatives even if they're packaged to appeal to men. In many instances, the difference is only a matter of marketing.

Women are disadvantaged by the kinds of taxes levied by state legislatures too. Though a growing number of states, including my native New Jersey, have exempted tampons and other menstruation-related products from sales tax, others, such as Indiana, which exempts barbecue-flavor sunflower seeds, and Wisconsin, which doesn't tax gun-club memberships, still charge a tax on women's-health items. Many states list these products as nonessential luxuries, while providing tax exemptions for other health and hygiene products like dandruff shampoo, razors, and even Viagra. But menstrual products are necessary items and shouldn't be taxed. Only individual state legislatures can remedy this obvious oversight, and at least twenty have already taken action. It's time for the rest to end this blatantly discriminatory tax.

A $175 BILLION MARKET

Of course, we must also speak out against discrimination toward people with disabilities, who suffer poverty at twice the rate as nondisabled people, and 25 percent of whom experience housing insecurity and homelessness, according to the Ford Foundation. The organization's president, and my friend and former colleague, Darren Walker, has been instrumental in extending the work of philanthropy to help bring Americans with disabilities into the economic mainstream, and what he and many others have accomplished gives us reason for optimism.

Consumers living with disabilities are now part of more than one-third of US households, and they represent market power of $175 billion in discretionary spending. So there's a compelling economic reason for companies to cater to them. Still, the physical marketplace has been historically inhospitable to people with disabilities, and we have to remain vigilant that the online world doesn't replicate the bias.

Sure enough, adaptive fashion received a blow in 2021 from an all-too-predictable source: a wayward algorithm. Facebook took down an advertisement from the apparel retailer Yarrow showing a woman in a wheelchair modeling a pair of pants, but kept online another model wearing the same pants who was shown walking. Retailers complained that similar snubs against adaptive fashion in other circumstances had occurred on TikTok, Amazon, and Facebook's Instagram. They were corrected, but clearly the artificial intelligence behind the algorithm-related discrimination needs correcting too.

Consumers have demanded that companies do more than just talk about diversity, equity, and inclusion, and retailers have responded by showing they care about their disabled customers, even if it's just with a gesture. The UK grocery chain Sainsbury's renamed one of its stores Signsbury's for four days in July 2019 to encourage people to learn and use sign language in the supermarket. Another UK retailer, Home Bargains, introduced a weekly "quiet hour" to provide a more welcoming environment for shoppers with autism. Other retailers offer products geared to a clientele that has specific needs. London-based lingerie maker Megami offers postmastectomy bras that feature discreet pockets for prostheses. Clothing manufacturer I Am Denim designs stretchy jeans for wheelchair users and people undergoing abdominal surgery.

In the US, Nike released its first hands-free athletic shoe in 2021. Prospective buyers of the Nike Go FlyEase include people who can't put on shoes independently. The shoe allows the wearer to slip in, step down, and get moving in one action, requiring no bending or unfastening.

Advocates hope that 3D printing will revolutionize fashion for disabled consumers. Whether to accommodate a specific leg length, an amputation, or the need for easy-access fastenings, printed garments can be made to order. Chances are, such an advancement will benefit all consumers in the way that closed-captioning, once an innovation for the hearing impaired, is now used by millions of Americans, including tweens and teens silently enjoying TikTok videos while they should be paying attention in class. We need to ensure that the marketplace is always making equitable treatment easier for disabled consumers, and that includes looking to design improvements that build accessibility into products, starting in their first days of development.

BROADBAND FROM THE MOUNTAINTOPS

From time to time I hear those who oppose the spread of a societal good such as broadband say they're against it because they don't want to have to pay for somebody else's internet. Many times, they're wrong. They don't have to pay for it, but even if they're forced to, such as through their taxes, maybe they can think of the pennies they contribute as an investment. Getting more people on the internet doesn't improve only those people's lives. It improves the lives of all of us because it expands markets and opens lines of communication with new individuals who contribute fresh perspectives.

Increasingly, Americans think of internet access not as a luxury but as a necessity. In a 2021 national poll, 76 percent said they considered internet service as important as electricity and running water, and three-quarters said they rely on the internet every day of the week.

Here's an example of how internet can transform lower-income, isolated communities. In 2001, as Matthew Rantanen and his team were just beginning the onerous task of piecing together a broadband network for a group of Native American villages in Southern California, 26 kids graduated from high school in that collection of communities. By 2020, after Rantanen and his team had figured out how to provide access to more than seven hundred homes over a sprawling, remote area and made it possible for shuttered public libraries and tribal resource centers to continue providing broadband during the COVID-19 pandemic, the graduating class had rocketed to 127. "It blew me away when I started tracking the numbers," Rantanen said.

The increase in graduates is a welcome sign of positive momentum for Native communities, where nearly one-third of adults nationwide were jobless in the worst days of the pandemic. Broadband offers an avenue out of poverty, a method of connecting with the wider world, and more fun for families.

Rantanen is director of technology for the Southern California Tribal Chairmen's Association in San Diego County and parts of Riverside County. He started out as a graphic designer and moved to broadband-network design because that's where he saw he was needed. Many Native communities are woefully behind on technology. Thirty percent of tribal homes in the US still didn't have emergency 911 service in 2021, according to Rantanen.

How Rantanen and his team were able to put up twenty-two towers in the rough desert terrain to wire an area that stretches 650 miles wide as the crow flies—and to rebuild the network three times, as the technology changed—is a lesson in ingenuity, improvisation, perseverance, and cobbling together a variety of funding sources. Their success shouldn't have taken so much hard work.

To help close the digital divide, Consumer Reports is supporting efforts in Congress to help connect more Americans to broadband. More than one-third of rural Americans lack the service, and Consumer Reports has long advocated that they get it.

The tally of Americans who are unconnected varies depending on the source. The Federal Communications Commission reports that forty-four million households don't have a standard broadband connection, either because they lack access or can't afford it. The data company LightBox claims that the number is more like sixty million. Money plays a big role. In 2019, Pew Research said that 44 percent of adults with household incomes below $30,000 didn't have home broadband.

Those families are missing out on both economic and social opportunities. Broadband makes it immeasurably easier to find a job, go shopping, or sell just about anything. Researchers have shown that where there's broadband, there are economic growth, higher incomes, and lower unemployment. Online access provides mental health support, combats isolation, allows medical professionals to see patients they otherwise might not be able to, and includes schoolchildren in remote learning. Think of how much more prosperous, informed, and connected the country would be with expanded broadband.

Back in 2001, when funding was more scarce than it is now, the Southern California Tribal Chairmen's Association was able to land an initial "digital village" grant from tech giant Hewlett-Packard. They discovered that linking the Native communities to the internet via their preferred method, fiber, meant negotiating rights of way with a long list of property owners—not exactly how they wanted to spend their time. So they decided to go wireless. That meant Rantanen had to educate himself not only on the process of building a network but also on marshaling the support, both financial and technical, that he needed.

Rantanen traveled to Washington to meet with members of Congress, worked his contacts in the Tribal Digital Village network, and tapped the expertise of amenable professors at various universities. On one memorable occasion, an employee received what Rantanen calls a "CliffsNotes version of how to build a network" from Hans-Werner Braun of the High Performance Wireless Research and Education Network of the University of California–San Diego, the tribal group's first mentor in microwave communications.

"Braun basically sat my network administrator down in his kitchen and put two radios across the room from each other and walked him through the configuration process without antennas on them, because you'll burn them up that close together, and said, 'Okay, here's how you connect them. Now, you do it,'" Rantanen recalls. "He played around with it. And then forty-five minutes later, Braun handed him all the stuff and said, 'Okay, now go do that on the mountaintops.' We were out there building the network before we even understood what we were actually doing."

Lack of access to broadband is a national problem. An estimated three million American pupils quit attending class in 2020. Many of them had problems connecting online and gave up. In Los Angeles, as many as 25 percent of students didn't have access to the school district's online educational materials. In Mississippi and Arkansas, about 40 percent of students lacked high-speed internet. In Florida's Miami-Dade County, sixteen thousand fewer students enrolled in fall 2020 compared with the previous year. The New York Times reported on a fifth grader in Mississippi who had to use his mother's cell phone to attend classes because their home had no internet. Mom worked the night shift and didn't come home till nine in the morning, so the fifth grader usually missed the first classes of the day.

Rantanen knows the benefits of broadband for education, but he also knows that Native families could be sold on the inexpensive entertainment available on the internet. "I think kids playing Fortnite is important," Rantanen said. "Kids are on a reservation that's a long ways from those types of entertainment services—movie theaters and arcades and such. Access to thirteen- or fourteen-dollar-a-month entertainment online is huge. Because people are like, 'Oh, you're just creating a Netflix network,' and I'm like, 'Well, so what if I am? We're solving a lot of problems with that Netflix network.'"

Economics and logistics are only two obstacles standing in the way of expanding broadband. Another is the desire of major internet service providers to maintain their status as lords of access. Large ISPs, such as Comcast and AT&T, spent $234 million in 2020 on lobbying, according to a study by Common Cause (a public-interest group) and the Communications Workers of America labor union. The companies want to keep control of broadband by making it illegal for municipalities to build their own networks. The groups said that eighty-three million Americans live under a broadband monopoly.

In 2021, Consumer Reports started a consumer-powered campaign to push for more accessible and affordable internet service by gathering data on prices and internet speeds from consumers across the country. The pandemic made the issue of connectivity even more urgent, and we wanted to get to the bottom of what people were really paying and the quality they were receiving. We succeeded in extending our reach by partnering with more than fifty organizations. Tens of thousands of consumers signed up to participate. People know that the issue is critical for our country and the millions being left behind.

Expanding broadband access is all about pushing America to be as fair and as prosperous as it can be. It's also about tapping all available resources for the good of everyone.

"That next person we connect could be the missing piece of the equation that solves a biological pandemic problem," Rantanen said. "Access is a right. It should be an opportunity that everybody has. It shouldn't be based on where you live, or how much money you make, or anything like that. There are so many brilliant minds out there that get caught in a situation where they never have that access to get out."

WHAT CAN I DO NOW?

Stand Up to Housing Discrimination

Housing discrimination can be based on race, ethnicity, sex, disability, or other federally protected categories. It doesn't only involve people trying to buy a home. The Fair Housing Act covers discrimination in renting, buying, getting a mortgage, seeking housing assistance, or "engaging in other housing-related activities."

If you think this has happened to you, file a federal complaint at the website of the US Department of Housing and Urban Development (hud.gov/fairhousing). Many local and state governments also have specific agencies where you can file a complaint, but the agency to contact changes depending on your location.

You can also turn to fair-housing organizations, like the National Fair Housing Alliance (NationalFairHousing.org), for more detailed resources.

Build Your Credit Score

Your credit score is based on a complicated algorithm whose secretive and potentially error-filled inputs make it difficult to build a good score and easy for a few mistakes to mess it up. Even so, it's used as a gatekeeper to many avenues of success for consumers. Start by monitoring your credit report and being timely with bill payments. Beyond that, here's some advice from experts at Consumer Reports on how to raise your scores.

- **Look out for certain common errors in credit reports.** Our experts suggest using AnnualCreditReport .com to request a free report from a different agency every four months. Some common errors to watch out for:
    » credit accounts that aren't reflected
    » duplicate credit accounts
    » debts incurred by a former spouse
    » bad debts older than seven years

- **Don't apply for several credit cards at once.** Doing so creates numerous inquiries into your credit history and reduces the average amount of time you've had credit cards. Both factors can lower your score.
- **Don't cancel unused cards.** Much of your score is based on total credit, so a canceled card only undermines you. The exception is if the cards carry an annual fee.
- **Keep balances low.** Most people with the highest scores owe less than $3,000 on their accounts.
- **Don't let your credit stay inactive.** Even if you have a credit history, it can become "stale" if you don't continue

to use credit regularly. Credit card companies could close inactive accounts, hurting your credit score.

- **Recognize that building your credit score can take time.** It won't happen overnight. Depending on the reason for low scores, it could take twelve to twenty-four months. But don't give up. Continuous care will help you get out of a credit score hole.

Advocate for Yourself Against Medical Discrimination

As we touched on in this chapter, biases in the medical field can lead to discriminatory results for many consumers. But that discrimination has a wide range, from medical devices that don't work as well for some people to medical professionals not taking some people's pain or accounts of symptoms seriously. Professional advocates are taking steps to change the system from within, but if you're part of a community that experiences this discrimination, experts agree that taking steps to advocate for yourself is the best immediate option. Below are a few pieces of advice from various medical professionals on how to do just that.

- **Be willing to challenge your doctor.** Many communities value deferring to authority figures, including medical professionals. But if you feel that you're not getting the care you need, speak up. As Rumay Alexander, a professor of nursing at University of North Carolina and president of the National League for Nursing, told MarketWatch, "What patients have to remember is they are the experts on themselves. Use 'I' statements to push back, like 'I'm sensing that you're not hearing me,' or 'I'm concerned that you believe I'm exaggerating the intensity of my pain' if you feel your concerns are being minimized." Consumer Reports worked with the American Board of Internal Medicine to come up with the five questions every patient should be ready to ask their doctor before agreeing to any test, treatment, or procedure:

» Do I really need this test or procedure?
» What are the risks and side effects?
» Are there simpler, safer options?
» What happens if I don't do anything?
» How much does it cost, and will my insurance pay for it?

• **Educate yourself on your health and treatment options.** Dr. Deborah Crabbe, a cardiologist and professor at the Lewis Katz School of Medicine at Temple University, says health literacy is one of her "biggest tips," especially for Black women, whose medical concerns are often disproportionately challenged. Kimberly McElroy-Jones, director of community partnerships for community health at Eskenazi Hospital in Indianapolis, also suggests researching your symptoms, the tests you may need, and any other treatments that might come up before you go for your appointment.

• **The health-care system is a marketplace—use it.** Dr. Leo Morales, chief diversity officer for the University of Washington School of Medicine, advises patients who have experienced discrimination to file a complaint with the medical practice and to switch medical professionals. Health care is part of the marketplace, and if you can, take advantage of the competition to get yourself the treatment you deserve.

MORE INFORMATION

For more references, details on these solutions, updates on these issues, and ways to get engaged in taking action, go to BuyerAware.CR.org, or use the QR code below.

CHAPTER FIVE

SAFETY

I LOVE SEAT BELTS.

I know it sounds corny to feel affection for a safety device, but I view them as a symbol, a turning point. Making seat belts standard equipment in American cars sent the message that people mattered and that car companies weren't going to profit without taking safety into account. Seat belts are one of the great things we've accomplished by bringing consumers, government, and manufacturers together to save lives.

It wasn't that long ago that Americans were left to rattle around in their cars. I have a vivid memory of being four or five years old and riding in my father's two-tone Chevy sedan. My grandfather sat in the middle of the front seat—remember bench seats?—and I sat between him and the passenger door. Another driver cut us off and my father jammed on the brakes, sending me toppling headfirst into the dashboard. My grand-father asked me if I was okay. I told him I was, but I remember my lip quivering because I didn't want anyone to see me cry. Still, I was lucky. I could have been hurt far worse.

Friends tell me they had similar experiences. Some of those two-tone Chevy sedans are still around, and every time I see one I remember crashing into the dashboard without a seat belt to stop me. That would never happen to a child today. A car without seat belts has become one of those bygone oddities from a distant era that make today's young people shake their heads and say, "How did you live like that?"

Safety is the quintessential consumer issue. People have a lot of questions about the products they use, but "Will I be safe?" is *the* question. What consumers have been able to achieve over the years is amazing. People are so much safer than they were at the turn of the twentieth century, and it took a lot of work to get to where we are today.

Leaders in the early 1900s laid the foundation, including Upton Sinclair through his book *The Jungle*. Sinclair described unimaginable working conditions that enabled a meatpacking worker to tumble into a vat of bubbling lard and perish. His body, mauled, chopped, and combined with animal by-products, presumably made its way to families' kitchen tables. The meat industry was incensed at such a grim portrayal, but so was the public. That's why Congress passed the Pure Food and Drug Act and created a federal agency, the Food and Drug Adminis-tration, to oversee the meat industry and many others.

The 1962 publication of Rachel Carson's *Silent Spring* ex-posed the death and devastation caused by chemical pesticides that harmed air, water, and all living things and nearly drove the

bald eagle to extinction. Carson's revelations eventually led to
the creation of the Environmental Protection Agency, an awak-
ened vigilance regarding the damage chemicals can inflict, and
the sentiment, still strong and still correct despite a barrage
of recent attacks, that science can both identify problems and
guide us to solutions.

Ralph Nader's 1965 exposé, *Unsafe at Any Speed*, ushered
in a time of breakthroughs in car safety. It also led to the establishment of a government regulator, the National Highway
Traffic Safety Administration, that has partnered with consumers and the auto industry to make driving safer. Since the book's
publication, fatalities per hundred-million vehicle miles traveled have dropped from 5.3 to 1.4, meaning roughly 3.5 million
lives have been saved.

These developments didn't just happen. Sinclair, Carson,
and Nader were visionaries who inspired consumers to pressure
companies and government to put people before profit. We've
required carmakers to adopt as routine safety features the seat
belt, the shoulder harness, power steering, engines fueled by
unleaded gasoline, stability control, airbags, antilock brakes,
backup cameras, and automatic emergency braking. We've
forced flammable clothing off the market. We've forced industry to stop the manufacture of many toxic contaminants, and
made efforts to keep them away from our drinking water, our
garden beds, our forests, and our dinner tables. We've helped
create standards for what's in our food and how it's grown, produced, and processed. These are fights that took decades of
sustained determination that continue to this day.

The work's not over. In this chapter, we'll focus on current
examples of advocates pushing for consumer safety and the

obstacles still in their way. Not only are we fighting to secure the newest method of protection (the "seat belts" of the modern age); we also need to prepare for those of the future.

One of the toughest obstacles to achieving a more consumer-focused marketplace is people's assumption that it already exists. Just about all respondents to a 2020 Consumer Reports survey—97 percent—said they believed that manufacturers safety-tested their products before sending them out to be sold. The truth is almost none are required to do so. We assume they do because we want to trust that someone is looking out for us. In reality, the government has created gaping holes where safety testing ought to be. Without government requirements or industry-wide rules, most manufacturers decide for themselves how much testing a product needs, if any, and what threshold of danger is acceptable. Manufacturers can often simply slap on a warning label to compensate for a dangerous design, in an attempt to shift the safety-monitoring burden to consumers and shield themselves from any responsibility for defective products.

A big part of our job going forward is convincing car manufacturers, food producers, furniture makers, baby-product companies, and others that it's in their best interests to make their products safer and to respond with openness when a question about a product arises. Some companies have embraced these standards. Others simply hunker down. It's an old public relations strategy to blame consumers for injuries and deaths, hoping that people will continue to believe the product is safe if users would only follow the manufacturer's instructions. In many cases, this is simply not true. If a product has a defect, it poses a hazard no matter how consumers use it. A company's defensive reaction to negative news only keeps deadly products on store shelves. Even when infants are at risk.

HOW MANY CHILDREN?

One universal truth about babies is they don't sleep through the night. They're not *supposed* to sleep through the night. They need to eat. Another universal truth is that babies' nighttime schedules will exhaust their parents in a soul-eroding way that feels as if it will last forever. There was a period of time when I barely had the opportunity to have a conversation with my brother Val. When he visited, he would nod off in the middle of our conversations. I tried not to take the sudden snoring personally. That lasted several years, until his girls slept through the night. When the Fisher-Price Rock 'n Play Sleeper burst onto the market in October 2009, parents like my brother who were desperate for a few hours of rest heralded it as a lifesaver.

As *Consumer Reports* reporter Rachel Rabkin Peachman tells us, the story of how this unsafe product was introduced, became a must-have item for new parents, and stayed on the market for more than a decade spotlights critical failures in the American product-safety system. It's a cautionary tale about how the government agency that's supposed to protect consumers from dangerous products keeps important information about injuries and deaths locked away from public scrutiny. It also illustrates just how much leeway manufacturers have to bring products to market without safety testing, and it outlines the marketplace changes we need to ensure that dangerous products don't spend years sitting on retail shelves, in American homes, and for sale on secondary markets such as Craigslist and Facebook Marketplace.

Brands like Fisher-Price have earned the trust of consumers over the course of decades. I was a babysitter in the 1970s, and every family I worked for had either the family-farm playset, the telephone pull toy, or that maddening xylophone. This brand was and continues to be everywhere that kids are. Generations of parents come to view companies like Mattel, its corporate parent, almost like friends. We don't expect friends to betray us.

In 2008, when Linda Chapman came up with the blueprint for the Rock 'n Play Sleeper, she was a Fisher-Price toy designer who had no experience with products aimed at infants. Chapman drew from her own days in the 1990s as the mother of an infant son who was kept awake by a persistent case of reflux. She remembered the feeling of bone-deep exhaustion. Her design for the product had children reclining at a thirty-degree angle on a frame with a restraint harness and sidewalls and head support made of soft bedding. At that angle, Chapman figured, reflux wouldn't bother infants, while the rocking motion would lull them to sleep and keep them asleep so Mom and Dad could get a break.

Unfortunately, Chapman and her employer didn't heed a 1994 directive from the American Academy of Pediatrics recommending that babies sleep alone on their backs on a firm, flat surface that's free of soft bedding and restraints. Babies' heads are too heavy for their developing neck muscles to control, the pediatricians said, and when a baby sleeps on an incline their head can loll forward or to the side and block the windpipe, creating an asphyxiation hazard. As for reflux, pediatric gastroenterologists say that sleeping on an incline doesn't help and can actually worsen the condition. This knowledge had been circulating since the early 1990s.

Even so, Mattel's hazard-analysis team didn't sound the alarm. No pediatricians with sleep expertise were consulted. Fisher-Price marketed the Rock 'n Play Sleeper in ads and in packaging as suitable for all-night sleep but did no testing to prove it was safe for that purpose. The thirty-degree angle they chose for the product was based on a hunch.

Less than a year after the Rock 'n Play Sleeper went on sale, the Consumer Product Safety Commission (CPSC), the federal agency responsible for policing dangerous products, created new standards based on medical recommendations that set a maximum incline of ten degrees for bassinets, which are small beds on legs that often rock and are meant for babies up to about five months old. Instead of recalling the Rock 'n Play Sleeper, with its thirty-degree angle, Fisher-Price asked the agency to create a new category for sleepers like the Rock 'n Play. That would ensure the new bassinet rules wouldn't apply to the Rock 'n Play. The agency complied. So the key feature that made the product unsafe, its angle, became the thing that essentially exempted it from government safety standards.

In 2011, the Australian government said the Rock 'n Play couldn't be sold there because of asphyxiation danger. Soon after, the Royal College of Midwives in the UK told Fisher-Price that it wouldn't endorse the product as a sleeper because it was only suitable for short periods of supervised wakefulness. Canada permitted the product to be marketed only as the Rock 'n Play Soothing Seat rather than as a sleeper.

Meanwhile, in the US, doctors raised alarms. When a Georgia pediatrician called and wrote to Fisher-Price in February 2013 to warn that the product was unsafe for infant sleep, the company emailed back that "the Rock 'n Play Sleeper complies with all applicable standards." At the time, however, there were no standards to comply with. The Rock 'n Play Sleeper no longer qualified as a bassinet, so it didn't need to adhere to bassinet standards, and the new "inclined sleeper" category wouldn't officially be created until 2015, two years in the future. It wasn't revealed until 2018, when a Fisher-Price employee was deposed for a lawsuit, that the company knew, even when communicating with the Georgia pediatrician, that the sleeper had been linked to fourteen infant deaths.

The public remained unaware of the dangers of the Rock 'n Play Sleeper, and its popularity grew. The product became a number one best seller on Amazon and was given a "Moms Love It" award by WhatToExpect.com and Babies R Us. The product's success inspired other companies to create similar items, spawning a series of knockoffs.

Meanwhile, the number of deaths related to the sleepers mounted. They weren't disclosed to the public by Fisher-Price but reported privately to the Consumer Product Safety Commission by manufacturers, hospitals, and consumers. A two-month-old girl in Hidalgo County, Texas, was found on her back in the sleeper with her chin on her shoulder, cutting off her airway; the mother of a two-month-old boy in Jacksonville, Florida, discovered him with blood coming out of his nose and mouth after a nap in his sleeper; a three-month-old boy in Leesville, Louisiana, was found with cheeks cold, pacifier in mouth, not breathing. Sara Thompson, of Nazareth, Pennsylvania, told the CPSC in December 2012 that her son had died in the Rock 'n Play Sleeper in September 2011. The agency passed the information to Fisher-Price's risk-management team, which documented the incident as an "injury flag."

Some babies, like five-month-old Ezra Overton of Alexandria, Virginia, were found dead on their bellies after rolling over in the Rock 'n Play. He'd been put to sleep on his back one evening shortly before Christmas 2017 and was found in the middle of the night with his face pressed against the sleeper's padding. "He was blue, and his body was, it was hard, and he didn't feel real," said Ezra's dad, Keenan Overton. Ezra had smothered to death.

As the death toll rose, Fisher-Price declined to pull its product from the market or make design changes. During a deposition, Kitty Pilarz, the director of product safety for Fisher-Price's parent company, Mattel, was asked to confirm that Fisher-Price had not changed how it marketed the Rock 'n Play Sleeper despite evidence of the deaths. Her reply: "Correct."

"Is there a particular number [of] children that have to die before that's going to be looked into?" the plaintiff's lawyer asked. Pilarz didn't answer.

Despite the lawsuits, the CPSC also stayed largely mum on the growing number of deaths. The reason: Section 6(b) of the Consumer Product Safety Act.

Section 6(b) requires the CPSC to seek permission from a manufacturer before it publicly releases information about the company or its products, even when it's warning about injuries or deaths. Section 6(b) also allows companies to negotiate the language the agency uses in press releases in the event of a safety alert or product recall. Proponents say that by giving companies a chance to review safety concerns first, the law prevents the government from unfairly damaging a company's reputation.

I think Section 6(b) is an abomination that allows defective products to continue to kill or injure consumers, as was the case with the Rock 'n Play. Congress ought to toss Section 6(b) in the trash. "People die because of Section 6(b)," said Elliot Kaye, a former CPSC chairman. "It's that simple."

Even without the constraints of Section 6(b), the CPSC doesn't have the ability to recall products on its own. The agency is required to get the company's approval or sue the company for a recall, an expensive, time-consuming step it rarely takes.

Eventually, on May 31, 2018, nearly nine years after the Rock 'n Play Sleeper's launch, the CPSC issued a mild warning in the form of an alert posted on its website titled, "Caregivers Urged to Use Restraints with Inclined Sleep Products." Its vague warning to consumers was to "be aware of the hazards when infants are not restrained in inclined sleep products," and to "always use restraints and stop using these products as soon as an infant can roll over."

Only in the alert's fourth paragraph was the possibility of death mentioned: "CPSC is aware of infant deaths associated with inclined sleep products. Babies have died after rolling over in these sleep products."

The announcement failed to list products by name, and many parents familiar with the Rock 'n Play Sleeper would have no idea what an "inclined sleep product" was.

In early 2019, Rachel Rabkin Peachman and the *Consumer Reports* team were reviewing data they'd requested from the CPSC. It included information on product failures, injuries, and deaths that manufacturers, health-care providers, and consumers had provided to the agency—data that *Consumer Reports* analyzes regularly. This time, there was something unusual: the manufacturers and product names were not edited out, as Section 6(b) requires.

The government agency had made a mistake by releasing unredacted information. There in plain view were details of as many as twenty-nine infant deaths linked to the Fisher-Price

Rock 'n Play Sleeper and other deaths in similar products, such as Kids II Rocking Sleepers. For the first time, the vast scope of the deaths, as well as the brands that caused them, were exposed to the public.

After *Consumer Reports* contacted the CPSC for comment, revealing the error, the agency's lawyers sent letters to *Consumer Reports* demanding that the data be destroyed and nothing be published based on it.

How absurd. I wouldn't have believed it except I read those letters, with their threatening tone, and backed the *Consumer Reports* team's desire to press forward.

On April 5, 2019, Fisher-Price and the agency issued a joint announcement. It was another alert, this one warning that ten infants had died in the Rock 'n Play Sleeper since 2015 after they had "rolled from their back to their stomach or side, while unrestrained."

Consumer Reports immediately went to Fisher-Price to set the record straight. The data showed that although ten infants had died in the specific circumstances cited in the alert, there were at least twenty-nine infants' deaths linked to the Rock 'n Play Sleeper. A Fisher-Price spokesperson confirmed to *Consumer Reports* that the company knew of "approximately thirty-two fatalities since the 2009 product introduction." They also noted that Fisher-Price did "not believe any deaths have been caused by the product."

They were blaming parents for the tragedies.

On April 8, 2019, a *Consumer Reports* investigative story tied the Rock 'n Play Sleeper to dozens of deaths, and we emphatically called for the product's recall. The findings aired nationally on every evening news program and were published online and in newspapers across the country.

Within two weeks, Fisher-Price went from downplaying a problem to recalling nearly five million sleepers. By the end of the month, Kids II recalled all of its nearly seven hundred thousand inclined infant sleepers.

As the controversy unfolded, Fisher-Price continued to maintain that its Rock 'n Play Sleeper was safe when used as directed. The company's April 5, 2019, alert said that "the reported deaths show that some consumers are still using the product when infants are capable of rolling and without using the three-point harness restraint."

It would later become clear that the restraints didn't prevent deaths, yet this misleading narrative continued even after the recall. In a message on its website describing the recall, Fisher-Price general manager Chuck Scothon said, "While we continue to stand by the safety of all of our products, given the reported incidents in which the product was used contrary to safety warnings and instructions, we've decided in partnership with the Consumer Product Safety Commission . . . that this voluntary recall is the best course of action."

The idea that parents were to blame for their babies' deaths still haunts Sara Thompson, the Pennsylvania mother who first contacted the government agency in December 2012. Her son Alex had never rolled over in the sleeper, she says. In fact, the morning he died, Thompson had placed him on his back and found him less than fifteen minutes later in the same position—not breathing. She'd only learned about the sleeper's connection to her son's death through the *Consumer Reports'* investigation, nearly eight years after Alex died.

In addition to her grief, Thompson has been burdened by attacks on social media from trolls who blame her for her son's death. "So many people believe what Fisher-Price said, that it's all deaths from babies rolling over," she said. "At what point is Fisher-Price forced to take ownership for publicly blaming all the parents of the babies who died?"

It took more time to ensure that secondary-market sellers stopped offering the sleepers even though recall laws forbid resale. While eBay uses filters and a team of employees that scours the site for illegal goods, resale platforms like Facebook and Craigslist rely on warnings, deep in their terms-of-service agreements, that urge users not to sell banned products.

Consumer Reports discovered one of the sleepers on sale for twenty-five dollars on Craigslist in August 2021,* more than two years after the original recall. "Very suitable for the first six months!" the seller wrote. Some sellers might have been unaware of the recalls, but others have used the hashtag #BlackMarket to flaunt their decision to continue selling the Rock 'n Play Sleeper after its ban, misleading parents with the promise that, as long as they follow the instructions, the product is safe.

In the eleven years of the sleeper's availability on the market, about one hundred infants died. The product might still be on the market today if it weren't for an embarrassing clerical error by the CPSC. It shouldn't take a fluke bureaucratic blunder to keep babies safe.

FINDING A MORAL PLACE

The Rock 'n Play saga illustrates so much about the dysfunction in America's product-recall system. That's one reason why I tell the story in such detail. Another reason, I have to confess,

---

* By October 2021, the listing was gone.

is how proud I am of Rachel's investigative reporting and how she and a team of colleagues were such bulldogs in pursuing the truth, despite sustained resistance from Fisher-Price and the Consumer Product Safety Commission. We worked hard to advocate with and for Rock 'n Play consumers, and we really made a difference for families who otherwise would never have known the hazards of the sleeper.

There are some who think Consumer Reports should stick to only giving advice to buyers of household items, but they may not know that working for a more fair and just marketplace has always been embedded in our DNA and always will be. Reviews and ratings are only part of what consumers need. This story is a great example of why we do what we do. We fight for and along with consumers however we can—and the stakes are high when we fight to save lives.

Another reason I tell the story is because the Rock 'n Play narrative shows in stark and unmistakable ways the hurdles we have to overcome in order to bring consumer power to the marketplace. We won this round, we've won many others, and we'll win many more. But we can't declare victory until all institutional obstacles are cleared.

That's why we push for broad changes to the marketplace that will make life better for all consumers even while battling over a single product. There's always a wider cause. We need standards, rules, and agencies that protect consumers and hold companies accountable. We can't allow them to hide behind perverse rules and shameless public relations tactics. We also need those agencies to be as fearless as Rachel was in safeguarding families.

Mattel and Fisher-Price aren't the only firms to use a timeworn strategy to defend their harmful product: claim all is well, blame the victims, and extend the product's time on store shelves. Companies must recognize that only a partnership with their customers and the government will bring about a marketplace that works for all Americans. Until then, we need to call out reckless behavior wherever we find it, or other businesses will think they can get away with it.

Thanks to campaigns like the one to recall the Rock 'n Play, they can't. Let's look at a case concerning Peloton, the interactive stationary-bike company that upended the at-home-fitness industry. The company's ultimate response to a safety crisis signaled that we've made some progress when it comes to corporate accountability and how quickly companies come clean.

On March 18, 2021, John Foley, Peloton's chief executive officer and cofounder, announced that a child had died in an accident involving Peloton's Tread+, a $4,295 treadmill that had been on the market only since November 2020.

"While we are aware of only a small handful of incidents involving the Tread+ where children have been hurt, each one is devastating to all of us at Peloton, and our hearts go out to the families involved," Foley said in a statement. The company urged Peloton users to take safety warnings seriously and asked them to keep their treadmills where children couldn't get to them. In PR speak, that's called a holding statement. You say as little as possible, buy time to figure out next steps, and hope the news cycle goes somewhere else. Peloton evidently failed to realize that it was dealing with a full-blown crisis.

Details about the fatal incident were hard to come by, and Peloton said it wouldn't disclose more about it "out of respect for the family and their privacy." The Consumer Product Safety Commission needed to issue a subpoena to get the company to give up contact information for the family of the child who died.

The next month, the safety commission released a harrowing video of a different child getting his head jammed between the floor and the open end of the treadmill. There were no adults in sight, and the moving treads of the device sucked the child deeper underneath the machine. It was excruciating to watch the boy struggle to extricate himself. Finally, to great relief, he was able to get free and walk away. The video was accompanied by what the agency called an "urgent warning": thirty-eight injuries and one death had been linked to the Tread+, and consumers with small children should stop using it. Those who insisted on continuing should do their treadmilling in a locked room inaccessible to children and pets.

Peloton chose to sacrifice its integrity by ignoring its moral compass. Instead of addressing the harm the product had done and working with the government agency to fix it, Peloton called the commission's urgent warning "inaccurate and misleading." The company took the view that consumers were to blame because they hadn't followed product instructions. "While Peloton knows that the Tread+ is safe for the home when used in accordance with warnings and safety instructions, the company is committed to taking whatever steps are necessary and appropriate to further inform members of potential risks," a Peloton press statement read. In other words, it wasn't a product problem; it was a people problem.

We denounced Peloton's reaction. My colleague William Wallace, Consumer Reports' manager of safety policy, called Peloton's handling of the situation "outrageous" and urged the company to take further action. "What Peloton should do is make sure that its customers know the company is putting safety first and that it's going to make them whole," Will told the *Wall*

Street Journal. That advice was picked up by other news outlets and social media and blasted all over the internet.

Between Fisher-Price and Peloton, you could see a pattern in corporate reactions to bad news. Seth Arenstein, editor of PRNEWS and *Crisis Insider*, said their responses followed an "outdated and ineffective crisis-response approach: Deny, deny, deny, and deflect." Both companies claimed that injuries caused by their products were the fault of consumers who had engaged in "unforeseeable misuse." The companies implied that they couldn't possibly plan for the crazy things consumers do with their products and shouldn't be held responsible. But as my Consumer Reports colleague Jen Shecter likes to say, "Every use is a foreseeable use." By fostering a new-age, rooting-for-each-other, community feel among its customers, Peloton had cultivated a well-established brand. When it aggressively shirked responsibility for the product's problems, the company not only chose a path inconsistent with that brand; it also lost its moral place. The deflections of blame reminded me of Wells Fargo, which didn't initially take responsibility for the millions of phony accounts its employees opened in the name of unaware customers in the 2010s. John Stumpf, the bank's CEO, pointed the finger at midlevel, bad-apple executives. But Stumpf was wrong. Wells Fargo had widespread ethical problems that upper management should have been aware of and put a stop to. He was soon out of a job.

Safety issues quickly become trust issues. And trust issues become issues of corporate reputation. It's simply sound business practice to own up to mistakes. Peddling dangerous products can mar a reputation carefully built over decades, but denying responsibility while blaming consumers can completely wreck it. There's nothing like a crisis to test a company's leadership. I spent years on the front lines of unpredictable events, whether it was in the US Senate or at a global philanthropic organization with offices in some of the most challenging regions of the world. Unfortunately, rather than seeing a crisis as a moment requiring leadership, Peloton chose a familiar path: try to avoid any ethical responsibility, focus on minimizing negative media attention instead of taking the higher moral ground, and assume that consumers have no power to think for themselves. Peloton failed to recognize that empathy is what will build its brand. In a corporate crisis, transparency equals caring, and authentic caring engenders trust.

Peloton executives couldn't help but sense public sentiment gathering like a storm against them. They reportedly engaged in intense discussions over the company's strategy regarding Tread+. At some point, a more consumer-friendly approach prevailed. On May 5, less than two months after it disclosed the child's death, and less than a month after calling the Consumer Product Safety Commission's urgent warning "inaccurate and misleading," Peloton reversed course and agreed to a recall. The company told owners of the Tread+ to stop using the product and offered refunds. The CPSC said Peloton was working on software that would automatically lock the Tread+ after use and require a four-digit passcode to unlock it.

"Peloton made a mistake in our initial response to the Consumer Product Safety Commission's request that we recall the Tread+," Foley, the CEO, said in a statement on the company's website. "We should have engaged more productively with them from the outset. For that, I apologize." In short, safety is not the enemy.

Foley continued, "Today's announcement reflects our recognition that, by working closely with the CPSC, we can increase safety awareness for our Members. We believe strongly in the future of at-home connected fitness and are committed to work with the CPSC to set new industry safety standards for treadmills. We have a desire and a responsibility to be an industry leader in product safety."

We don't know what happened behind closed doors in the Peloton C-suite. Did Peloton find its moral place? We do know that while the company was denying responsibility, its share price was tanking. The Peloton saga may one day become a case study for MBA students to debate, but my hope is that the story won't be limited to a playbook on public relations strategy, and that it will instruct us on business ethics and a more profound meaning of success. Judy Samuelson, my former colleague at the Aspen Institute, has been thinking about these issues for over twenty years and working with business executives and scholars to align business decisions and investments with the long-term health of society and the planet. She advises corporate leaders to disrupt the tried and true and go beyond profits to arrive at a purpose. Visit any corporate website and you will see that companies have their mission statements written out for all to see. But those manifestos shouldn't be bare-minimum, performative attempts to connect with consumers who tell marketing surveys that they'll reward companies that take a stand. They need to be rooted in an authentic desire to put consumers first. Executives should devote less time to shallow purpose-positioning and more time to thinking about ethics and morality. They could reflect on the impact their products might have on consumers and transparently share their thoughts on morality as both an internal value and an external, consumer-focused principle that drives their actions before and after a crisis. I'm proposing a different way of seeing risk. You don't get points for playing the blame game at a time when people's lives and, as Judy might say, the planet's well-being may hang in the balance.

While Peloton's initial response was shortsighted and might have resulted in more injuries and death, I applaud the company's pivot and eventual apology. It's hard to say you were wrong and ask for forgiveness. Let's set aside an obvious motive for the apology—corporate self-preservation—and be grateful for the expression of regret. Many companies and individuals would never go that far. Behavioral economists will tell you that apologies have to be costly to be meaningful, and Peloton's stock sank to an eight-month low the day of Foley's confession (it has rebounded since). It's imperative that companies work with consumers, and the apology positions Peloton to be a partner in creating and maintaining a more consumer-focused marketplace. Let's hope that the next time consumers are injured, the responsible company will learn the lesson offered by Peloton, ignore Mattel's playbook of full-court defensiveness, and in the process help save lives.

As for the government's role, this is an example of progress, especially given a 2019 congressional staff report questioning whether the Consumer Product Safety Commission could "adequately protect American consumers" given a "pattern of inappropriate deference to industry." Apparently the agency learned from its mistakes with Rock 'n Play. By releasing the video and warnings about the Peloton Tread+, it took an active and powerful role in defense of consumers. Positive change can happen in Washington too, but it's often at the mercy of the political yo-yo that shifts direction every four or eight years. It's hard to be consistent when policies are altered with each presidential election. That's why we need Congress to codify a new, more responsible path for the commission whose work is so important to consumers—who are, after all, their constituents.

SOMEONE ELSE TO BLAME

Blaming consumers isn't the only way companies try to evade responsibility for threatening our safety. In online marketplaces, third-party sellers are a perennial problem. In 2017, for instance, Consumer Reports discovered that Amazon and eBay were selling carbon monoxide detectors that didn't effectively detect carbon monoxide in our tests. Consumer Reports rated the devices "Don't Buy: Safety Risk." When we asked Amazon about its process for evaluating the safety of the alarms, Amazon said it had an algorithm that screened out products that weren't up to its standards. After my colleagues pointed out that the algorithm was broken, Amazon fixed it and removed the defective products from the site, but our monitoring showed that other off-brand models were still available for sale. The incident highlights the game of whack-a-mole played by platforms like Amazon, which have argued they're not responsible in cases where they're the seller and not the manufacturer of the defective product.

The issue of liability came up in a 2021 legal complaint filed against Amazon by the Consumer Product Safety Commission, which was seeking a recall of hundreds of thousands of items, including the carbon monoxide detectors, because the agency alleged they were defective and posed a risk of serious injury or death. The legal action was considered a welcome example of government finally standing up to one of tech's Big Four. But think about the possible harm of the defective detectors. Every year, more than four hundred Americans die from accidental carbon monoxide poisoning, and another fifty thousand visit the emergency room. We can't be satisfied with bad actors being punished only after the harm is done.

The third-party sellers who use Amazon's platform, of course, aren't innocent little lambs. Many of them are savvy enough to have designed ways to outwit Amazon's algorithms. The Markup, a watchdog-journalism site that *Consumer Reports* has partnered with on investigations, showed how a maker of gun accessories was able to sell a gunsmithing tool as a "paperweight desk organizer." This was despite the fact that the banned product was linked to other gun-related items through Amazon's "frequently bought together" tool, and even though the comments section was filled with jokey references from customers who knew exactly what they were buying. It wasn't until the Markup notified Amazon of what was going on that the "desk organizer" was taken off the online marketplace.

Amazon doesn't have to be reactive, with a shrugging approach to product-safety enforcement almost guaranteed to let some dangerous or prohibited items slip through. Apple's App Store, which Consumer Reports has criticized for other reasons, combines human expertise with automated systems to conduct extensive reviews of programs before it lists them on the site. Amazon must add more human experts to the safety-review process so it can ensure that the products it sells are systematically and thoroughly vetted before they're made available to customers. If Amazon can't do that, government regulators should punish the company in a way that makes Amazon feel the injury. A mere nine-figure fine is just a cost of doing business for a company whose market value is on its way to $2 trillion. People's lives are at stake.

THE NOTORIOUS SECTION 6(B)

As I've pointed out, certain policy hurdles also undercut consumer safety. Have I emphasized my loathing for Section 6(b) of the Consumer Product Safety Act enough? It directs the CPSC to get a company's approval before the commission alerts consumers to a problem with a product. It's a license to kill. In one example of many, there's evidence that the provision may have prevented consumers from knowing the risks of another popular product, IKEA's Malm dresser.

A surprisingly high number of injuries and deaths are caused by poorly designed furniture. Adults can be injured and occasionally killed if they handle these items unsafely, but the most threatened group are children who get hurt while climbing on them. Every sixty minutes, a child is treated in a hospital emergency room for injuries related to a furniture tip-over. Between 2000 and 2019, 351 people were killed following a furniture tip-over incident; 286 of them were children. These deaths were preventable. Design adjustments could dramatically reduce the risks, and the fact that such adjustments aren't consistently implemented makes these numbers infuriating.

Nevertheless, to this day, there are no federal mandatory standards governing the stability of dressers and other furniture prone to toppling, and many businesses remain opposed to changing the status quo, in which they set their own standards and police themselves.

The Malm dresser had already caused many injuries before 2016, when the death of twenty-two-month-old Ted McGee of Apple Valley, Minnesota, finally spurred IKEA to recall the dresser four months later.

In a familiar twist, the Consumer Product Safety Commission and IKEA were aware of safety concerns surrounding the Malm, including at least two prior deaths, but Section 6(b) forced the CPSC to largely stay silent, pending IKEA's approval of any messaging. It also emerged that IKEA had ignored the voluntary safety standards for furniture makers, which required each dresser drawer to be able to hold a fifty-pound weight without causing the dresser to tip over. Voluntary standards are, of course, unenforceable. There's nothing we can do when companies disregard them. Testing by Consumer Reports determined that even this industry-driven standard was inadequate, since the weight of a child likely to be climbing on dressers was greater than fifty pounds, and in many cases there's more than one drawer open.

To determine what could make a dresser safer, Consumer Reports developed its own series of progressively more rigorous evaluations. From the results, CR was able to not only rank the dressers' safety performance but also share with the industry a new set of standards companies could use to evaluate future furniture designs.

Coming to such conclusions through scientific study is a positive force in making the marketplace safer. A number of consumer groups have helped bring about change by channeling the righteous anger and grief of parents into the grinding advocacy work required to keep pressure on manufacturers of dangerous products. Shane's Foundation, named for Shane Siefert, whose mother, Lisa, became a consumer advocate after his 2011 death due to a furniture tip-over, is one such group, along with Kids in Danger, Parents Against Tip-Overs, and others. These organizations have been instrumental in making the marketplace safer for everyone.

The good news is that the Consumer Reports investigation showed it was possible to build a stable dresser at an affordable price.

In 2019, IKEA announced that some future dressers would have a mechanism that keeps multiple drawers from opening at the same time, which was a clear safety improvement. They also introduced a design that would require furniture to be anchored to the wall before drawers will function. This solution poses another problem, however. It places the burden on consumers to correctly assemble the product by requiring them to fasten it to the wall. Wall anchors can be an effective way to secure furniture, but installing them can be tricky. The executive director of Kids in Danger, Nancy Cowles, who has spent decades working as a consumer advocate to prevent childhood injuries, says that anchors are often ignored. "Frankly, I rarely talk to someone who anchors their furniture," she says. "People say, 'No, my child is never alone.' Everyone thinks their dresser is not going to tip over—until it happens."

Consumer Reports agrees that while wall anchors can act as an effective backup to stop a potentially dangerous tip-over, relying on them to do most of the safety work is a flawed approach. Our survey research shows that a clear majority of people buy furniture expecting that it will be sturdy and resist tipping over. The solution isn't to push an additional burden for safety onto consumers by requiring them to anchor it. We know designing stable furniture is possible. To prevent tip-overs, companies just need to build sturdier furniture. You can't get around this, or as Consumer Reports' chief scientific officer, Dr. James Dickerson, put it, "It's just the physics."

Designing for safety needs to be completed before a product hits the market. If we want to protect people once a safety risk develops, we have to get rid of Section 6(b). The provision makes it far too difficult to recall a dangerous product and relies on companies to do the right thing when their economic interests might oppose it. That's an obstacle consumers shouldn't have to fight to overcome. The Consumer Product Safety Commission needs to be able to warn the public of danger and start the recall process on its own, even as the agency negotiates with the company over what actions the company can take. Requiring the prior approval of the company is a needless obstacle to public safety. Congress needs to cut the red tape that endangers lives and repeal Section 6(b) so the government can do its most basic job: keeping its citizens from harm.

Of course, there are a number of other reforms the CPSC can and should implement on its own. Once it determines that a recall is necessary to protect the public, an independent monitor should be installed to make sure the company is complying and taking steps to assure that another dangerous product won't land on store shelves. If the CPSC decides to punish the company with a fine, the agency should hold the company accountable in a way that doesn't make it more profitable for the business to pay the penalty and continue as if no regulatory action had been taken. In other words, the fine should be high enough that a company can't write it off as the cost of doing business. That could mean handing down bigger penalties to bigger companies.

Companies want recalls conducted faster so they can assess the financial damage and, hopefully, move on to bigger profits by putting consumers first. We, too, want speedier recalls when they're called for. An important step would be to establish common guidelines on recalls and not negotiate a new process each time one is necessary.

The CPSC doesn't have to wait for congressional action to implement some of these changes. The dedicated people running the agency can take more assertive action on their own. It's past time they do.

GOVERNMENT CATFISHING

We've all heard the comparison of laws to sausage and how it's wise to avoid watching either of them being made. I've got a story that illustrates that all too well.

When it comes to food safety, our reliance on government is nearly complete. No individual consumer can be expected to inspect packs of freshly slaughtered chicken for pathogens or to make sure *E. coli* hasn't infested a crop of leafy greens bound for supermarkets. We need government to ensure the health of Americans, and for that, two agencies split the task. The US Department of Agriculture inspects meat, poultry, processed egg products, and catfish, while the Food and Drug Administration keeps watch over everything else. You might ask why catfish is on the USDA's list. It doesn't fit with beef and chicken, and it's the only kind of fish the department inspects. Why does catfish get special treatment? Why does the USDA have oversight of any fish at all? These are all good questions, and they're where this particular sausage-and-law story begins.

In the 2000s, after the US and Vietnam reestablished trade relations, the Southeast Asian nation began exporting catfish to the US and quickly gained ground on domestic producers. The Vietnamese variety wasn't better than the American kind, but it wasn't any worse, and it was a lot cheaper to produce. American consumers responded. In 2002, imported catfish made up 20 percent of the US market, but the product was steadily growing in popularity.

Domestic catfish farmers were worried about the competition, so they went hunting for an advantage. They settled on switching oversight of catfish to the USDA from the FDA. The USDA conducts regular inspections and the FDA does not, so if the USDA became the country's catfish sheriff, the Vietnamese farmers would have to adopt the same rules on cleanliness and safety as their American counterparts. The thinking went that it would cost overseas competitors a lot of money to comply with USDA standards, if they could comply at all, and the extra expense would level the playing field for domestic producers. Fish farmers from Mississippi, Alabama, Louisiana, Arkansas, and other big production areas lobbied their representatives in Washington to put Vietnamese catfish under USDA surveillance with the goal of crippling the import business.

As the late Senator John McCain said at the time, in opposition to the changeover, the catfish is a "bottom feeder with friends in high places." McCain and others argued that the transfer would cost US taxpayers millions of dollars a year to put American inspectors in Southeast Asia to enforce the higher safety standards. They said the transfer of catfish oversight was an unnecessary taxpayer gift to domestic farmers that would benefit only a single industry. It's a relatively small industry too.

The average American eats about a pound of catfish per year, compared with just under one hundred pounds of chicken. No matter. Led by Thad Cochran, a US senator from Mississippi, Congress included the transfer of catfish oversight to the USDA in the 2008 farm bill. It took another few years for the turnover to be finalized.

Proponents cited public health concerns as a good reason to support the change, and Consumer Reports was among the advocates that hailed the USDA takeover as a positive move for food safety. But let's be honest. Congress didn't make this change with your safety in mind. As the Government Accountability Office pointed out, there had been only one recorded instance of a catfish-related outbreak of salmonella, a potentially deadly microorganism. The outbreak occurred in 1991 and "was not clearly linked to catfish," the GAO said. Since then, there have been no salmonella problems related to catfish.

It was trade protection that was at stake. Domestic catfish producers wanted an artificial barrier to protect them against imported catfish, and they got it.

The legislation didn't work as American fisheries had planned. The Vietnamese farmers and other overseas producers cleaned up their act—a win for consumers. For farmers in the catfish-raising region of the US, however, the USDA hasn't been the solution they envisioned. Consumption of imported catfish soared to 76 percent of the American market in 2019 while domestic sales have been heading straight for the bottom— swamped by the competition.

The lesson I want to highlight is that strange and behind-the-scenes reasons exist for the passage of certain pieces of legislation, and when something doesn't make sense, following the money remains the best way to sort things out. But this story also shows how consumer issues are frequently not priorities for lawmakers, and how a law that helped clean up an industry did so by accident. That's another reason why we have to push harder for what we need.

TOXIC CHEMICALS IN BABY FOOD

In early 2021, a panel of the House Committee on Oversight and Reform released a staff report on the dangerous levels of toxic heavy metals in popular brands of baby food. Arsenic, lead, cadmium, and mercury are naturally found in the environment, but there are steps companies can take to keep them out of our food. A heavy metal like lead is so dangerous that the best amount to ingest is zero, but, with few exceptions, the US Food and Drug Administration doesn't have any enforceable limits for heavy metals in food.

"The FDA is almost completely AWOL on this issue," Representative Raja Krishnamoorthi of Illinois, chair of the House subcommittee responsible for the study, told *Consumer Reports*.

Lead, cadmium, and arsenic have destructive effects on the developing infant mind, brain, cardiovascular system, and immune system. Those effects can lower IQ and are linked to behavior problems and attention deficit disorders as well as an increased risk for skin and bladder cancers. But showing harm from trace amounts of toxic chemicals can take a long time, and it's impossible to know for sure if a developmental disorder can be traced directly to any particular product.

The subcommittee contacted seven companies, and four responded to the request for data: Nurture (which sells Happy Family Organics and Happy Baby products), Beech-Nut Nutrition Company, Hain Celestial Group (which sells Earth's Best organic products), and Gerber. Walmart, Sprout, and the Campbell Soup Company (which sells Plum Organics products) didn't respond. All companies that sent data to the subcommittee reported finding inorganic arsenic, lead, and cadmium in their products. Only one company, Nurture, tested regularly for mercury.

The levels of all heavy metals were often far above what experts consider safe. For example, the FDA set a limit in August 2020 for inorganic arsenic in infant rice cereal at 100 parts per billion. Using 100 ppb as a reference, a quarter of finished products tested by Nurture went over that level, according to the report. Hain usually tested only ingredients as opposed to the finished products, and some came in as high as 309 ppb. Certain ingredients used by Beech-Nut tested as high as 913 ppb, and Gerber used at least sixty-seven batches of rice flour that tested at more than 90 ppb.

There's no lead standard for baby foods. None. But the FDA's safe limit for bottled water is 5 ppb lead. Twenty percent of Nurture's finished products contained more than 10 ppb lead, and many ingredients used by Beech-Nut, Hain, and Gerber contained more than 20 ppb lead.

The report stated the obvious: Any internal standards the companies had devised were insufficient. And the method followed by some companies of testing only ingredients routinely underestimated the amount of arsenic in final products, possibly due to additives like vitamins or the manufacturing process. What's more, companies used ingredients with higher levels of metals than their own standards allowed. Nurture told congressional investigators that it sold all the products it tested, regardless of the results.

Federal agencies need to take stronger action on this issue by incentivizing better corporate behavior, but consumer advocates recognized that they couldn't wait. That's why the Environmental Defense Fund and Healthy Babies Bright Futures, a national alliance of scientists, government officials, and child-health-advocacy organizations, are working with baby-food producers to change the status quo. Through an initiative known as the Baby Food Council, they're developing standards for heavy metals in baby food and ways to certify foods that comply with those standards. What they come up with will more than likely be stricter standards than the government would implement, says Tom Neltner, chemical policy director for the Environmental Defense Fund. "We've been working with the companies to develop baby-food standards partly because we think the industry is willing to do more than what FDA will expect," he told *Consumer Reports*.

It's a good thing consumer groups took the lead. Eight months after the initial report on toxins in baby food, a follow-up study by the same congressional subcommittee found that Gerber and Beech-Nut failed to properly test and remove dangerous products from the market, while Sprout, Walmart's Parent's Choice, and Campbell's Plum Organics were lax in testing and failed to control the amounts of heavy metals in their baby food.

One company learned its lesson from the bad publicity surrounding toxins in its product. In 2012, Nature's One made headlines after a university study found arsenic in its organic baby formula. Consumers were furious, and business "went to zero," CEO Jay Highman told CBS News. "It was a difficult time, it really was. It's emotional."

It was also a turning point, Highman said. Since then, he's dedicated himself to keeping toxins out of the company's baby foods. "It's up to me to have a conscience for my consumer," he said. "It's cost us more to go through this process, but is there really any price you wouldn't pay to remove a toxin that's harmful to a child? I say no."

LETHAL LETTUCE

So how do we shift the burden for food safety to government and industry, where it belongs? Clearly, we need them to put consumer safety first. That hasn't been a priority in the periodic outbreaks of *E. coli* in vegetables that have vexed the country for years.

E. coli is a bacterium naturally found in livestock feces that can be fatal if eaten. There were at least forty-five outbreaks of *E. coli* exposure linked to leafy vegetables in the US between 1998 and 2016. *E. coli* infections lead to around 265,000 illnesses and about one hundred deaths every year.

Romaine lettuce was implicated in four different *E. coli* eruptions from 2017 to 2019, with the spring 2018 outbreak the widest and deadliest in decades. In the lone 2019 episode, there was no mechanism to trace the origin of the produce grown in large-scale farms, so no one could pinpoint where the contamination was coming from, a prerequisite for government action. Neither the FDA nor the Centers for Disease Control and Prevention gave any clear guidance to consumers. After the number of sickened people rose to thirty-four, Consumer Reports decided to take action. Out of an abundance of caution, we did the right thing and encouraged people to stop eating all romaine lettuce. In essence, we conducted our own recall, almost a year before the government made the same recommendation.

As you can imagine, that didn't make romaine growers happy, and they slammed us for our "unfair attacks." We asked the lettuce growers to identify where the bad lettuce was coming from, but they were unable to or didn't respond. Nor could they explain how *E. coli* was getting into their lettuce.

Consumer Reports scientists concluded that the *E. coli* had probably contaminated the lettuce through irrigation ditches that connected the growing fields to nearby cattle-feeding bins. In the end, they proved to be correct. Soil from a factory farm two miles uphill from the growing fields was linked to the strain of *E. coli*.

Preventing *E. coli* outbreaks would seem to require huge changes in the way feeding lots keep watch on where their livestock waste ends up, how vegetable fields defend against contaminated water seeping into their irrigation, and widespread testing of water used on food crops. These are big jobs usually left to government, which should mandate protective consumer measures and enforce them.

Stemming ongoing outbreaks is another story. Tracking contaminated produce and tracing it to its origins are jobs that can be handled capably by the private sector through innovation. For example, Walmart, the world's biggest retailer, developed a track-and-trace system with computer maker IBM that can follow food from the field, through washing and cutting, to the warehouse, then to the store. It's even possible to pinpoint which part of a field and at what time the vegetables were harvested. The system is based on blockchain, the electronic ledger that's used to record sales of cryptocurrency. Blockchain takes away the guesswork on the whereabouts of a head of lettuce. In one test, Walmart employees without the benefit of blockchain took seven days to locate the farm in Mexico that grew certain mangoes. Walmart claims that for the same task the blockchain could identify the origin of the mangoes in just over two seconds.

Some skeptics argue that blockchain doesn't have magical powers, and that the Walmart program is a public relations stunt. I prefer to wait and see how well the procedure works. I'm rooting for any company that finds a solution to a complex task. When corporations take these kinds of steps, trust is enhanced throughout the marketplace. For Walmart, the use of blockchain to trace bad vegetables can save millions of dollars in recalls, destruction of contaminated plants, and a damaged reputation. For consumers, it can save lives.

UPSTREAM IMPACT

Even as we push companies and government agencies to intensify their consumer-safety efforts, advocates such as Consumer Reports need to take stock of our own methods. The opportunity to reimagine how consumers can amplify their impact was one of the reasons why I was so eager to step into a leadership role in developing the next generation of marketplace-shaping innovations at Consumer Reports.

Traditionally, rigorous evaluation of products and services takes place when they hit the market, and it's been a reliable and effective way to improve consumer safety, quality, and value. But the pace of the marketplace is so much faster than it was just a few years ago. How do we prevent dangerous products like an ill-conceived infant sleeper from reaching consumers in the first place? In a world of connected products powered by software, how do we make sure the latest car, cell phone, or security camera is designed with consumers in mind?

Consider, for example, the automotive industry, for which Consumer Reports ratings are an especially trusted and popular way for consumers to get help deciding on a major purchase. Think of all the time and expense it takes manufacturers to shepherd a new vehicle from sketch pad to dealer showroom. Testing a vehicle for safety only after it's waxed and gleaming in the customer's driveway misses countless opportunities to step in during the development process, when engineers and designers can make changes to ensure that the vehicles are safe and driver friendly.

A road test provides great feedback on features such as handling, comfort, braking, and acceleration, but Consumer Reports' product ratings are unique in the marketplace. They combine testing information with owner-satisfaction data gathered from millions of consumers over many years, allowing us to credibly track categories such as product durability across the lifetimes of many vehicle models. When we say "consumer reports," we're saying, in part, that it's consumers who are doing the reporting. Their real-world experiences with vehicles they've owned give us unique insight into a car's performance. By combining that with the expertise of our test-track staff, we offer the most complete information on what can be expected from a wide array of products.

Imagine offering similar data to carmakers and other manufacturers, with the goal of helping them build the safest, best-performing, most efficient, and most appealing products they can. Imagine making that information available to them during the product-design process so they can incorporate the

values of Consumer Reports—safety, security, better performance, and quality for consumers—before the product rolls off
the assembly line.

We call this initiative Consumer Reports Data Intelligence,
and it's up and running.

When I first proposed this idea, some suggested that manufacturers would "game" the consumer insights to get higher
ratings. But that's precisely what we want them to do. We
want them to act on our recommendations. Why not work
proactively with manufacturers to more efficiently achieve our
goals? Why not provide them with new tools to make better
consumer-driven and safety-based decisions? Every year, we
independently test thousands of products and regularly survey millions of consumers. We continue to use our critical
research to write reviews for consumers, and we'll never shy
away from calling out bad products and bad actors, but we
must strive to also help develop products, standards, and policies that prioritize safety and quality. We believe that Data
Intelligence can be an exciting new way to leverage trusted
data and consumer insights gleaned over nearly ten decades of
testing and research.

Here's how it works. For a fee, manufacturers, regulators,
and research professionals can participate in working-group forums, subscribe to a steady flow of our consumer-driven data
insights, and access studies and reports written specifically for
them. Our aim is to achieve what we call upstream impact:
improving products and services before they reach the market.
In the two years since the launch of the program, a majority of
appliance makers and car companies operating in the US have
participated. We've kept track of instances where we can verify

that our consumer insights have had a direct impact on a company's decision-making process. Since we began, the number of those incidents has more than doubled. Examples include very specific changes in products, such as rearranging the duct structure of a clothes dryer so it dries faster, or recalibrating the height of a stove's cooktop surface so it's less likely to crack.

Esther Han, Consumer Reports' vice president of new products and services, who moved mountains to start the program, points out that companies maintain lots of their own data, and our consumer insights can validate and sometimes add weight to theirs. Our data can also be used to, for example, settle disagreements among company engineers in favor of improved safety mechanisms, or help sway an overseas home office about the preferences of American consumers. But Data Intelligence makes a mark simply by offering information to a new and receptive audience. In one example, the opinions of Consumer Reports members concerning cars' advanced driver-assistance systems—specifically, automatic lane-centering, lane-keeping, and lane-departure warnings—have been downloaded nearly six hundred times by manufacturers, auto-safety groups, and other industry experts.

One large appliance manufacturer has used both the testing and survey data across multiple categories to make specific improvements in its next generation of products. Another has been analyzing Data Intelligence's long-term reliability data to help determine ways to prolong the life of its appliances, including the addition of new tests during its product-development cycle. Consumer Reports gives consumers a place at the table where timely corporate decisions are made, and does so in a way that prevents trouble rather than responding to it.

SAFETY IN THE DIGITAL AGE

Our efforts at driving impact farther upstream are an example of just how much the market has transformed since Ralph Nader's *Unsafe at Any Speed* was published more than fifty years ago. Change is accelerating, and the marketplace doesn't wait for us to perfect safety measures. It used to be that consumer advocates worried only about hardware, such as IKEA furniture and infant sleepers. Today, we have to keep a close watch on software problems too.

With the digital world come dangers we've never seen before. A tragic example is the Boeing 737 MAX fiasco of 2018. After two 737 MAX airplane crashes killed a total of 646 people, the main culprit turned out to be a software glitch, made worse by management's decision to rush the safety-overview process, prioritizing their bottom line. Passengers on the 737 MAX had put their trust in Boeing, a longtime global leader in aviation, but the reality is that our society hasn't updated the way we oversee connected products and the software that powers them. In other words, there's nobody enforcing standards in the digital world or standing behind rules that guarantee security, safety, and control for consumers. As the Boeing debacle reveals, the result can be catastrophic.

Still, signs of hope peek through the dark clouds. Digital advancements can enhance the potential for consumer safety. When Samsung's Galaxy Note 7 phones started exploding while charging, Consumer Reports pressured the company to issue a recall. Eventually, Samsung complied, recalling 2.5 million phones, the largest smartphone recall in history. But what was most remarkable wasn't the number of phones in the recall.

It was how Samsung did it. They made the phones unusable. Although most phones were returned, for the tens of thousands that weren't, Samsung simply issued a software update that made them inoperable. Usually, dangerous items can be found on a secondary market months after a recall, still risking lives. Not this time. While I can't officially confirm this figure, it could be considered the first 100 percent recall ever. That's the positive potential of the shift to digital. Addressing problems by sending software updates will increasingly become the norm. Peloton and Tesla have both included software changes as part of solving their consumer-safety issues. Carmakers are turning more and more often to software to make their systems work, a process known as telematics—which is also a growth industry making use of wireless devices to transmit data in real time. Nowadays, cars are computers on wheels that can be reprogrammed by "over-the-air" updates from manufacturers and third parties. In many cases, no physical recall is needed. A mechanic doesn't have to so much as touch the car with a wrench. By 2025, an estimated 90 percent of new vehicles will be pre-equipped with telematics. This means, however, that today's vehicles are data guzzlers. Large amounts of information are collected and stored in modules installed in the cars. As the technology matures and grows, so will the market for telematics data.

Using telematics to improve vehicle safety is a tantalizing possibility. Still, the privacy implications are daunting. Whom does the data belong to? How can we track cars securely and share driving information with third-party vendors? How would consumers be able to make informed decisions if the telematics data is proprietary? Telematics is a tool that can't be left to parties looking to profit from your data.

It's imperative that as the world changes, consumer advocates aren't left in the dust. We need a set of digital standards, like the ones created by Consumer Reports' Digital Lab, to set a moral compass of safety, security, and protection of freedom of expression for the industry to navigate by. Consumers should be at the top of the priority list, above profits. Trusting companies to self-police is not the answer. There's too much at stake.

It's why we need to modernize government regulators, whether by ending dangerous provisions like Section 6(b) of the Consumer Product Safety Act, improving the structure of the regulatory agencies to clarify their duties, or giving them the mandate to take action even where they haven't before.

It's why we need advocates, companies, and government leaders thinking about consumer safety in the world as it is now and as it will be tomorrow. We must contend with the digital reality and its impact on people and families, adopting consumer-safety guidelines that will stay relevant or will be flexible enough to change in order to stay current, for two, ten, and twenty years down the line.

If we don't continue to adapt, it won't just be the policies of government agencies or the corporate safety measures that become relics of the past. So will the civil and economic rights of consumers. More people will be hurt. More people will feel the sting of discrimination. More people will be stripped of power. And they'll be left behind.

We're at a new frontier of consumer safety, with daunting obstacles and unprecedented puzzles. But our goal is the same as it was for those who fought for seat belts decades ago. We want a future world in which young Americans will shake their heads and say, "How did you live like that?" We don't want them hanging their heads, realizing they still do.

WHAT CAN I DO NOW?

Be Aware of the Dangers of Recalled Products

Recalls are an important part of consumer safety, but unfortunately some recalled products aren't ever returned, fixed, or thrown away by their owners. For example, about one of every four recalled vehicles on US roads right now hasn't been repaired. Part of this can be explained by the fact that many people don't hear about a recall when it happens or don't know what to do when there is one. Others didn't own the products when they were recalled—and it makes sense that people don't retain recall information that doesn't, at least at the time, apply to them.

This chapter focuses a good deal on the safety of children. It's critical for parents and guardians to always check the recall status of products they purchase for their young ones. But it's also important for all consumers to know what some of the most commonly recalled products are, including child safety seats, cosmetics, toys, and vehicles. Check for a recall before you buy such products, especially if you're buying used.

Some government sites that will help:

- Recalls.gov: Lists of recalls from federal agencies (This is the best spot to check for recalls of infant sleepers, loungers, and other products. You can even sign up for email alerts.)
- NHTSA.gov: Safety information on vehicles and their equipment, including child car seats
- FSIS.USDA.gov and FoodSafety.gov: For listings of many, though not all, food recalls
- FDA.gov: For recalls of food, medicine, pet items, and other products

In addition, be sure to register your new purchase with the manufacturer, so there's a way for the company to communicate with you. You can look at *Consumer Reports* articles for recent recall information and even take advantage of our Car Recall Tracker at CR.org/CarRecallTracker. Just enter your car's data, and you'll be alerted of any recalls. We also offer a Food Recall Tracker at CR.org/FoodRecallTracker.

Report Product Safety Concerns

As you read in the chapter, sometimes the only reason the public learns about dangerous products is because individuals have stepped up and reported incidents. But often people don't know what to do when they witness a safety concern.

The first place to report any potentially risky product is to the federal government. There are multiple websites you can turn to, including:

- FoodSafety.gov: For unsafe food products, including pet food and restaurant food
- NHTSA.gov/report-a-safety-problem: For defective vehicles and accessories
- SaferProducts.gov: For more general consumer products

Once you tell the federal government about a concern, you should also let Consumer Reports know by visiting our website, CR.org, and clicking either "Report a Safety Problem" or "Give a Confidential News Tip." I recognize that this is another step for you to take, but know that it will help us investigate concerns, report trends, and fight for consumers across the country. Working together, we can help save lives.

MORE INFORMATION

For more references, details on these solutions, updates on these issues, and ways to get engaged in taking action, go to BuyerAware.CR.org, or use the QR code below.

CHAPTER SIX

BUILDING A CONSUMER-FIRST MARKETPLACE

YOU WAKE UP IN THE MORNING AND CHECK YOUR PHONE. Fourteen texts were sent to you overnight, but due to the freedom-from-harassment section of a comprehensive consumer-digital-rights law, thirteen of them have crackled and ignited in a virtual spam bonfire. The one that got through to you is an advertisement for lawn furniture. You're delighted. You're looking to buy a patio set, and you had directed your controls to show you deals as they became available. You take a look at the message, and you love the table and chairs you see, so you hit a button that stops all further ads from reaching you. The convenience is terrific, and you don't feel guilty about shopping at a big internet company because there are twenty others competing with it for your business.

You put on your fitness tracker and go for a run. The tracker monitors your vital signs as you fall into a rhythm. Because of the new data-privacy law, the manufacturer's setting prohibits that information from being sent anywhere, but you did program it to summon medical help if something goes wrong. You finish your run in excellent time, so you celebrate with a selfie near your favorite coffee shop. When you post the photo, it goes to your followers and no one else, and the only way to identify your location is to guess. When you walk past a neighbor you don't particularly like, you don't even notice them, and they don't notice you. The two of you will live the rest of your lives never being bothered by People You May Know notifications suggesting over and over that you hang out together because, hey, it's never going to happen.

Before you order a coffee, you do a search for the difference in calories between a mocha and a cappuccino. Your search is shared with nobody. When you use your phone to pay for your order, the money comes from the account you've designated. No one else knows about the transaction but the coffee shop. They send you a thank-you text, and after you glance at it, it melts into the ether.

As you walk away, sipping your drink, a hacker causes a data breach at one of the countless companies you've interacted with. Because you use a security app developed by a trusted nonprofit organization that didn't try to sell you anything and didn't have any undisclosed connections to anybody who would, your data isn't included in the breach. You're safe. You go home and shower.

You've been unhappy at your job for a while, and you have an interview with the recruiter from a rival company who's already intimated that you could be in for a big pay raise if you left your current employer and went to work for them. You have no tracker on your phone, so you never had to disable one, and since bypassing any command that a person doesn't want to be tracked is now against the law, you're doubly protected. Nobody has to know where you're heading, and nobody will.

If all of this sounds too good to be true, it's not. It's a future that's possible if consumers keep demanding digital and economic rights and a more level playing field. Government and corporations have critical roles to play, and the obstacles are big and systemic, but the most important change agents are consumers. You and me.

AN AFFLICTION OF AFFECTION

It can be daunting to consider the powerful forces that block the way to a future like the one envisioned above. Corporations possess the power of wealth, and tech's Big Four are among the wealthiest companies in history. They've put their thumbs on the scale, and today their influence is part of a drastic imbalance that needs to be corrected. There are other reasons, however, they became as rich and formidable as they are: We love their products. We buy them and use them every day.

I'm certainly not immune. Like two hundred million other people every month, I shop on Amazon. I grew to rely on the company during the coronavirus pandemic. My parents, both in their nineties, came to live with us, and I was afraid of bringing COVID-19 into our home. Shopping online kept us safe. When my mother took a fall, I went to Amazon to buy grab bars for the bedroom and a chair for the shower. Each time I visit the site, I feel conflicted. Many times, I float my cursor over the Place Your Order button and argue with myself about which is more important: the tranquil ease of buying from The Everything Store or the larger issue of standing with the Davids against the Goliath that Amazon has become. Sometimes I close out the Amazon window and shop on other websites or at a local business. Sometimes I don't.

I recognize, as many of us do, that we've given up something of immeasurable value in the exchange. We enjoy the convenience, but we've traded control of the marketplace to get it. While we've been mesmerized by the magic of free next-day shipping, the online giant has used our affection to lull us into trusting it, and in our distraction we may have failed to notice how Amazon exploits us and how bloated in money and influence it has become. The same goes for the other companies in the Big Four. The iPhone is so addictive it seems surgically attached to the hands of many Americans, and Apple has taken advantage of that. And what's easier than default Google searches? Google now has a big presence in mapping, cloud storage, email, and web browsing. Posting on Facebook becomes routine and a stress-free way to connect with friends and family. The company, however, can't be counted on to help society if it means sacrificing revenue. We pay dearly for the convenience these companies offer. We shouldn't have to.

We don't necessarily need to break free from the intoxicating allure and amazing power of technology to accomplish the goal of a consumer-first marketplace. We want the businesses to succeed. We don't want to do away with Amazon, even if we could. We do, however, want competitors to have a fighting chance against the behemoth businesses. We want dozens more Amazons. And Googles. And Apples. That way, they can win our business by competing against each other to be the company that best protects our privacy, that partners with us, that holds itself to better environmental, labor, and other conscientious practices, and that's most enthusiastic about putting our needs first. They can be rivals who'll win by making our lives easier without exacting such a steep price. If this sort of competition is impossible, we may need to use a hammer to break up the companies into smaller businesses that will operate that way.

Obstacles such as a lack of competition among the biggest tech companies and outdated government regulations to rein them in undercut and dwarf consumer power. There's another hurdle we can do something about: complacency. We've all likely assumed that of course the government will require the maker of an infant sleeper to test its product before selling it to new parents desperate for rest. Of course a company will have the best interests of consumers in mind when its terms of service require arbitration instead of the US legal system to settle disputes. Of course a lender would never sell a mortgage to a borrower who can't afford it. It's natural to think that the entity on the other side of a transaction is only looking to earn a reasonable profit and won't rip you off. It's just as natural to feel betrayed when you discover they aren't.

The founders of Consumer Reports believed that consumers needed an honest broker, and that's why we've fought so hard since 1936 to earn and keep Americans' trust. We've been fighting battles for nine decades. Our history speaks to who we are and informs how we've evolved to stand with and for consumers. When we say Consumer Reports, we mean that literally. We amplify the consumer voices we hear in the many surveys and direct engagements we have with people across the country. We're nonpartisan, with millions of members, and what defines our nonpartisanship is that we rely on facts and science to improve people's lives. Our bias is putting consumers first.

CONSUMER RIGHTS ARE CIVIL RIGHTS

I'm aware that the word "consumerism" can have a negative connotation. When it's defined as a preoccupation with acquiring things, in a world where there's so much competition for resources, it can be cast as part of the problem. But there's another definition of the word, and that's fighting for and promoting the interests of buyers. Consumer power involves the harnessing of everyone's market influence for common benefit. It's about galvanizing people to take an active role in improving the world.

With discretion over the spending of trillions of dollars, consumers have unique clout and can do incredible things. Consumer power saves lives by keeping deadly products and toxic foods off store shelves and by insisting on accountability for companies that prioritize profit over safety and well-being. It elevates the importance of women in the marketplace by, for example, ensuring that cars are designed so that women won't be killed in a crash that men would likely survive. It guarantees that Black and Latino Americans have an equal chance of surviving a medical emergency by demanding devices that function as well for them as they do for others. It expands access to the internet, and the opportunities that come with it, to all Americans, regardless of where they live, how much money they have, or who they are. It flips the financial landscape so that transactions are transparent and fair and not laden with traps to bury borrowers in suffocating piles of debt. And it respects the lives of everyone everywhere by insisting on basics like gas stoves that don't leak noxious fumes, face-recognition algorithms that don't discriminate based on skin color, and a college education that won't bury young people in debt before they've even started their adult lives.

Civil rights, human dignity, economic opportunity, environmental justice, education, ensuring our health, and keeping us alive—they're all about putting people ahead of profit. There's universality in what we fight for. We can't separate these causes; they're part of the same battle. In 1936, the year that Consumer Reports was founded, President Franklin D. Roosevelt made the link between civil rights and consumer rights explicit. "We stand committed to the proposition that freedom is no half-and-half affair," he said. "If the average citizen is guaranteed equal opportunity in the polling place, he must have equal opportunity in the marketplace."

The marketplace is where all Americans go to chase their dreams, to buy a home or car, to pay for school, to start or expand a business—to live our lives to the fullest. If we discover that we can't do those things, or they're harder or more expensive than they should be, or there are unfair barriers, or we get hurt or killed in the process, the marketplace is broken. It doesn't have to be this way. Consumer Reports works not only to fix what needs repair but also to transform the marketplace, to alter its orientation, to change prevailing attitudes so that our economy puts people like you and me ahead of corporate dominance and bureaucratic inaction.

These issues are bigger than Consumer Reports, and they don't stop at the US border. By nature of its reliance on the internet, the opportunities and risks of the digital marketplace affect people in every country, but so do many of the other issues we've discussed: the quality of the food and water families rely on, the need for honesty in advertising, the concern that discrimination skews how companies operate, the safety of everyday household products. The average person needs representation at any negotiation where economic decisions are made. Too often, government task forces and international forums, like the one held every year in Davos, Switzerland, are dominated by other interests. Some recognize this need and are working to meet it. For example, Consumers International, a group of two hundred organizations, including Consumer Reports, from one hundred countries, is committed to making sure everyday people are seen and have a voice in these critical discussions around the world. We're a global movement, and while the specific issues of every community or country might differ, we're connected through the need for a greater presence at the highest levels and through the goal of a global marketplace that prioritizes people.

To match up against corporate influence and governments that can be too slow to act, we must establish ourselves as a real force within our communities and around the world. As we've learned over the years, consumer power springs from buyers who are aware and ready to demand their rights.

#CONSUMERSDEMAND

Those rights can be asserted through vigilance. In 2016, Consumer Reports found security flaws in the mobile app Glow, which is used by women to track their monthly menstruation cycles and pregnancies. A vulnerability in the software might have allowed someone with zero hacking skills access to personal data, making it easier for stalkers, online bullies, or identity thieves to exploit the information they gathered to harm some of Glow's roughly four million users. Consumer Reports shared its concerns with the company, and Glow moved quickly to correct the problems, though the state of California fined Glow $250,000 for its carelessness.

Glow's openness to Consumer Reports' feedback shows that some companies reject the traditional knee-jerk defensive response to legitimate criticism, the kind we saw from Mattel's Fisher-Price. It's not as though companies suddenly discovered the morality of putting people's needs before their own profits. It's that profits are getting tougher to earn without considering those needs. Consumers are demanding that companies be good citizens, and evidence suggests that businesses are listening. Paul Polman was correct when he said that companies failing to respond to social and environmental challenges risk going out of business. "The power is in the hands of the consumers, and they will not give us a sense of legitimacy if they believe the system is unfair or unjust," Polman said in 2011, when he was CEO of global retail giant Unilever. "Some people sometimes accuse me of being a socialist, but I'm a capitalist at heart. But what I want is a sustainable and equitable capitalism. Why can't we have that as a model?" I strongly agree that, despite the many roadblocks that corporate America throws in our way, it's possible to create such a system.

Investors, too, increasingly demand that companies look beyond the balance sheet to measure success. In 2020, they had placed $17 trillion in so-called ESG funds, which only buy shares in companies that take into account factors like environmental impact, social improvements, and ethical governance standards. That was a 42 percent increase over 2018. If Wall Street is insisting on those principles, you know that consumers' demands have penetrated the culture. *Fortune* magazine reported in 2021 that there was "clear support among corporate leaders" for the Securities and Exchange Commission to require companies to disclose sustainability and diversity metrics. The B Corps certification, for companies that lead the way in building a sustainable and inclusive economy, is also gaining momentum. In 2021, there were more than four thousand B Corps–verified companies in over seventy countries. Businesses have shown they can take a broader view by considering the well-being of employees, communities, and consumers—prioritizing stakeholder capitalism over shareholder capitalism—as long as they have incentives to do so. The incentive for these improvements, and for others that include lower or no fees on retirement accounts and wider investment options, is mostly coming from consumers, especially younger generations.

Unlike their grandparents, the members of Gen Z, born between 1995 and 2012, don't form opinions of a company solely based on the quality of its products and services. Seventy-seven percent say they also consider ethics and social impact and want the companies to practice what they preach. Before you attribute that attitude to the idealism of the very young, you should know that millennials, born between 1981 and 1994, feel similarly. Whereas one in ten Baby Boomer consumers act on their values by, for example, switching brands due to a company's labor practices, the number of millennials who does so is one in four. According to business-services consultant Deloitte, which has surveyed millennials for a decade, the most consistent finding during that time is the cohort's belief that "business has both a responsibility to improve society and the greatest potential to drive change—but that it's not living up to that potential or their expectations." In the five-year span ending in 2021, the number of millennials who felt that business was a "force for good" dropped from three-quarters to one-half. It's not as if companies are getting worse. Evidence suggests that millennial and Gen Z consumers are demanding more. So should the rest of us.

These are the first generations coming of age in the internet marketplace, with its trolls, its pop-ups, its bots, its haters, its constant tracking, and its lightning-fast feedback loops, where a company or business icon (or athlete or pop star) can go from villain to hero to villain in the course of a TikTok scroll session. Many young people were deeply affected by movements such as #MeToo and #BlackLivesMatter. A March 2021 Harvard poll found that 36 percent of young Americans are politically active, a 12-percentage-point jump in just two years, with young Black voters (41 percent) the most active. We now have two generations of young people who take their politics with them wherever they go, and that includes to the marketplace, where they're fearless and much less likely than their parents and grandparents to allow companies to bully them. They're less shy about demanding what they want.

That's the key, really, and why I wrote this book. If you come away with just one thought, I hope it's this: *nothing will change unless we demand it.*

We demanded that the Consumer Product Safety Commission do a better job for customers of potentially dangerous products than it did for owners of Mattel's Fisher-Price Rock 'n Play. And it did. In a victory for the most vulnerable among us, the CPSC approved a new rule that requires any product intended or marketed for infant sleep to meet strong safety standards, covering a number of unregulated products like inclined sleepers, sleep hammocks, in-bed sleepers, and others that have fallen through the cracks of safety regulations.

It's a landmark win, but now all of us have to demand that Congress get rid of Section 6(b) of the Consumer Product Safety Act. This provision forbids the CPSC from recalling a product without company approval and requires the agency to consult with companies before giving consumers the information they need to avoid injury and death. It's a license to kill. It's got to go.

We demanded that Congress fund the expansion of broadband so that schoolchildren everywhere, regardless of the abilities of their families to pay for it or where they live, could have access to the internet during a global pandemic. Now all of us must demand that the money be fairly distributed to all communities that need access, and that internet companies be clear and fully transparent about the services they provide and at what cost.

We demanded that government attorneys seriously consider the extraordinary influence of tech's Big Four—Amazon, Apple, Facebook, and Google—and quit using outdated models as indications of possible violations of antitrust law. Lina Khan, who for years has highlighted the need to scale back the power of big tech, is in charge of the Federal Trade Commission, the government's main antitrust agency. All of us need to demand that Khan's political opponents get out of the way and allow her to make her case, the consumer's case. If Khan falters in that mission, we need to be there to let her know.

We demanded that internet sites such as Facebook take more responsibility for the misinformation and hate speech spread on their platforms. Congress is taking a close look at Section 230 of the Communications Decency Act, which insulates internet platforms from liability for the content that others post. Americans are starting to agree with us. While only 41 percent favor the right to sue media companies over posts on their platforms, 53 percent say discourse would be improved if we could, and 81 percent support labels for misleading content. Now all of us have to demand that lawmakers require social networks to do more to stem the lies that are tearing our country apart.

We demanded that lawmakers across the country mandate reductions of harmful chemicals called PFAS (per- and polyfluoroalkyl substances) in our drinking water. They are linked to birth defects, cancer, thyroid disease, and other serious health issues. PFAS are known as "forever chemicals" because they don't break down easily. Three states have banned PFAS in food packaging, and California is among several other states considering similar moves. Now all of us have to demand that Congress make drinking-water monitoring and remediation a national requirement, invest in rural water systems, and fund wastewater disposal so people everywhere can live in dignity.

After Consumer Reports engineers were able to trick a Tesla Model Y into using its autopilot driver-assistance feature without a person behind the wheel—a dangerous scenario if repeated outside CR's testing facility—we raised the volume on demands that carmakers improve the safety of their products by adding technology that makes sure drivers keep their eyes on the road even when automatic driving systems are activated, so they'll be ready to intervene when needed. The National Highway Traffic Safety Administration launched an investigation into the Tesla incident, and the auto industry is creating a set of standards for driver-assist safety. Now all of us need to demand that Congress make those performance guidelines into law, so we don't sacrifice safety on the road.

We know we can create change. We already have! Think of the struggle for vehicle emissions standards and the tough battles against carmakers and fossil fuel companies, who argued that fighting pollution and climate change would send auto prices through the roof, cause job losses, and force us to change our lives in ways we wouldn't like. People, ordinary consumers in large numbers, told them no, we want cleaner air, we won't tolerate smog or asthma or a drastically warming planet. We wouldn't stop fighting. We wouldn't back down.

Think of Rachel Carson and how she and her landmark book *Silent Spring* were the targets of vicious attacks from the people, companies, and institutions that profited from the widespread use of hazardous chemicals. Her work is credited with paving the way for creating critical watchdogs like the Environmental Protection Agency and saving countless lives. But readers in 1962 first needed to be made aware that they were surrounded by toxins. They didn't see the harm that was all around them. Once they knew, they dug in. They fought. They got government scientists to prove her work, which led to vital policy changes. That was how the impossible became the possible.

I hope this book has revealed the toxins that surround us today: exploitation in the digital world, lack of accountability in corporate America and government, discrimination in the market. Despite the fear and the frenzy our opponents may stir up to confuse us, we can raise our voices and build on our successes. We need to keep shaping the marketplace we have into the marketplace we need. We've been there before. We can do it again. We *will* do it again. It will require growing our ranks by creating a broader coalition—one that includes champions in business and government—to take on the challenges of tomorrow.

A PEOPLE-POWERED MOVEMENT

So how do we maximize consumer power and expand the movement?

One step is to continually reimagine how we engage, connecting in new ways and to more communities, including with digital tools that are used by the people we're trying to reach. In the last two decades, we've seen how organizations and politicians have built online communities that are mobilized for petitions, fundraising, and actions, both virtual and real-life.

In 2015, when an American dentist on safari in Zimbabwe trophy-hunted a popular lion called Cecil, activists at SumOfUs.org organized an online petition drive to pressure airlines to rewrite their policies on transporting the bodies of endangered animals. A number of international airlines complied immediately. When Delta Airlines was slow to act, SumOfUs .org targeted it with more than 250,000 signatures, and Delta gave in, followed immediately by United, American, and Virgin Atlantic.

One of the most visible of the online-based activist groups, Color of Change, focuses on issues of criminal justice, technology, and the ways Black and brown people are represented in pop culture. It was instrumental in getting the TV show *Cops* booted off the air in 2020 because of the program's portrayal of racial stereotypes, has waged campaigns for emergency debt relief for Black and Indigenous farmers, and uses public pressure and the hashtag #NoBloodMoney to dissuade credit card companies and payment start-ups from processing money for white-supremacist organizations. With Consumer Reports and a number of other groups and companies, it demanded that

Facebook take a stand against hate speech. By 2020, Color of Change's email list had ballooned from 1.7 million members to more than 7 million, and its text-message list grew from around 100,000 people to nearly 6 million.

Online activism that fights for principles such as transparency, networking, and participation—what activists and authors Jeremy Heimans and Henry Timms call "new power"—has exciting potential. Combined with strategic use to focus on real, obtainable, and meaningful goals, and not simply changing profile pictures in support of the latest popular cause, this new power can carry us further down the road toward our desired destination: a fair marketplace.

We also need to see more of what my friend Micah Sifry calls "civic tech." An author of books on improving American democracy, Micah is a Consumer Reports board member and a cofounder of Civic Hall, a hub for change-minded technology professionals in New York City. He defines civic tech as any use of technology for the public good. Over the past few years, a number of tech companies with missions of improving the world have sprouted. Code for America is one. Nearly $60 billion in government benefits go unclaimed each year by eligible people, and programmers at Code for America work to link those individuals with the assistance available.

Another, SeeClickFix, is a social network that enables community members to report issues like an abandoned pet, a broken sidewalk, or an overflowing trash can at a public park and receive a response from someone who can address the matter. The network, which can work with local government or stay neighbor to neighbor, gives people a tighter connection with what's going on in their towns and stronger engagement with their neighbors.

"Civic tech is still in its early days," says Micah, who cautions against what he calls "solutionism"—the belief that programmers know best and can right all wrongs. "Civic tech builds solutions *with* communities instead of *for* them."

Micah is right. Technology alone can't build civic muscle. We also have to widen the avenues that bring new people and communities to the consumer cause. We have to extend ourselves through new relationships that connect to other movements. We have to ask ourselves: Who's being left out?

During my last semester of college, I was a summer intern in Washington, DC, with Ralph Nader's organization, Public Citizen. I first saw Ralph on TV when I was young. I admired the way he stood up to power. He, too, was the child of immigrants—his parents were from Lebanon. Nader wasn't only the country's foremost consumer advocate; he also promoted an idea of civic engagement in which individuals use their unique skills to solve problems identified not by government or industry but by the people themselves. This vision spoke to me.

The internship was eye-opening for a college student eager to learn how to make change happen in people's lives. At that time there wasn't a great deal of diversity among Nader's Raiders, the nickname the media gave to Ralph's staff of public-interest lawyers. In fact, I was the only minority among the interns. That wasn't unusual when I was a student. But thirty-five years later, and what feels like a million years since that internship, not enough relationships with people from different and diverse communities have been forged. When I spoke at a consumer conference in 2015, I was disappointed that I still didn't see many people in the audience who looked like me—and I said so. The only other Latina at the event was a college student who came up to me after I spoke and told me how glad she was that I'd mentioned the lack of diversity among the consumer activists at the event.

When it comes to people who haven't seen themselves represented, we need to invite them into the consumer movement and help make their important issues, vital needs, personal dreams, and individual communities more visible in our work. We're not yet doing that. Consumer issues are everyone's issues. In the 1960s, when my family arrived from Cuba, Latino and African American buying power was negligible. Today, each group accounts for more than $1 trillion in consumer spending, with the total approaching $3 trillion and rising. If Latinos in the US were their own country, they'd represent the eleventh-largest economy in the world. Our movement hasn't done enough to empower them, to connect our work to their challenges in the marketplace, and to build trust. The same is true for all underrepresented groups in our consumer-first movement, whether they're Black, Latino, Native American, Asian American, LGBTQ, disabled people, younger people—everyone.

In addition to reaching out to more communities, we have to make clear there isn't just one way to be a part of the consumer movement. When I was an intern, most consumer advocates were lawyers fighting the legal fights. Many battles were won because of that work, including the establishment of the Consumer Product Safety Commission, the National Highway Transportation Safety Administration, and the Environmental Protection Agency.

But today, we can't afford to limit our movement to those with law degrees or those who are ready to march down city streets carrying signs and chanting slogans. There are different roles for different people—from the reformer ready to join local government to promote better policies, to the online activist using their web power to spread information and to create communities for change, to the technologist who wants to make the internet work for people, to the business student who wants to bring ethical and consumer-focused standards into their work and corporate culture, to the doctor committed to fighting discriminatory practices and treatments. Everyone can be a part of this movement. Everyone can help make a difference.

Over the years, when I attended conferences and took part in panels focused on consumer activism, people would often ask me, "Where's the movement we need?" It seems we've been looking for it for decades. But we've got to stop trying to find it. Because it's here. It's all of us. We are the movement we've been waiting for.

We can do the everyday things. Stick up for ourselves. Speak up for others. We can call a company to complain about a mystery fee on a monthly bill, write an email to a member of Congress urging them to take action, or tell our friends or strangers online about how they can help a worthy cause. These small actions are the sparks that ignite a larger fire. Because the movement doesn't stop there. We aim to dramatically transform an entire marketplace to bring fair standards, consumer-friendly laws, and justice for those injured or abused.

How will we know we've succeeded?

When we have strong product-safety rules, so consumers can buy with confidence.

When companies responsible for a problem are held accountable regardless of their wealth or influence.

When all financial transactions are transparent and fair and don't pull consumers into debt traps.

When consumers have access to data-control solutions and the keys to their own online privacy and security.

When we know the items we buy won't hurt our own health or our environment.

When higher education is a path to social and economic mobility, not a lifetime of debt.

When a family isn't confronted with discrimination while purchasing a home.

When children can play at home without the risk of being hurt by the items around them.

That's the world we're fighting for. When you ask for it—when you demand it—know that millions of others are demanding it too. Millions of voices alongside yours.

You're part of something bigger. You're transforming things. You're making a better world. Welcome to the consumer movement—the people's movement. Let's get to work.

Acknowledgments

MANY PEOPLE WARNED ME THAT WRITING A BOOK CAN BE A solitary endeavor, but working on this project was far from that, even during a global pandemic that required most interactions on this journey to be virtual. It began with Matt Latimer and Keith Urbahn at Javelin, who believed in the story I wanted to tell. They introduced me to my editor Colleen Lawrie and the marvelous folks at PublicAffairs, who supported every aspect of the development, writing, and production of *Buyer Aware*. Colleen's perpetual enthusiasm and positive spirit helped me push through even as COVID shifted the professional and personal realities of how we conduct our lives.

So many of the stories, research, thinking, and knowledge that inform these pages build on the work and legacy of many in the consumer movement. Navigating my way through that history and the fast-changing consumer marketplace was a weighty task made lighter only by a terrific team that worked tirelessly through it all with me. I was fortunate to work closely with Bob Ivry, a gifted author and writer who helped me bring shape, substance, and simplicity to an otherwise unruly set of ideas. Long hours and late nights of writing did not diminish his good cheer and ear for what I was struggling to convey. Joshua Cinelli showed an unshakable steadiness while he advised me and organized a process that had many moving parts. He kept them all moving forward. Phil Cardarella's eagle eye and meticulous review of every detail allowed us to sleep at night. The indispensable Lina Vitarelli magically found the time and protected the space for me to stay on task. Thanks as well to board members of Consumer Reports, whose encouragement was indispensable to the completion of the book.

There were also so many others who played a vital role in making this book possible, including Jeff Alexander, Joaquin Alvarado, Nikitra Bailey, Bill Bradley, Justin Brookman, David Butler, Camille Calman, Dan Cluchey, Syed Ejaz, Jake Fisher, David Friedman, Heath Grayson, Esther Han, Michael Hubner, Karen Kelly, Sally Kohn, Suzanne Martindale, Ben Moskowitz, Cathy O'Neil, Jon Schwantes, Sumit Sharma, Jen Shecter, Micah Sifry, Jenny Sucov, Shar Taylor, Jenny Toomey, Will Wallace, and Leonora Wiener. *Buyer Aware* is a culmination of great minds, and any flaws in the book are mine alone. Thank you all.

My gratitude to my family is without limit. I want to thank my parents, Marta Rodriguez and Ibrahim Tellado, whose courage and fortitude in leaving their homeland created a new life full of opportunities for me. Curling up next to me every day was four-legged Coquito, reminding me that breaks were essential. And a mere thank-you doesn't seem adequate to express my love and appreciation to my husband, David Maddox, for supporting me and feeding me delicious meals throughout the hours of our lives that writing this book filled. Te amo.

Bibliography

INTRODUCTION: CONSUMER RIGHTS ARE CIVIL RIGHTS

Angwin, Julia, Jeff Larson, Lauren Kirchner, and Surya Mattu. "Minority Neighborhoods Pay Higher Car Insurance Premiums than White Areas with the Same Risk." ProPublica/Consumer Reports, April 5, 2017. www.propublica.org/article/minority-neighborhoods-higher-car-insurance-premiums-white-areas-same-risk.

Bosman, Julie, Sophie Kasakove, and Daniel Victor. "U.S. Life Expectancy Plunged in 2020, Especially for Black and Hispanic Americans." *New York Times*, July 21, 2021. www.nytimes.com/2021/07/21/us/american-life-expectancy-report.html.

Chase, Stuart, and F. J. Schlink. *Your Money's Worth: A Study in the Waste of the Consumer's Dollar.* New York: MacMillan, 1927.

Consumer Reports. "A Long History of Standing Up for American Consumers." Accessed January 10, 2022. https://trustcr.org/.

Korman, Hailly T. N., Bonnie O'Keefe, and Matt Repka. "Missing in the Margins: Estimating the Scale of the COVID-19 Attendance Crisis." Bellwether Education Partners, October 21, 2020. https://bellwethereducation.org/publication/missing-margins-estimating-scale-covid-19-attendance-crisis.

Molotsky, Irvin. "Esther Peterson Dies at 91; Worked to Help Consumers." *New York Times*, December 22, 1997. www.nytimes.com/1997/12/22/us /esther-peterson-dies-at-91-worked-to-help-consumers.html.

National Consumers League. "A Look Back on 100+ Years of Advocacy." Accessed January 10, 2022. https://nclnet.org/about-ncl/about-us /history/.

Randolph, A. Philip. "Mission Statement." A. Philip Randolph Campus High School, accessed February 14, 2022. www.aprandolph.com/apps /pages/index.jsp?uREC_ID=846867&type=d&pREC_ID=1216142.

Science History Institute. "Ellen H. Swallow Richards." Last updated December 15, 2017. www.sciencehistory.org/historical-profile/ellen-h-swallow -richards.

US Consumer Product Safety Commission. "CPSC Sues Amazon to Force Recall of Hazardous Products Sold on Amazon.com." Press release, July 14, 2021. www.cpsc.gov/Newsroom/News-Releases/2021/CPSC-Sues -Amazon-to-Force-Recall-of-Hazardous-Products-Sold-on-Amazon-com.

CHAPTER ONE: YOUR LIFE, THEIR PROFIT

Apple, Inc. *A Day in the Life of Your Data*. April 2021. www.apple.com /privacy/docs/A_Day_in_the_Life_of_Your_Data.pdf.

Brookman, Justin. *Understanding the Scope of Data Collection by Major Technology Platforms*. Consumer Reports Digital Lab, May 2020. https://digital-lab.consumerreports.org/wp-content/uploads/2021/02 /Understanding-the-scope-of-data-collection-by-major-platforms_2020 _FINAL.pdf.

Valentino-DeVries, Jennifer, Natasha Singer, Michael H. Keller, and Aaron Krolik. "Your Apps Know Where You Were Last Night, and They're Not Keeping It Secret." *New York Times*, December 10, 2018. www.nytimes .com/interactive/2018/12/10/business/location-data-privacy-apps.html.

How Free Is Free?

Zuboff, Shoshana. *The Age of Surveillance Capitalism: The Fight for a Human Future at the New Frontier of Power*. New York: PublicAffairs, 2019.

"We Can't Have Both"

Byrnes, Nanette. "Tim Cook: Technology Should Serve Humanity, Not the Other Way Around." *MIT Technology Review*, June 9, 2017.

www.technologyreview.com/2017/06/09/151322/tim-cook-technology
-should-serve-humanity-not-the-other-way-around/.

Ceglowski, Maciej. "The Internet with a Human Face." *Idle Words*
(blog), May 20, 2014. https://idlewords.com/talks/internet_with_a_human
_face.htm.

Ghaffary, Shirin, and Alex Kantrowitz. "Should We Break Up Google?"
Land of the Giants podcast, season 3, episode 7. Recode and the Vox Media
Podcast Network, March 30, 2021. https://podcasts.apple.com/my/podcast
/should-we-break-up-google/id1465767420?i=1000514996566&l=ms.

Global Stats: Stat Counter. "Search Engine Market Share North America:
July 2009–July 2021." Updated December 2021. https://gs.statcounter.com
/search-engine-market-share/all/north-america/#monthly-200907-202107.

Heilweil, Rebecca. "Why the U.S. Government Wants Facebook
to Sell Off Instagram and WhatsApp." Vox/Recode, December 9, 2020.
www.vox.com/recode/22166437/facebook-instagram-ftc-attorneys-general
-antitrust-monopoly-whatsapp.

Khan, Lina. "Amazon's Antitrust Paradox." *Yale Law Journal*, January
2017. www.yalelawjournal.org/note/amazons-antitrust-paradox.

Kohan, Shelley E. "Amazon's Net Profit Soars 84% with Sales Hitting
$386 Billion." *Forbes*, February 2, 2021. www.forbes.com/sites/shelleykohan
/2021/02/02/amazons-net-profit-soars-84-with-sales-hitting-386-billion
/?sh=7c41c3011334.

Leswing, Kif. "Apple Can No Longer Force Developers to Use In-App
Purchasing, Judge Rules in Epic Games Case." CNBC, September 10, 2021.
www.cnbc.com/2021/09/10/epic-games-v-apple-judge-reaches-decision-.html.

Manjoo, Farhad. "The Apple Tax Is Rotten." *New York Times*, May 26, 2021.
www.nytimes.com/2021/05/26/opinion/apple-app-store-fortnite-lawsuit
.html?action=click&module=Opinion&pgtype=Homepage.

Molla, Rani, and Adam Clark Estes. "Google's Three Antitrust Cases,
Briefly Explained." Vox/Recode, December 17, 2020. www.vox.com
/recode/2020/12/16/22179085/google-antitrust-monopoly-state-lawsuit
-ad-tech-search-facebook.

Statt, Nick. "Google Is Still Paying Apple Billions to Be the Default
Search Engine in Safari." Verge, July 1, 2020. www.theverge.com/2020
/7/1/21310591/apple-google-search-engine-safari-iphone-deal-billions
-regulation-antitrust.

US Congress (House), Judiciary Committee, Subcommittee on Antitrust, Commercial, and Administrative Law. *Investigation of Competition*

in Digital Markets. October 2020. https://judiciary.house.gov/uploadedfiles
/competition_in_digital_markets.pdf?utm_campaign=4493-519.

Zakrzewski, Cat, and Tyler Pager. "Biden Taps Big Tech Critic Lina Khan
to Chair the Federal Trade Commission." *Washington Post*, June 15, 2021.
www.washingtonpost.com/technology/2021/06/15/khan-ftc-confirmation
-vote/.

Digital Fingerprinting

Bohn, Dieter. "Google to 'Phase Out' Third-Party Cookies in Chrome,
but Not for Two Years." Verge, January 14, 2020. www.theverge.com
/2020/1/14/21064698/google-third-party-cookies-chrome-two-years-privacy
-safari-firefox.

Brookman, Justin. *Understanding the Scope of Data Collection by Major
Technology Platforms*. Consumer Reports Digital Lab, May 2020. https://digital
-lab.consumerreports.org/wp-content/uploads/2021/02/Understanding-the
-scope-of-data-collection-by-major-platforms_2020_FINAL.pdf.

Cox, Joseph. "Hundreds of Bounty Hunters Had Access to AT&T,
T-Mobile, and Sprint Customer Location Data for Years." Motherboard, February 6, 2019. www.vice.com/en/article/43z3dn/hundreds-bounty-hunters
-att-tmobile-sprint-customer-location-data-years.

Germain, Thomas. "DuckDuckGo's Solution to Google's Latest Privacy Controversy." *Consumer Reports*, April 12, 2021. www.consumer
reports.org/privacy/duckduckgo-solution-to-latest-google-privacy-controversy
-a7122636451/.

Iati, Marisa, and Michelle Boorstein. "Case of High-Ranking Cleric
Allegedly Tracked on Grindr App Poses Rorschach Test for Catholics." *Washington Post*, July 21, 2021. www.washingtonpost.com/religion/2021/07/21
/catholic-official-grindr-reaction/.

Lapowsky, Issie. "FLoC Is Dead. But Topics Won't Fix Google's Ad-
Targeting Problems." Protocol, January 26, 2022. www.protocol.com/bulletins
/floc-topics-google.

Lomas, Natasha. "Europe's Cookie Consent Reckoning Is Coming."
TechCrunch, May 31, 2021. https://techcrunch.com/2021/05/30/europes
-cookie-consent-reckoning-is-coming/.

Tanner, Adam. "Starting Today, Jealous Lovers Can Buy NSA-Like Monitoring Powers." *Forbes*, March 12, 2014. www.forbes.com/sites/adamtanner
/2014/03/12/starting-today-jealous-lovers-can-buy-nsa-like-monitoring
-powers/?sh=1103d8c56148.

From the Personal to the Political

Coldewey, Devin. "Facebook Bans First App Since Cambridge Analytica, MyPersonality, and Suspends Hundreds More." TechCrunch, August 22, 2018. https://tcrn.ch/3kB2iX2.

Grassegger, Hannes, and Mikael Krogerus. "The Data That Turned the World Upside Down." Motherboard, January 28, 2017. www.vice.com/en/article/mg9vvn/how-our-likes-helped-trump-win.

Issenberg, Sasha. "Cruz-Connected Data Miner Aims to Get Inside U.S. Voters' Heads." Bloomberg, November 12, 2015. www.bloomberg.com/news/features/2015-11-12/is-the-republican-party-s-killer-data-app-for-real-.

Mosley, Tonya. "Developer of MyPersonality App Fires Back Against Facebook's Allegations." KQED, August 23, 2018. www.kqed.org/news/11688419/developer-of-mypersonality-app-fires-back-against-facebooks-allegations.

Tobias, Manuela. "Comparing Facebook Data Use by Obama, Cambridge Analytica." PolitiFact, March 22, 2018. www.politifact.com/factchecks/2018/mar/22/meghan-mccain/comparing-facebook-data-use-obama-cambridge-analyt/.

The Spy in My Living Room

Bridges, Lauren. "Amazon's Ring Is the Largest Civilian Surveillance Network the U.S. Has Ever Seen." *The Guardian*, May 18, 2021. www.theguardian.com/commentisfree/2021/may/18/amazon-ring-largest-civilian-surveillance-network-us.

Federal Trade Commission. "Vizio to Pay $2.2 Million to FTC, State of New Jersey to Settle Charges It Collected Viewing Histories on 11 Million Smart Televisions Without Users' Consent." Press release, February 6, 2017. www.ftc.gov/news-events/press-releases/2017/02/vizio-pay-22-million-ftc-state-new-jersey-settlecharges-it.

Germain, Thomas. "How a Photo's Hidden 'Exif' Data Exposes Your Personal Information." *Consumer Reports*, December 6, 2019. www.consumerreports.org/privacy/what-can-you-tell-from-photo-exif-data/.

Hill, Kashmir. "'People You May Know': A Controversial Facebook Feature's 10-Year History." Gizmodo, August 8, 2018. https://gizmodo.com/people-you-may-know-a-controversial-facebook-features1827981959.

Horcher, Gary. "Woman Says Her Amazon Device Recorded Private Conversation, Sent It Out to Random Contact." KIRO 7 News, May 25,

2018. www.kiro7.com/news/local/woman-says-her-amazon-device-recorded
-private-conversation-sent-it-out-to-random-contact/755507974/.

Kim, Eugene. "This Guy Turned His Failure on 'Shark Tank' into a $28 Million Investment from Richard Branson." *Business Insider*, August 19, 2015. www.businessinsider.com/ring-from-shark-tank-to-richard-branson-2015-8.

Priest, David. "Ring Will Stop Sending Video Requests from Police to Neighbors App Users." CNET, June 3, 2021. www.cnet.com/home/security /ring-will-stop-sending-video-requests-from-police-to-neighbors-app-users/.

_____. "Ring's Police Problem Didn't Go Away. It Just Got More Transparent." CNET, June 6, 2021. www.cnet.com/home/security/rings -police-problem-didnt-go-away-it-just-got-more-transparent/.

St. John, Allen. "Smart Speakers That Listen When They Shouldn't." *Consumer Reports*, August 29, 2019. www.consumerreports.org/smart -speakers/smart-speakers-that-listen-when-they-shouldnt/.

When Hackers Attack

Associated Press. "Data of More than 40 Million Exposed in T-Mobile Breach." *Los Angeles Times*, updated August 18, 2021. www.latimes.com /business/story/2021-08-18/data-of-more-than-40-million-exposed-in-t -mobile-data-breach#:~:text=T%2DMobile%20says%20about%207.8,in %20a%20recent%20data%20breach.

Hill, Michael, and Dan Swinhoe. "The 15 Biggest Data Breaches of the 21st Century." CSO, July 16, 2021. www.csoonline.com/article/2130877 /the-biggest-data-breaches-of-the-21st-century.html.

Security Planner, Consumer Reports, accessed January 10, 2022. https://securityplanner.consumerreports.org/.

St. John, Allen. "Stopping the Data Breach Epidemic." *Consumer Reports*, December 21, 2018. www.consumerreports.org/data-theft/stopping-the-data -breach-epidemic-a2767478423/.

Digital Standard

Consumer Reports. "The Digital Standard." Accessed January 10, 2022. https://digital-lab.consumerreports.org/the-digital-standard/.

Apple's Gambit

Barrett, Brian. "Don't Buy into Facebook's Ad-Tracking Pressure on iOS 14.5." *Wired*, May 3, 2021. www.wired.com/story/facebook-ad-tracking -pressure-ios-14-5/.

Facebook, Inc. "Facebook Report Fourth Quarter and Full Year 2020 Results." Press release, January 27, 2021. https://investor.fb.com/investor -news/press-release-details/2021/Facebook-Reports-Fourth-Quarter-and -Full-Year-2020-Results/default.aspx.

———. "How the Apple iOS 14 Release May Affect Your Ads and Reporting." Accessed January 10, 2022. www.facebook.com/business /help/331612538028890?id=428636648170202.

Fowler, Geoffrey A., and Tatum Hunter. "When You 'Ask App Not to Track,' Some iPhone Apps Keep Snooping Anyway." *Washington Post*, September 23, 2021. www.washingtonpost.com/technology/2021/09/23 /iphone-tracking/.

Germain, Thomas. "What the New iPhone Tracking Setting Means, and What to Do When You See It." *Consumer Reports*, April 26, 2021. www .consumerreports.org/privacy/what-the-new-iphone-tracking-setting -means-and-what-to-do-when-you-see-it-a8018618269/.

Gruber, John. "Online Privacy Should Be Modeled on Real-World Privacy." *Daring Fireball* (blog), September 3, 2020. https://daringfireball .net/2020/09/online_privacy_real_world_privacy.

Ha, Anthony. "Apple's App Tracking Transparency Feature Has Arrived—Here's What You Need to Know." TechCrunch, April 26, 2021. https://techcrunch.com/2021/04/26/apples-app-tracking-transparency -feature-has-arrived-heres-what-you-need-to-know/.

Jansen, Bernard J., Kathleen Moore, and Stephen Carman. "Evaluating the Performance of Demographic Targeting Using Gender." *Information Processing and Management*, July 17, 2012. https://faculty.ist.psu.edu/jjansen /academic/jansen_gender_ppc.pdf.

John, Leslie K., Tami Kim, and Kate Barasz. "Ads That Don't Overstep." *Harvard Business Review*, January–February 2018. https://hbr.org/2018/01 /ads-that-dont-overstep.

Laziuk, Estelle. "iOS 14.5 Opt-in Rate—Daily Updates Since Launch." *Flurry* (blog), April 29, 2021. www.flurry.com/blog/ios-14-5-opt-in-rate-att -restricted-app-tracking-transparency-worldwide-us-daily-latest-update/.

Levy, Dan. "Speaking Up for Small Businesses." Facebook, December 16, 2020, last updated June 30, 2021. www.facebook.com/business/news/ios -14-apple-privacy-update-impacts-small-business-ads.

Matsakis, Louise. "Online Ad Targeting Does Work—as Long as It's Not Creepy." *Wired*, May 11, 2018. www.wired.com/story/online-ad-targeting -does-work-as-long-as-its-not-creepy/?utm_source=WIR_REG_GATE.

O'Dea, S. "Share of Smartphone Users That Use an Apple iPhone in the United States from 2014 to 2021." Statista, March 31, 2021. www.statista .com/statistics/236550/percentage-of-us-population-that-own-a-iphone -smartphone/.

Statista Research Department. "U.S. Digital Advertising, Statistics and Facts." Statista, November 4, 2021. www.statista.com/topics/1176/online -advertising/.

Warren, Tom. "Facebook Hits Back at Apple with Second Critical Newspaper Ad." Verge, December 17, 2020. www.theverge.com/2020/12 /17/22180102/facebook-new-newspaper-ad-apple-ios-14-privacy-prompt.

Technology in the Public Interest

Alphabet, Inc. "Alphabet Announces Third Quarter 2021 Results." Press release, October 26, 2021. https://abc.xyz/investor/static/pdf/2021Q3 _alphabet_earnings_release.pdf.

Amazon.com, Inc. "Amazon.com Announces Third Quarter Results." Press release, October 28, 2021. https://s2.q4cdn.com/299287126/files /doc_financials/2021/q3/Q3-2021-Earnings-Release.pdf.

Apple, Inc. "Condensed Consolidated Statements of Operations (Un-audited)," through June 26, 2021. Accessed January 11, 2022. www.apple .com/newsroom/pdfs/FY21_Q3_Consolidated_Financial_Statements .pdf.

DataGrail. *The State of CCPA: 2021 Consumer Privacy Report.* Accessed January 11, 2022. https://bit.ly/2XMdWG0.

Facebook, Inc. "Facebook Reports Third Quarter 2021 Results." Press release, October 25, 2021. https://s21.q4cdn.com/399680738/files /doc_financials/2021/q3/FB-09.30.2021-Exhibit-99.1.pdf.

Lohr, Steve. "Once Tech's Favorite Economist, Now a Thorn in Its Side." *New York Times*, May 20, 2021. www.nytimes.com/2021/05/20/technology /tech-antitrust-paul-romer.html?referringSource=articleShare.

McCabe, David. "Maryland Approves Country's First Tax on Big Tech's Ad Revenue." *New York Times*, February 12, 2021. www.nytimes.com/2021 /02/12/technology/maryland-digital-ads-tax.html.

Myrstad, Finn, and Oyvind H. Kaldestad. "International Coalition Calls for Action Against Surveillance-Based Advertising." ForbrukerRadet, June 22, 2021. www.forbrukerradet.no/side/new-report-details-threats-to-consumers -from-surveillance-based-advertising/.

Perzanowski, Aaron. "Consumer Perceptions of the Right to Repair." *Indiana Law Journal*, November 16, 2020, page 29. https://papers.ssrn.com/sol3/papers.cfm?abstract_id=3584377.

Waddell, Kaveh. "An Interview with Tech Activist and Author Cory Doctorow." *Consumer Reports*, June 15, 2021. www.consumerreports.org/digital-rights/an-interview-with-tech-activist-and-author-cory-doctorow-a1943952645/.

White House. "Fact Sheet: Executive Order on Promoting Competition in the American Economy." Press release, July 9, 2021. www.whitehouse.gov/briefing-room/statements-releases/2021/07/09/fact-sheet-executive-order-on-promoting-competition-in-the-american-economy/.

Wikipedia. "Office of Technology Assessment." Last edited January 9, 2022. https://en.wikipedia.org/wiki/Office_of_Technology_Assessment.

CHAPTER TWO: THE MISINFORMATION MARKETPLACE

Liberty Center for God and Country. "The Communist Democrats Created Massive Election Fraud." Facebook, November 6, 2020. https://www.facebook.com/libertycgc/.

Office of the District Attorney, Harris County, Texas. "Former Houston Police Captain Charged with Holding Repairman at Gunpoint in Bogus Voter-Fraud Conspiracy." Press release, December 15, 2020. https://app.dao.hctx.net/former-houston-police-captain-charged-holding-repairman-gunpoint-bogus-voter-fraud-conspiracy.

Salcedo, Andrea. "An Ex-Cop Held an A/C Repairman at Gunpoint over a False Claim He Had 750,000 Fake Ballots, Police Said." *Washington Post*, December 16, 2020. www.washingtonpost.com/nation/2020/12/16/aguirre-texas-cop-election-fraud/.

Shay, Miya, and Jessica Willey. "Former HPD Capt. Mark Anthony Aguirre Charged with Holding Air Conditioning Man at Gunpoint in Fake Voter-Fraud Conspiracy." ABC13, December 19, 2020. https://abc13.com/mark-anthony-aguirre-former-houston-police-department-captain-arrested-aggravated-assault-liberty-center/8802235/.

Magic Beans

Chase, Stuart, and F. J. Schlink. *Your Money's Worth: A Study in the Waste of the Consumer's Dollar*. New York: MacMillan, 1927.

Woodward, Helen. *Through Many Windows*. New York: Harper's Modern Classics, 1925.

Wu, Tim. *The Attention Merchants: The Epic Scramble to Get Inside Our Heads*. New York: Vintage Books, 2017.

Online Reviews

Baker, Trevor, and Josh Robbins. "Five-Star Fakes." Which?, September 2019.

Consumer Reports. "A User's Guide to User Reviews." April 2014. www.consumerreports.org/cro/magazine/2014/05/a-user-s-guide-to-user-reviews/index.htm.

eBay. "Top Rated Seller Program." Accessed January 11, 2022. https://pages.ebay.com/seller-center/service-and-payments/top-rated-program.html.

Hart, Robert. "Amazon and Google Face U.K. Investigation into Fake Reviews." *Forbes*, June 25, 2021. www.forbes.com/sites/roberthart/2021/06/25/amazon-and-google-face-uk-investigation-into-fake-reviews/?sh=7949ed424340.

He, Sherry, Brett Hollenbeck, and Davide Proserpio. "The Market for Fake Reviews." SSRN, August 20, 2020. https://papers.ssrn.com/sol3/papers.cfm?abstract_id=3664992.

Hickman, Arvind. "More than Half of Instagram Influencers 'Engaged in Fraud,' with 45 Percent of Accounts 'Fake.'" PR Week, April 15, 2021. www.prweek.com/article/1712976/half-instagram-influencers-engaged-fraud-45-per-cent-accounts-fake.

Morris, Richard L. D., ed. *The Consumer Movement: Lectures by Colston E. Warne*. Yonkers, New York: Consumer Reports, 2014.

Nguyen, Nicole. "Her Amazon Purchases Are Real. The Reviews Are Fake." *BuzzFeed News*, November 20, 2019. www.buzzfeednews.com/article/nicolenguyen/her-amazon-purchases-are-real-the-reviews-are-fake.

Stone, Brad. *The Everything Store: Jeff Bezos and the Age of Amazon*. New York: Little, Brown, 2014.

Swearingen, Jake. "Hijacked Reviews on Amazon Can Trick Shoppers." *Consumer Reports*, August 26, 2019. www.consumerreports.org/customer-reviews-ratings/hijacked-reviews-on-amazon-can-trick-shoppers/.

Misinformation Strikes Back

Chang, Ailsa. "How Facebook Wants to Handle Misinformation Around the Coronavirus Epidemic." *All Things Considered*, NPR, March 25, 2020.

www.npr.org/2020/03/25/821591134/how-facebook-wants-to-handle
-misinformation-around-the-coronavirus-epidemic.

Germain, Thomas. "How Social Platforms Are Scrambling to Slow the
Spread of Election Falsehoods." *Consumer Reports*, October 30, 2020. www
.consumerreports.org/election-day/how-social-platforms-are-scrambling-to
-slow-the-spread-of-election-falsehoods-a5253312422/.

Sesin, Carmen. "Spanish-Language Covid Disinformation Is Aimed at
Latinos as Delta Surges." NBC News, September 6, 2021. www.nbcnews
.com/news/latino/spanish-language-covid-disinformation-aimed-latinos-delta
-surges-rcna1809.

Daily Doses of Bleach

Dwoskin, Elizabeth. "Russia Is Still the Biggest Player in Disinformation, Facebook Says." *Washington Post*, May 26, 2021. www.washingtonpost
.com/technology/2021/05/26/facebook-disinformation-russia-report/.

Ingram, David. "Facebook Says 126 Million Americans May Have Seen
Russia-Linked Political Posts." Reuters, October 30, 2017. www.reuters
.com/article/us-usa-trump-russia-socialmedia/facebook-says-126-million
-americans-may-have-seen-russia-linked-political-posts-idUSKBN1
CZ2OI.

Kornbluh, Karen, Eli Weiner, and Adrienne Goldstein. "New Study by
Digital New Deal Finds Engagement with Deceptive Outlets Higher on
Facebook Today than Run-Up to 2016 Election." German Marshall Fund
of the United States, October 12, 2020. https://www.gmfus.org/news/new
-study-digital-new-deal-finds-engagement-deceptive-outlets-higher-facebook
-today-run-2016.

Linddara, Dara. "Facebook's 'I Voted' Sticker Was a Secret Experiment
on Its Users." Vox, November 4, 2014. www.vox.com/2014/11/4/7154641
/midterm-elections-2014-voted-facebook-friends-vote-polls.

McGregor, Jena. "What Mark Zuckerberg Got Wrong with His 1300-
Word Facebook Memo." *Forbes*, October 7, 2021. www.forbes.com/sites
/jenamcgregor/2021/10/06/what-mark-zuckerberg-got-wrong-facebook
-memo/?sh=3d3dea106d7f.

Meyer, Robinson. "Everything We Know About Facebook's Secret
Mood-Manipulation Experiment." *The Atlantic*, June 28, 2014. www
.theatlantic.com/technology/archive/2014/06/everything-we-know-about
-facebooks-secret-mood-manipulation-experiment/373648/.

Pelley, Scott. "Facebook Whistleblower Frances Haugen: The 60 Minutes Interview." Video, YouTube, October 3, 2021. www.youtube.com/watch?v=_Lx5VmAdZSI.

Salinas, Sara. "The Top Trending Video on YouTube Was a False Conspiracy That a Survivor of the Florida School Shooting Was an Actor." CNBC, February 21, 2018. www.cnbc.com/2018/02/21/fake-news-item-on-parkland-shooting-become-top-youtube-video.html.

Schultz, Colin. "In the Wake of the Boston Marathon Bombing, Twitter Was Full of Lies." *Smithsonian*, October 24, 2013. www.smithsonianmag.com/smart-news/in-the-wake-of-the-boston-marathon-bombing-twitter-was-full-of-lies-5294419/.

Sullivan, Margaret. "Facebook Is Harming Our Society. Here's a Radical Solution for Reining It In." *Washington Post*, October 5, 2021. www.washingtonpost.com/lifestyle/media/media-sullivan-facebook-whistleblower-haugen/2021/10/04/3461c62e-2535-11ec-8831-a31e7b3de188_story.html.

Waddell, Kaveh. "Facebook Approved Ads with Coronavirus Misinformation." *Consumer Reports*, April 7, 2020. www.consumerreports.org/social-media/facebook-approved-ads-with-coronavirus-misinformation/.

Wagner, Kurt, and Naomi Nix. "Facebook Disables Accounts Tied to NYU Research Project." Bloomberg, August 3, 2021. www.bloomberg.com/news/articles/2021-08-03/facebook-disables-accounts-tied-to-nyu-research-project.

Wells, Georgia, Jeff Horwitz, and Deepa Seetharaman. "Facebook Knows Instagram Is Toxic for Teen Girls, Company Documents Show." *Wall Street Journal*, September 14, 2021. www.wsj.com/articles/facebook-knows-instagram-is-toxic-for-teen-girls-company-documents-show-11631620739.

Zuboff, Shoshana. *The Age of Surveillance Capitalism: The Fight for a Human Future at the New Frontier of Power*. New York: PublicAffairs, 2019.

Correcting the Record

Bond, Shannon. "In 1st Big Test, Oversight Board Says Facebook, Not Trump, Is the Problem." NPR, May 7, 2021. www.npr.org/2021/05/07/994436847/what-we-learned-about-facebook-from-trump-decision.

Clegg, Nick. "In Response to Oversight Board, Trump Suspended for Two Years; Will Only Be Reinstated if Conditions Permit." Facebook, June 4, 2021. https://about.fb.com/news/2021/06/facebook-response-to-oversight-board-recommendations-trump/.

Conger, Kate. "Twitter's Revenue Jumps 28 Percent in Its First Post-Trump Quarter." *New York Times*, April 29, 2021. www.nytimes.com/2021/04/29/business/twitter-growth-trump-ban.html.

Dwoskin, Elizabeth, and Craig Timberg. "Misinformation Dropped Dramatically the Week After Twitter Banned Trump and Some Allies." *Washington Post*, January 16, 2021. www.washingtonpost.com/technology/2021/01/16/misinformation-trump-twitter/.

Goldmacher, Shane. "Trump Sues Tech Firms for Blocking Him, and Fund-Raises off It." *New York Times*, July 7, 2021. www.nytimes.com/2021/07/07/us/politics/trump-lawsuit-facebook-google-twitter.html.

Kornbluh, Karen, Eli Weiner, and Adrienne Goldstein. "New Study by Digital New Deal Finds Engagement with Deceptive Outlets Higher on Facebook Today than Run-Up to 2016 Election." German Marshall Fund of the United States, October 12, 2020. www.gmfus.org/news/new-study-digital-new-deal-finds-engagement-deceptive-outlets-higher-facebook-today-run-2016.

Lehman, Laurel. "CR's Section 230 2020 Legislative Round-Up." Digital Lab at Consumer Reports, February 8, 2021. https://medium.com/cr-digital-lab/crs-section-230-2020-legislative-round-up-4683c309fcb3.

Romm, Tony, and Elizabeth Dwoskin. "Trump Banned from Facebook Indefinitely, CEO Mark Zuckerberg Says." *Washington Post*, January 7, 2021. www.washingtonpost.com/technology/2021/01/07/trump-twitter-ban/.

St. John, Allen. "What Congress' Section 230 Debate Means for the Future of Online Speech." *Consumer Reports*, February 8, 2021. www.consumerreports.org/federal-laws-regulations/what-is-section-230-communications-decency-act-a3205342497/.

Swisher, Kara. "Good Riddance, Donald Trump?" *New York Times*, May 5, 2021. www.nytimes.com/2021/05/05/opinion/trump-facebook-oversight-board.html.

Twitter, Inc. "Permanent Suspension of @realDonaldTrump." January 8, 2021. https://blog.twitter.com/en_us/topics/company/2020/suspension.

US Code, Title 47, Telecommunications, Section 230. Accessed January 11, 2022. https://uscode.house.gov/view.xhtml?req=(title:47%20section:230%20edition:prelim).

News of the World

Grieco, Elizabeth. "Fast Facts About the Newspaper Industry's Financial Struggles as McClatchy Files for Bankruptcy." Pew Research Center,

February 14, 2020. www.pewresearch.org/fact-tank/2020/02/14/fast-facts -about-the-newspaper-industrys-financial-struggles/.

Harris, Lauren. "Local Newsrooms Can Combat Polarization, if Only They Have the Margins." *Columbia Journalism Review*, June 9, 2021. www .cjr.org/the_media_today/local-news-can-combat-polarization.php.

Notarangelo, Liz White. Interview with author, November 19, 2021.

The Net's Huckster Houseguests

FBI. "Elder Fraud." Accessed February 3, 2022. www.fbi.gov/scams-and -safety/common-scams-and-crimes/elder-fraud.

What Can I Do Now?

Hardee, Howard. "Stick Up for Truth: How to Fact-Check Friends and Family on Social Media." *Cap Times*, September 26, 2020. https:// captimes.com/news/local/govt-and-politics/stick-up-for-truth-how-to-fact -check-friends-and-family-on-social-media/article_61874df5-bc62-522c -a182-022ee45bc34a.html.

CHAPTER THREE: FINANCIAL FAIRNESS

Brancaccio, David. "Elizabeth Warren on Credit Card Tricks and Traps.'" *Now on PBS*, January 9, 2009. www.shoppbs.pbs.org/now/shows/501/credit -traps.html.

Consumer Financial Protection Bureau. "Enforcement by the Numbers." January 2021. www.consumerfinance.gov/enforcement/enforcement-by-the -numbers/.

Federal Trade Commission. *Consumer Sentinel Network, Data Book 2020.* February 2021. www.ftc.gov/system/files/documents/reports /consumer-sentinel-network-data-book-2020/csn_annual_data_book_2020 .pdf.

Graves, Steven. "Think Payday Lending Isn't Out of Control in the United States?" California State University Northridge, accessed January 11, 2022. www.csun.edu/~sg4002/research/mcdonalds_by_state.htm.

Thou Shalt Not

Americans for Financial Reform. *Private Equity Piles into Payday Lending and Other Subprime Consumer Lending.* December 2017. https://

pestakeholder.org/wp-content/uploads/2017/12/PE-Investment-in-Payday
-Installment-Lending-AFR-PESP-121117-with-links.pdf.

 Amscot Financial. "Amscot Financial Sponsors 40th Annual Calle Ocho
Festival." Press release, Business Wire, March 9, 2017. www.businesswire
.com/news/home/20170309006106/en/Amscot-Financial-Sponsors-40th
-Annual-Calle-Ocho-Festival.

 ————. "Amscot Financial to Partner with Local Law Enforcement Dis-
tributing Bike Helmets in 18 Florida Counties." Press release, Business Wire,
October 17, 2018. www.businesswire.com/news/home/20181017005594
/en/Amscot-Financial-to-Partner-with-Local-Law-Enforcement-Distributing
-Bike-Helmets-in-18-Florida-Counties.

 Baker, Dean. "This Is What Minimum Wage Would Be if It Kept Pace
with Productivity." Center for Economic and Policy Research, January 21, 2021.
https://cepr.net/this-is-what-minimum-wage-would-be-if-it-kept-pace
-with-productivity/.

 Balancing Everything. "Payday Loan Statistics." December 31, 2021.
https://balancingeverything.com/payday-loan-statistics/.

 Center for Responsible Lending. "Map of U.S. Payday Interest Rates."
March 23, 2021. www.responsiblelending.org/research-publication/map-us
-payday-interest-rates.

 ————. "Payday and Car Title Lenders Drain Nearly $8 Billion in
Fees Every Year." April 25, 2019. www.responsiblelending.org/research
-publication/payday-and-car-title-lenders-drain-8-billion-fees-every
-year.

 CNN Business. "EZCORP Inc." Accessed January 11, 2022. https://
money.cnn.com/quote/shareholders/shareholders.html?symb=EZPW
&subView=institutional.

 Consumer Affairs. "Amscot—The Money Superstore." Customer reviews, updated December 29, 2021. www.consumeraffairs.com/finance
/amscot-financial.html.

 Credit Summit. Payday Loan Debt Statistics in the US (Updated
2021)." Accessed January 11, 2022. www.mycreditsummit.com/payday-loan
-debt-statistics/.

 Fox, Jean Ann, Tom Feltner, Delvin Davis, and Uriah King. *Driven to Di-
saster: Car-Title Lending and Its Impact on Consumers.* Center for Responsible Lending, February 28, 2013. www.responsiblelending.org/other-consumer
-loans/car-title-loans/research-analysis/CRL-Car-Title-Report-FINAL.pdf.

FRED Economic Data. "10-Year High Quality Market (HQM) Corporate Bond Spot Rate." Updated December 10, 2021. https://fred.stlouisfed.org/series/HQMCB10YR.

Gordon, Mark. "Pay Day." *Business Observer*, October 28, 2016. www.businessobserverfl.com/article/pay-day

Gray, Michael. "Obama Orchestrated a Massive Transfer of Wealth to the 1 Percent." *New York Post*, January 17, 2016. https://nypost.com/2016/01/17/occupy-obama-he-orchestrated-a-massive-transfer-of-wealth-to-the-1-percent/.

InCharge Debt Solutions. "How Do Payday Loans Work?" Updated December 6, 2021. www.incharge.org/debt-relief/how-payday-loans-work/.

Open Secrets. "Payday Lenders." Accessed January 11, 2022. www.opensecrets.org/industries/indus.php?cycle=2020&ind=F1420.

Sherman, Erik. "How Great Recession Bank Rescue Profited the Wealthy and Hurt Lower Income People." *Forbes*, August 30, 2019. www.forbes.com/sites/eriksherman/2019/08/30/how-great-recession-bank-rescue-profited-the-wealthy-and-hurt-lower-income-people/?sh=157fb5f654e6.

Stempel, Jonathan. "U.S. Returns $505 Million to Victims of Giant Payday Lending Scheme." Reuters, September 27, 2018. www.reuters.com/article/us-usa-paydaylending/u-s-returns-505-million-to-victims-of-giant-payday-lending-scheme-idUSKCN1M72BX.

US Naval Criminal Investigative Service. *Security Clearance Appeals Process*. Accessed January 11, 2022. www.secnav.navy.mil/dusnp/Security%20Documents/NAVY%20GMT%20Training.pdf.

"Hearse Chasers"

Felton, Ryan. "How an Obscure Industry Makes Money off the Dead." *Consumer Reports*, April 15, 2021. www.consumerreports.org/predatory-lending/how-an-obscure-industry-makes-money-off-the-dead/.

Lazarus, David. "Sorry for Your Loss—Would a Cash Advance Ease Your Pain?" *S.F. Gate*, October 8, 2004. www.sfgate.com/business/article/Sorry-for-your-loss-would-a-cash-advance-ease-2719166.php.

House of Games

Fredman, Catherine. "Health Insurance Marketplace Scam Alert." *Consumer Reports*, March 4, 2016. www.consumerreports.org/consumer-protection/health-insurance-marketplace-scam/.

Nickel and Dimed

Board of Governors of the Federal Reserve System. "Federal Reserve Board Announces Temporary Actions Aimed at Increasing the Availability of Intraday Credit Extended by Federal Reserve Banks." Press release, April 23, 2020. www.federalreserve.gov/newsevents/pressreleases/other20200423a.htm.

Consumer Reports Advocacy. "South Carolina Rejects Duke Energy Fee Hike After 'What the Fee?!' Outcry." Press release, May 2, 2019. https://advocacy.consumerreports.org/press_release/south-carolina-rejects-duke-energy-fee-hike-after-what-the-fee-outcry/.

Mariner Finance. "Itemized Schedule of Charges (DE): Closed End Loans." Accessed January 11, 2022. www.marinerfinance.com/wp-content/uploads/2017/06/Delaware-Schedule-of-Fees-Closed-End-Loans-06_2017.pdf.

Ponciano, Jonathan. "Sen. Warren Grills Billionaire JPMorgan CEO for Collecting $1.5 Billion in Overdraft Fees During Pandemic." *Forbes*, May 26, 2021. https://bit.ly/2ZZfTzw.

Schwantes, Jonathan. *What the Fee?! How Cable Companies Use Hidden Fees to Raise Prices and Disguise the True Cost of Service: CR Cable Bill Report 2019.* Consumer Reports, October 2019. https://advocacy.consumerreports.org/wp-content/uploads/2019/10/CR-Cable-Bill-Report-2019.pdf.

US Congress. H.R. 5035: Television Viewer Protection Act of 2019. Accessed January 11, 2022. www.congress.gov/bill/116th-congress/house-bill/5035/text.

Wang, Penelope. "Protect Yourself from Hidden Fees." *Consumer Reports*, May 29, 2019. www.consumerreports.org/fees-billing/protect-yourself-from-hidden-fees/.

Warburg Pincus. Home page, updated December 22, 2021. https://warburgpincus.com/.

Companies Embracing Ethics

Business Roundtable. "Business Roundtable Redefines the Purpose of a Corporation to Promote 'An Economy That Serves All Americans.'" August 19, 2019. www.businessroundtable.org/business-roundtable-redefines-the-purpose-of-a-corporation-to-promote-an-economy-that-serves-all-americans.

Gurdus, Lizzy. "ESG Investing to Reach $1 Trillion by 2030, Says Head of iShares Americas as Carbon Transition Funds Launch." CNBC, May 9,

2021. www.cnbc.com/2021/05/09/esg-investing-to-reach-1-trillion-by-2030
-head-of-ishares-americas.html.

Murray, Alan, and Katherine Dunn. "Two Years After the Business
Roundtable Statement on Stakeholder Capitalism, Has Anything Changed?"
Fortune, August 18, 2021. https://fortune.com/2021/08/18/ceo-daily-two
-years-business-roundtable/.

Riding, Siobhan. "Majority of ESG Funds Outperform Wider Market over 10 Years." *Financial Times*, June 13, 2020. www.ft.com/content
/733ee6ff-446e-4f8b-86b2-19ef42da3824.

Forced into Arbitration

Berliner, Uri. "Wells Fargo Admits to Nearly Twice as Many Possible
Fake Accounts—3.5 Million." NPR, August 31, 2017. www.npr.org/sections
/thetwo-way/2017/08/31/547550804/wells-fargo-admits-to-nearly-twice-as
-many-possible-fake-accounts-3-5-million.

Corkery, Michael. "Amazon Ends Use of Arbitration for Customer
Disputes." *New York Times*, July 22, 2021. www.nytimes.com/2021/07/22
/business/amazon-arbitration-customer-disputes.html.

Medintz, Scott. "Forced Arbitration: A Clause for Concern." *Consumer
Reports*, January 30, 2020. www.consumerreports.org/mandatory-binding
-arbitration/forced-arbitration-clause-for-concern/.

Randazzo, Sara. "Amazon Faced 75,000 Arbitration Demands. Now
It Says: Fine, Sue Us." *Wall Street Journal*, June 1, 2021. www.wsj.com
/articles/amazon-faced-75-000-arbitration-demands-now-it-says-fine-sue
-us-11622547000.

Warren, Elizabeth. "Senator Elizabeth Warren Questions Wells Fargo
CEO John Stumpf at Banking Committee Hearing." Video, YouTube, September 20, 2016. www.youtube.com/watch?v=xJhkX74D10M.

The Stickiest Debt

Barnard, Julia. "New Bipartisan Poll Shows Strong Support for Student Loan Debt Cancellation During COVID-19 Pandemic." Center for
Responsible Lending, May 12, 2020. www.responsiblelending.org/media
/new-bipartisan-poll-shows-strong-support-student-loan-debt-cancellation
-during-covid-19.

Board of Governors of the Federal Reserve System. "Report on the
Economic Well-Being of U.S. Households in 2020." May 2021. www

.federalreserve.gov/publications/2021-economic-well-being-of-us
-households-in-2020-dealing-with-unexpected-expenses.htm.

CBS News. "Military Borrowers Express Frustration over Public Service Loan Forgiveness Program." *60 Minutes*, September 30, 2021. www
.cbsnews.com/video/military-borrowers-express-frustration-over-public
-service-loan-forgiveness-program/.

Consumer Reports. "Degrees of Debt and Regret." June 28, 2016. www
.consumerreports.org/student-loan-debt-crisis/degrees-of-debt-and-regret/.

Cowley, Stacy. "The Education Department Ends Its Effort to Stop States from Suing Federal Student Loan Servicers." *New York Times*, August 9, 2021. www.nytimes.com/2021/08/09/business/states-federal-student
-loan-services.html.

Duffin, Erin. "College Enrollment in Public and Private Institutions in the U.S., 1965–2029." Statista, September 10, 2021. www.statista.com
/statistics/183995/us-college-enrollment-and-projections-in-public-and
-private-institutions/.

Executive Office of the President of the United States. *Investing in Higher Education: Benefits, Challenges, and the State of Student Debt.* July 2016. https://obamawhitehouse.archives.gov/sites/default/files/page/files
/20160718_cea_student_debt.pdf.

Friedman, Zack. "Student Loan Debt Statistics in 2021: A Record $1.7 Trillion." *Forbes*, February 20, 2021. www.forbes.com/sites/zackfriedman
/2021/02/20/student-loan-debt-statistics-in-2021-a-record-17-trillion/?sh
=4d9fc03c1431.

H&R Block. "I Have a Student Loan Debt Offset. Can the IRS Take This Debt Out of My Refund Money, Including the Amount I Receive for the Earned Income Credit (EIC)?" Accessed January 12, 2022. www.hrblock
.com/tax-center/lifestyle/education/student-loan-debt-offset/.

Hanson, Melanie. "Student Loan Debt Statistics." Education Data Initiative, last updated November 17, 2021. https://bit.ly/3Ahkolx.

Helhoski, Anna. "Biden's Student Loan Forgiveness Could Wipe Out Debt for 15 Million Borrowers." NerdWallet, August 6, 2021. www.nerdwallet
.com/article/loans/student-loans/bidens-student-loan-forgiveness-could-wipe
-out-debt-for-15-million-borrowers.

Livingston, Gretchen. "Is U.S. Fertility at an All-Time Low? Two of Three Measures Point to Yes." Pew Research Center, May 22, 2019. www
.pewresearch.org/fact-tank/2019/05/22/u-s-fertility-rate-explained/.

Mitchell, Michael, Michael Leachman, and Matt Saenz. "State Higher Education Funding Cuts Have Pushed Costs to Students, Worsened Inequality." Center on Budget and Policy Priorities, October 24, 2019. www.cbpp.org/research/state-budget-and-tax/state-higher-education-funding-cuts-have-pushed-costs-to-students.

Nau, Michael, Rachel E. Dwyer, and Randy Hodson. "Can't Afford a Baby? Debt and Young Americans." *Research in Social Stratification and Mobility*, December 2015. www.sciencedirect.com/science/article/abs/pii/S0276562415000402.

O'Neil, Cathy. *Weapons of Math Destruction: How Big Data Increases Inequality and Threatens Democracy*. New York: Crown, 2016. (See Chapter 3, "Arms Race: Going to College.")

Rosato, Donna. "How to Qualify for Public Service Loan Forgiveness." *Consumer Reports*, October 25, 2018. www.consumerreports.org/student-loans/how-to-qualify-for-public-service-loan-forgiveness/.

Sherman, Erik. "College Tuition Is Rising at Twice the Inflation Rate—While Students Learn at Home." *Forbes*, August 31, 2020. www.forbes.com/sites/zengernews/2020/08/31/college-tuition-is-rising-at-twice-the-inflation-rate-while-students-learn-at-home/?sh=53ad165c2f98.

Turner, Cory. "Borrowers Say They Were Wrongly Denied Loan Forgiveness. Now, Help Is on the Way." NPR, November 4, 2021. www.npr.org/2021/11/04/1051463060/student-loan-forgiveness-overhaul-fedloan-public-service-borrowers.

Walton Family Foundation and Echelon Insights. *Opening Doors to Opportunity: Generation Z and Millennials Speak*. October 2020. https://bit.ly/3mrcEs1.

Wermund, Benjamin. "The Red State That Loves Free College." *Politico*, January 16, 2019. www.politico.com/agenda/story/2019/01/16/tennessee-free-college-000867/.

Whitford, Emma. "State Higher Ed Funding Looks Positive." *Inside Higher Ed*, August 10, 2021. www.insidehighered.com/news/2021/08/10/after-year-cuts-state-funding-looks-positive-fiscal-2022.

Credit Mysteries

Ejaz, Syed. "A Broken System: How the Credit Reporting System Fails Consumers and What to Do About It." *Consumer Reports*, June 10, 2021. https://advocacy.consumerreports.org/wp-content/uploads/2021/06/A

-Broken-System-How-the-Credit-Reporting-System-Fails-Consumers-and
-What-to-Do-About-It.pdf.

Gill, Lisa L. "The Hidden Costs of Credit Karma, Credit Sesame, and Other Credit Score Apps." *Consumer Reports*, September 30, 2021. www.consumerreports.org/credit-protection-monitoring/hidden-costs-of -credit-score-apps-a5900455243/.

_____. "How to Fix Your Credit Score." *Consumer Reports*, June 10, 2021. www.consumerreports.org/credit-scores-reports/how-to-fix-your-credit -score/.

_____. "More than a Third of Volunteers in a Consumer Reports Study Found Errors in Their Credit Reports." *Consumer Reports*, June 10, 2021. www.consumerreports.org/credit-scores-reports/consumers-found-errors -in-their-credit-reports-a6996937910/.

CHAPTER FOUR: BIAS IN, BIAS OUT

George, Alice. "The 1968 Kerner Commission Got It Right, but No-body Listened." *Smithsonian*, March 1, 2018. www.smithsonianmag.com /smithsonian-institution/1968-kerner-commission-got-it-right-nobody -listened-180968318/.

McLaughlin, Kevin, director. *Riot*. 2015. http://riotthefilm.com/.

Ms., cover image from vol. 1, no. 1. National Museum of American History, accessed January 17, 2022. https://s.si.edu/2WT2Dv0.

Mumford, Kevin. *Newark: A History of Race, Rights, and Riots in America*. New York: NYU Press, 2007.

Rojas, Rick, and Khorri Atkinson. "Five Days of Unrest That Shaped, and Haunted, Newark." *New York Times*, July 11, 2017. www.nytimes.com /2017/07/11/nyregion/newark-riots-50-years.html.

Drawing Red Lines Between Us

Calderon, Melanie. "No Place to Call Home: Latinos Suffer Housing Discrimination in U.S." Committee on U.S.–Latin American Relations, April 7, 2020. https://cuslar.org/2020/04/07/no-place-to-call-home-latinos -suffer-housing-discrimination-in-u-s/.

Coates, Ta-Nehisi. "The Case for Reparations." *The Atlantic*, June 2014. www.theatlantic.com/magazine/archive/2014/06/the-case-for-reparations /361631/.

FRED Economic Research, Federal Reserve Bank of St. Louis. "Housing and Homeownership: Homeownership Rate." Accessed January 17, 2022. https://fred.stlouisfed.org/release/tables?rid=296&eid=784188.

Harvard T. H. Chan School of Public Health. "Poll Finds One-Third of Latinos Say They Have Experienced Discrimination in Their Jobs and When Seeking Housing." Press release, November 1, 2017. www.hsph.harvard.edu/news/press-releases/poll-latinos-discrimination/.

Ivry, Bob. "Wall Street Kept Winning on Mortgages Upending Homeowners." Bloomberg, November 19, 2012. www.bloomberg.com/news/articles/2012-11-19/wall-street-kept-winning-on-mortgages-upending-homeowners.

Kamin, Debra. "Black Homeowners Face Discrimination in Appraisals." *New York Times*, August 25, 2020. www.nytimes.com/2020/08/25/realestate/blacks-minorities-appraisals-discrimination.html.

O'Neil, Cathy. *Weapons of Math Destruction: How Big Data Increases Inequality and Threatens Democracy*. New York: Crown, 2016.

Perry, Andre M., Jonathan Rothwell, and David Harshbarger. "The Devaluation of Assets in Black Neighborhoods." Brookings Institution, November 27, 2018. www.brookings.edu/research/devaluation-of-assets-in-black-neighborhoods/.

Rothstein, Richard. "A 'Forgotten History' of How the U.S. Government Segregated America." Interview by Terry Gross. *Fresh Air*, May 3, 2017. www.npr.org/2017/05/03/526655831/a-forgotten-history-of-how-the-u-s-government-segregated-america.

Credit Deserts

Aponte-Diaz, Graciela. "State Research Shows That Payday Lending Stores Are Heavily Concentrated in African American and Latino Communities Across California." Center for Responsible Lending, December 9, 2016. www.responsiblelending.org/media/state-research-shows-payday-lending-stores-are-heavily-concentrated-african-american-and.

Consumer Financial Protection Bureau. *Consumer Use of Payday, Auto Title, and Pawn Loans*. May 2021. https://files.consumerfinance.gov/f/documents/cfpb_consumer-use-of-payday-auto_title-pawn_loans_research-brief_2021-05.pdf.

Gill, Lisa L. "How to Fix Your Credit Score." *Consumer Reports*, June 10, 2021. www.consumerreports.org/credit-scores-reports/how-to-fix-your-credit-score/.

Mayer, Robert N., and Nathalie Martin. *The Power of Community Action: Anti-Payday Loan Ordinances in Three Metropolitan Areas.* Silicon Valley Community Foundation, January 24, 2017. www.siliconvalleycf.org/sites/default/files/publications/mayer-martin-payday-ordinances.pdf.

Remor, Isabella, and Caleb Quakenbush. "Americans' Credit Health Improved During the Pandemic, but There's More to the Story." *Urban Institute* (blog), February 17, 2021. www.urban.org/urban-wire/americans-credit-health-improved-during-pandemic-theres-more-story.

Scigliuzzo, Davide. "Charging 589% Interest in the Pandemic Is a Booming Business." Bloomberg, May 17, 2021. www.bloomberg.com/graphics/2021-payday-loan-lenders/.

Algorithms Have a Race Problem

ACLU of Northern California. "Facial Recognition Technology Falsely Identifies 26 California Legislators with Mugshots." Press release, August 13, 2019. www.aclunc.org/news/facial-recognition-technology-falsely-identifies-26-california-legislators-mugshots.

Agre, Philip E. "Your Face Is Not a Bar Code." Department of Information Studies, UCLA, updated September 10, 2003. https://pages.gseis.ucla.edu/faculty/agre/bar-code.html.

Dastin, Jeffrey. "Amazon Extends Moratorium on Police Use of Facial Recognition Software." Reuters, May 18, 2021. www.reuters.com/technology/exclusive-amazon-extends-moratorium-police-use-facial-recognition-software-2021-05-18/.

Duranton, Sylvain. "How Humans and AI Can Work Together to Create Better Businesses." TED Talk, September 2019. www.ted.com/talks/sylvain_duranton_how_humans_and_ai_can_work_together_to_create_better_businesses?language=en.

Hao, Karen. "The Two-Year Fight to Stop Amazon from Selling Face Recognition to the Police." *MIT Technology Review*, June 12, 2020. www.technologyreview.com/2020/06/12/1003482/amazon-stopped-selling-police-face-recognition-fight/.

Mac, Ryan. "Facebook Apologizes After A.I. Puts 'Primates' Label on Video of Black Men." *New York Times*, September 3, 2021. www.nytimes.com/2021/09/03/technology/facebook-ai-race-primates.html.

National Institute of Standards and Technology. "NIST Study Evaluates Effects of Race, Age, Sex on Face Recognition Software." December 19, 2019.

www.nist.gov/news-events/news/2019/12/nist-study-evaluates-effects-race
-age-sex-face-recognition-software.

Williams, Robert. "I Did Nothing Wrong. I Was Arrested Anyway."
ACLU, July 15, 2021. https://bit.ly/2WSIlSi.

Algorithms Have a Race Problem 2.0

Angwin, Julia, Jeff Larson, Lauren Kirchner, and Surya Mattu. "Minority Neighborhoods Pay Higher Car Insurance Premiums than White Areas with the Same Risk." ProPublica/Consumer Reports, April 5, 2017. www.propublica.org/article/minority-neighborhoods-higher-car-insurance -premiums-white-areas-same-risk.

Belson, Ken. "Black Former N.F.L. Players Say Racial Bias Skews Concussion Payouts." *New York Times*, August 25, 2020. www.nytimes .com/2020/08/25/sports/football/nfl-concussion-racial-bias.html.

Dastin, Jeffrey. "Amazon Scraps Secret AI Recruiting Tool That Showed Bias Against Women." Reuters, October 10, 2018. www.reuters.com/article /us-amazon-com-jobs-automation-insight/amazon-scraps-secret-ai-recruiting -tool-that-showed-bias-against-women-idUSKCN1MK08G.

Lima, Cristiano. "The Technology 202: Democrats Urged Google to Get Itself Vetted for Racial Biases. It Hasn't Budged." *Washington Post*, August 10, 2021. www.washingtonpost.com/politics/2021/08/10/technology -202-democrats-urged-google-get-itself-vetted-racial-biases-it-hasnt -budged/.

Stanger, Tobie. "The Smart Way to Save on Car Insurance." *Consumer Reports*, September 26, 2019. www.consumerreports.org/car-insurance/the -smart-way-to-save-on-car-insurance/.

Vincent, James. "Twitter Taught Microsoft's AI Chatbot to Be a Racist Asshole in Less than a Day." Verge, March 24, 2016. www.theverge .com/2016/3/24/11297050/tay-microsoft-chatbot-racist.

Vyas, Darshali A., Leo G. Eisenstein, and David S. Jones. "Hidden in Plain Sight: Reconsidering the Use of Race Correction in Clinical Algorithms." *New England Journal of Medicine*, August 27, 2020. www.nejm.org /doi/pdf/10.1056/NEJMms2004740.

Waddell, Kaveh. "Medical Algorithms Have a Race Problem." *Consumer Reports*, September 18, 2020. www.consumerreports.org/medical-tests /medical-algorithms-have-a-race-problem/.

Discrimination Costs Lives

Centers for Disease Control and Prevention. "Risk for COVID-19 Infection, Hospitalization, and Death by Race/Ethnicity." September 9, 2021. www.cdc.gov/coronavirus/2019-ncov/covid-data/investigations-discovery /hospitalization-death-by-race-ethnicity.html.

DeGuire, Peter, Binxin Cao, Lauren Wisnieski, Doug Strane, Robert Wahl, Sarah Lyon-Callo, and Erika Garcia. *Detroit: The Current Status of the Asthma Burden*. Michigan Department of Health and Human Services Bureau of Disease Control, Prevention and Epidemiology. March 2016. www. michigan.gov/documents/mdhhs/Detroit-AsthmaBurden_516668_7.pdf.

Fox 2 Detroit. "Beaumont Worker Turned Away 4 Times with COVID-19 Symptoms Before Dying." April 22, 2020. www.fox2detroit.com/news /beaumont-worker-turned-away-4-times-with-covid-19-symptoms-before -dying.

Han, Nydia, and Cheryl Mettendorf. "Woman Shares Emotional Story of COVID-19's Impact on Family, Latino Community." *ABC 6 Action News*, November 20, 2020. https://6abc.com/coronavirus-covid-19-deaths -latino/8129625/.

Hoffman, Kelly M., Sophie Trawalter, Jordan R. Axt, and M. Norman Oliver. "Racial Bias in Pain Assessment and Treatment Recommendations, and False Beliefs About Biological Differences Between Blacks and Whites." *Proceedings of the National Academy of Sciences of the United States of America*, April 19, 2016. www.pnas.org/content/113/16/4296.

Koons, Cynthia, and Bob Ivry. "Covid Plus Decades of Pollution Are a Nasty Combo for Detroit." *Bloomberg Businessweek*, October 20, 2020. www .bloomberg.com/news/features/2020-10-21/covid-pandemic-southwest -detroit-faces-pollution-covid-19-outbreaks.

National Comprehensive Cancer Network. "Latino Men Are Much Less Likely to Receive Optimal Treatment for High Risk Prostate Cancer than White Men, According to New Research in JNCCN." Press release, November 15, 2018. https://prn.to/30ftgM6.

Shamus, Kristen Jordan. "Family Ravaged by Coronavirus Begged for Tests, Hospital Care, but Was Repeatedly Denied." *Detroit Free Press*, April 19, 2020. www.freep.com/story/news/local/michigan/wayne/2020/04/19 /coronavirus-racial-disparity-denied-tests-hospitalization/2981800001/.

US Department of Health and Human Services, Office of Minority Health. "Minority Population Profiles: Hispanic/Latino Americans." Last modified October 12, 2021. www.minorityhealth.hhs.gov/omh/browse.aspx?lvl =3&lvlid=64.

Blood Makes Noise

Brodwin, Erin, and Nicholas St. Fleur. "FDA Issues Alert on 'Limitations' of Pulse Oximeters, Without Explicit Mention of Racial Bias." *STAT*, February 19, 2021. www.statnews.com/2021/02/19/fda-issues-alert-on -limitations-of-pulse-oximeters-without-explicit-mention-of-racial-bi/.

Moran-Thomas, Amy. "Oximeters Were Once Designed for Equity. What Happened?" *Wired*, June 4, 2021. www.wired.com/story/pulse-oximeters -equity/.

Sjoding, Michael W., Robert P. Dickson, Theodore J. Iwashyna, Steven E. Gay, and Thomas S. Valley. "Racial Bias in Pulse Oximetry Measurement." *New England Journal of Medicine*, December 17, 2020. www .nejm.org/doi/10.1056/NEJMc2029240.

Valley, Thomas, Michael W. Sjoding, and Susan Goold. "Commentary: More Health Inequality: Black People Are 3 Times More Likely to Experience Pulse Oximeter Errors." University of Michigan Institute for Healthcare Policy and Innovation, January 18, 2021. https://ihpi.umich.edu/news/commentary -more-health-inequality-black-people-are-3-times-more-likely-experience-pulse.

Designed by Men, for Men

Bajorek, Joan Palmiter. "Voice Recognition Still Has Significant Race and Gender Biases." *Harvard Business Review*, May 10, 2019. https://hbr. org/2019/05/voice-recognition-still-has-significant-race-and-gender-biases.

Barry, Keith. "The Crash Test Bias: How Male-Focused Testing Puts Female Drivers at Risk." *Consumer Reports*, October 23, 2019. www.consumer reports.org/car-safety/crash-test-bias-how-male-focused-testing-puts-female -drivers-at-risk/.

———. "New Data Expands on Why Women Have a Greater Risk of Injury in Car Crashes." *Consumer Reports*, February 11, 2021. www .consumerreports.org/car-safety/new-data-expands-on-why-women-have-a -greater-risk-of-injury-in-car-crashes-a7451402105/.

Belluck, Pam. "Chilly at Work? Office Formula Was Devised for Men." *New York Times*, August 3, 2015. www.nytimes.com/2015/08/04/science /chilly-at-work-a-decades-old-formula-may-be-to-blame.html.

Dinamani, Pavi, and Rich Shibley. "Why Aren't Smartphones Designed for a Woman's Hand Size?" *Digital Trends*, October 15, 2020. www.digital trends.com/mobile/smartphone-size-design-for-woman-hand/.

Olson, Mary. "Females Exposed to Nuclear Radiation Are Far Likelier than Males to Suffer Harm." Pass Blue, July 5, 2017. www.passblue.com /2017/07/05/females-exposed-to-nuclear-radiation-are-far-likelier-than-males -to-suffer-harm/.

Price, Jay. "Female Soldiers Are Getting New Body Armor Designed Just for Them." *Morning Edition*, NPR, July 22, 2021. www.npr.org/2021 /07/19/1017774038/female-soldiers-are-excited-about-new-body-armor-that -is-designed-for-them.

Wei-Haas, Maya. "First All-Woman Space Walk Puts Spotlight on Spacesuit Design." *National Geographic*, October 18, 2019. www.national geographic.com/science/article/first-all-women-spacewalk-suit-design.

The Pink Tax

Fried, Carla. "Pink Tax Repeal Act Aims to Make Pricing Fair to Women." *Consumer Reports*, July 11, 2016. www.consumerreports.org/ shopping/pink-tax-repeal-act-aims-to-make-pricing-fair-to-women/.

Miller, Walli. "How Payday Loan Lenders Target Women of Color." *Clever Girl Finance* (blog), September 1, 2021. www.clevergirlfinance.com /blog/how-payday-loan-lenders-target-women-of-color/.

New York City Department of Consumer Affairs. *From Cradle to Cane: The Cost of Being a Female Consumer*. December 2015. www1.nyc .gov/assets/dca/downloads/pdf/partners/Study-of-Gender-Pricing-in-NYC .pdf.

Office of US Congresswoman Jackie Speier. "Speier Reintroduces Pink Tax Repeal Act to End Gender-Based Pricing Discrimination." Press release, June 11, 2021. https://speier.house.gov/press-releases?id=C2F060D1 -0D84-4824-B9E5-40F879F22CFA.

Wakeman, Jessica. "Pink Tax: The Real Cost of Gender-Based Pricing." Healthline, August 6, 2020. www.healthline.com/health/the-real-cost -of-pink-tax#The-tampon-tax.

A $175 Billion Market

Ford Foundation. "Disability Inclusion." Accessed February 14, 2022. www.fordfoundation.org/work/challenging-inequality/disability-inclusion /us-disability-rights-program/.

Friedman, Vanessa. "Why Is Facebook Rejecting These Fashion Ads?" *New York Times*, February 11, 2021. www.nytimes.com/2021/02/11/style /disabled-fashion-facebook-discrimination.html.

Jackson, Lottie. "'It's a Basic Human Right': The Fight for Adaptive Fashion." *The Guardian*, February 26, 2021. www.theguardian.com /fashion/2021/feb/26/its-a-basic-human-right-the-fight-for-adaptive-fashion.

Nielsen. *Reaching Prevalent, Diverse Consumers with Disabilities*. 2016. www.nielsen.com/wp-content/uploads/sites/3/2019/04/reaching-prevalent -diverse-consumers-with-disabilities.pdf.

Sillitoe, Ben. "Disabled Consumers Left Logged Out of Retail's Digital Revolution." *Computer Weekly*, October 2, 2019. www.computerweekly.com /feature/Disabled-consumers-left-logged-out-of-retails-digital-revolution.

Broadband from the Mountaintops

Balingit, Moriah. "'A National Crisis': As Coronavirus Forces Many Schools Online This Fall, Millions of Disconnected Students Are Being Left Behind." *Washington Post*, August 16, 2020. www.washingtonpost .com/education/a-national-crisis-as-coronavirus-forces-many-schools-online -this-fall-millions-of-disconnected-students-are-being-left-behind/2020 /08/16/458b04e6-d7f8-11ea-9c3b-dfc394c03988_story.html.

Callimachi, Rukmini. "'I Used to Like School': An 11-Year-Old's Struggle with Pandemic Learning." *New York Times*, May 5, 2021. www .nytimes.com/2021/05/05/us/remote-learning-education-pandemic.html.

Common Cause Education Fund. *Broadband Gatekeepers: How ISP Lobbying and Political Influence Shapes the Digital Divide*. July 2021. www .commoncause.org/wp-content/uploads/2021/07/CCBroadbandGatekeepers _WEB1.pdf.

Consumer Reports. "Consumer Reports Launches Let's Broadband Together—A Nationwide Search for the Truth About Your Internet Service." Press release, July 13, 2021. www.consumerreports.org/media-room/press-releases /2021/07/consumer-reports-launches-broadband-together—a-nationwide -sea/.

Feir, D. L., and Charles Golding. "Native Employment During COVID-19: Hit Hard in April but Starting to Rebound?" Federal Reserve Bank of Minneapolis, August 5, 2020. www.minneapolisfed.org/article /2020/native-employment-during-covid-19-hit-hard-in-april-but-starting-to -rebound.

Kamanetz, Anya. "Enrollment Is Dropping in Public Schools Around the Country." NPR, October 9, 2020. www.npr.org/2020/10/09/920316481 /enrollment-is-dropping-in-public-schools-around-the-country.

Korman, Hailly T. N., Bonnie O'Keefe, and Matt Repka. "Missing in the Margins 2020: Estimating the Scale of the COVID-19 Attendance Crisis." Bellwether Education Partners, October 21, 2020. https://bellwether education.org/publication/missing-margins-estimating-scale-covid-19 -attendance-crisis#How%20did%20you%20estimate%201-3%20million %20missing%20students.

LightBox. "LightBox Digital Divide Mapping." Accessed January 18, 2022. www.lightboxre.com/solutions/connectivity-map/.

Morris, Traci. Letter to Representative Teresa Leger Fernandez. American Indian Policy Institute, April 1, 2021. https://naturalresources.house .gov/imo/media/doc/SCIP%2004.21.21%20Testimony%20-%20Dr.%20Morris %20(AIPI).pdf.

PBS SoCal, KCET, KLCS-TV, and Los Angeles Unified School District. "Los Angeles Unified Partnership with PBS SoCal and KCET Plans to Provide Educational Content to Students." Press release, March 12, 2020. https://kcet-brightspot.s3.amazonaws.com/legacy/sites/kl/files/atoms /document/los_angeles_unified_partnership_with_pbs_socal_and_kcet _031220finalrevised.pdf.

Rantanen, Matthew. Interview with author, July 13, 2021.

Shelton, Chris, and Angela Siefer. "Many Americans Still Don't Have Internet Access—Congress Should Help." *The Hill*, October 28, 2020. https://thehill.com/opinion/technology/523179-many-americans-still-dont -have-internet-access-congress-should-help.

Tomer, Adie, Lara Fishbane, Angela Siefer, and Bill Callahan. *Digital Prosperity: How Broadband Can Deliver Health and Equity to All Communities*. Brookings Institution, February 27, 2020. https://brook.gs/3GasBfp.

Vogels, Emily A. "Digital Divide Persists Even as Americans with Lower Incomes Make Gains in Tech Adoption." Pew Research, June 22, 2021. www.pewresearch.org/fact-tank/2021/06/22/digital-divide-persists-even-as -americans-with-lower-incomes-make-gains-in-tech-adoption/.

Whitacre, Brian, Roberto Gallardo, and Sharon Strover. "Broadband's Contribution to Economic Growth in Rural Areas: Moving Towards a Causal Relationship." *Telecommunications Policy*, December 2014. www .sciencedirect.com/science/article/abs/pii/S0308596114000949.

What Can I Do Now?

Affo, Marina. "Come Prepared, Speak Up, Take Notes: How to Advocate for Yourself at the Doctor's Office." *Delaware News Journal*, October 20, 2020. www.usatoday.com/story/news/health/2020/10/20/heres-how-doctors -say-advocate-yourself-appointments/5989178002/.

Cabotaje, Angela. "Blocking Bias: How to Speak Up for Your Health." *Right as Rain*, February 20, 2020. https://rightasrain.uwmedicine.org/well /health/minority-health-bias.

Jagannathan, Meera. "Bias in Health Care Isn't Limited to Race, Religion or Gender: How to Protect Yourself Against This Common Medical Practice." MarketWatch, September 3, 2019. www.marketwatch.com/story /how-to-protect-yourself-against-medical-bias-2019-09-03.

Yousry, Farah. "Self-Advocacy Can Improve Health Outcomes for Black Women." WFYI, May 12, 2021. www.wfyi.org/news/articles/self-advocacy -can-improve-health-outcomes-for-black-women.

CHAPTER FIVE: SAFETY

National Highway Traffic Safety Administration. "Motor Vehicle Traffic Fatalities and Fatality Rates, 1899–2019." May 2021. https://cdan.nhtsa .gov/tsftables/Fatalities%20and%20Fatality%20Rates.pdf.

———. "2020 Fatality Data Show Increased Traffic Fatalities During Pandemic." June 3, 2021. www.nhtsa.gov/press-releases/2020-fatality-data -show-increased-traffic-fatalities-during-pandemic.

Peachman, Rachel Rabkin. "Is This Safe to Buy? How Dangerous Products Get—and Stay—on the Market." *Consumer Reports*, May 4, 2021. www.consumerreports.org/product-safety/is-this-safe-to-buy-how-dangerous -products-get-and-stay-on-the-market/.

How Many Children?

Peachman, Rachel Rabkin. "Buyer Beware: Recalled Products Are Being Sold on Craigslist and Facebook Marketplace." *Consumer Reports*, November 6, 2019. www.consumerreports.org/product-safety/recalled-products-are -being-sold-on-craigslist-facebook-marketplace/.

———. "While They Were Sleeping." *Consumer Reports*, December 30, 2019. www.consumerreports.org/child-safety/while-they-were-sleeping/.

US Consumer Product Safety Commission. CPSA Section 6(b) Fact Sheet, accessed January 19, 2022. www.cpsc.gov/s3fs-public/pdfs/blk_pdf _CPSA6bFactSheet.pdf.

Finding a Moral Place

Arenstein, Seth. "Lessons from Peloton's Treadmill Recall Reminiscent of Other Crises." PR News, May 6, 2021. www.prnewsonline.com/peloton -crisis-lessons/.

Consumer Product Safety Commission. "Frightening Video Showing Child Being Pulled Under Peloton Treadmill." Video, YouTube, April 19, 2021. www.youtube.com/watch?v=F0GquqGzl1U. (Warning: It's unsettling.)

Peloton. "CPSC and Peloton Announce: Recall of Tread+ Treadmills After One Child Death and 70 Incidents; Recall of Tread Treadmills Due to Risk of Injury." Press release, May 5, 2021. www.onepeloton.com/press /articles/tread-and-tread-recall.

_____. "Peloton Refutes Consumer Product Safety Commission Claims." Press release, April 17, 2021. https://investor.onepeloton.com/news -releases/news-release-details/peloton-refutes-consumer-product-safety -commission-claims.

Samuelson, Judy. *The Six New Rules of Business: Creating Value in a Changing World.* New York: Penguin Random House, 2021.

Staff Report for Ranking Member Mara Cantwell. *Failed Recalls: The U.S. Consumer Product Safety Commission Must Take New Steps to Improve Recall Effectiveness.* December 19, 2019. www.cantwell.senate.gov/imo /media/doc/CPSC%20report%20-%20failed%20recalls.pdf.

Terlep, Sharon. "Peloton Faces Mounting Pressure to Recall Treadmills After One Death, Dozens of Injuries." *Wall Street Journal*, April 19, 2021. www.wsj.com/articles/peloton-faces-mounting-pressure-to-recall-treadmills -after-one-death-dozens-of-injuries-11618873584.

Thomas, Lauren. "Peloton Says It Has Been Subpoenaed by DOJ, DHS over Reporting of Treadmill Injuries." CNBC, August 27, 2021. www .nbcnews.com/business/business-news/peloton-says-it-has-been -subpoenaed-doj-dhs-over-reporting-n1277777.

Victor, Daniel. "Peloton Recalls Treadmills After Injuries and a Child's Death." *New York Times*, May 5, 2021. www.nytimes.com/2021/05/05 /business/peloton-recall-tread-plus.html.

Waller, Allyson. "Child Dies in Accident Involving Peloton Treadmill." *New York Times*, March 18, 2021. www.nytimes.com/2021/03/18/business /peloton-tread-death.html?action=click&module=RelatedLinks&pgtype =Article.

Warren, Elizabeth. "Senator Elizabeth Warren Questions Wells Fargo CEO John Stumpf at Banking Committee Hearing." Video, YouTube, September 20, 2016. www.youtube.com/watch?v=xJhkX74D10M.

Someone Else to Blame

Centers for Disease Control and Prevention. "Carbon Monoxide (CO) Poisoning Prevention." January 19, 2021. www.cdc.gov/nceh/features/copoisoning /index.html.

Gibson, Kate. "U.S. Regulator Sues Amazon to Force Recalls of Dangerous Products." MoneyWatch, July 15, 2021. www.cbsnews.com/news /amazon-products-recall-lawsuit-cpsc-safety-risk/.

Hope, Paul. "3 Carbon Monoxide Alarms Named 'Don't Buy: Safety Risk' by Consumer Reports." *Consumer Reports*, March 14, 2017. www.consumer reports.org/carbon-monoxide-alarms/consumer-reports-rates-off-brand-carbon -monoxide-alarms-purchase/.

Morris, Sam, and Jon Keegan. "Quiz: Can You Spot the Banned Amazon Item?" Markup, July 9, 2020. https://themarkup.org/banned-bounty /2020/07/09/amazon-content-moderation-banned-items-quiz.

The Notorious Section 6(b)

Amato, Kimberly. "My Daughter Should Have Been the Last Child to Die from a Furniture Tip-Over." *USA Today*, September 4, 2020. www .usatoday.com/story/opinion/voices/2020/09/04/furniture-tip-over-children -child-safety-fall-column/5702084002/.

Consumer Reports. "Furniture Tip-Overs: A Hazard in Your Home." August 2, 2021. www.consumerreports.org/furniture/furniture-tip-over -investigation/.

DiClerico, Daniel. "After Child Deaths, Ikea Recalls 29 Million Dressers." *Consumer Reports*, June 28, 2016. www.consumerreports.org/safety -recalls/ikea-dresser-recall/.

_____. "Safety Groups Urge Government to Recall Ikea Dresser." *Consumer Reports*, April 27, 2016. www.consumerreports.org/home-garden /ikea-dresser-tip-overs-.

Nadolny, Tricia L. "Commission Probes 3rd Child Ikea Dresser Death." *Philadelphia Inquirer*, April 15, 2016. www.inquirer.com/philly /news/20160417_Commission_probes_3rd_child_Ikea_dresser_death .html.

Peachman, Rachel Rabkin. "Furniture Anchors Not an Easy Fix, as Child Tip-Over Deaths Persist." *Consumer Reports*, November 5, 2018. www.consumerreports.org/furniture/furniture-anchors-not-an-easy-fix-as -child-tip-over-deaths-persist/.

———. "Furniture Tip-Overs: A Hidden Hazard in Your Home." *Consumer Reports*, March 22, 2018. www.consumerreports.org/furniture /furniture-tip-overs-hidden-hazard-in-your-home/.

Government Catfishing

Acheson, David. "Catfish Regulation: A Perfect Example of Wasted Resources in the U.S. Government." *Forbes*, June 6, 2016. www.forbes .com/sites/davidacheson/2016/06/06/catfish-regulation-a-perfect-example -of-wasted-resources-in-the-us-government/?sh=189f15f03be5.

Giamo, Cara. "Why the U.S. Government Treats Catfish Unlike Any Other Fish." *Atlas Obscura*, January 5, 2017. www.atlasobscura.com /articles/why-the-us-government-treats-catfish-unlike-any-other-fish.

Jones, Llewellyn. "Flood of Catfish Imports Continues Despite USDA Oversight." Mississippi Center for Investigative Reporting, July 4, 2021. www.clarionledger.com/story/news/2021/07/05/catfish-wars-foreign -catfish-imports-affecting-local-output-prices/5298289001/.

———. "Flood of Catfish Imports Continues Despite USDA Oversight." *Clarion Ledger* (Jackson, MS), July 4, 2021. www.clarionledger.com /story/news/2021/07/05/catfish-wars-foreign-catfish-imports-affecting-local -output-prices/5298289001/.

McCain, John. "The Fishy Deal on Catfish." *Politico*, June 7, 2013. www.politico.com/story/2013/06/the-fishy-deal-on-catfish-092415.

National Chicken Council. "Per Capita Consumption of Poultry and Livestock, 1965 to Forecast 2022, in Pounds." Updated December 2021. www.nationalchickencouncil.org/about-the-industry/statistics/per-capita -consumption-of-poultry-and-livestock-1965-to-estimated-2012-in-pounds/.

Seafood Health Facts. "Overview of the U.S. Seafood Supply." Accessed January 23, 2022. https://sites.udel.edu/seafoodhealthfacts/?s =annual+consumption+.

Toxic Chemicals in Baby Food

"High Levels of Toxins Found in More Baby Food Brands, Government Report Says." CBS News, September 29, 2021. www.cbsnews.com/news /baby-food-toxins-government-report/.

LaMotte, Sandee. "Manufacturers Allowed Baby Food Contaminated with Heavy Metals to Remain on Shelves, Lawmakers Say." CNN, September 29, 2021. www.cnn.com/2021/09/29/health/baby-food-toxins-update -wellness/index.html.

Loria, Kevin. "Baby Food and Heavy Metals: What Parents Should Do Now." *Consumer Reports*, February 5, 2021. www.consumerreports.org /baby-food/baby-food-and-heavy-metals-advice-for-parents/.

Subcommittee on Economic and Consumer Policy, US House Committee on Oversight and Reform. *Baby Foods Are Tainted with Dangerous Levels of Arsenic, Lead, Cadmium, and Mercury*, February 4, 2021. https://oversight .house.gov/sites/democrats.oversight.house.gov/files/2021-02-04%20ECP %20Baby%20Food%20Staff%20Report.pdf.

Lethal Lettuce

Calvo, Trisha. "Don't Eat Romaine Lettuce, Consumer Reports' Experts Advise." *Consumer Reports*, December 20, 2019. www.consumerreports.org /food-safety/dont-eat-romaine-lettuce-consumer-reports-experts-advise/.

Corkery, Michael, and Nathaniel Popper. "From Farm to Blockchain: Walmart Tracks Its Lettuce." *New York Times*, September 24, 2018. www .nytimes.com/2018/09/24/business/walmart-blockchain-lettuce.html.

Loria, Kevin. "FDA Discloses New *E. Coli* Romaine Outbreak After It Ends." *Consumer Reports*, November 1, 2019. www.consumerreports.org /e-coli/fda-discloses-new-e-coli-romaine-outbreak-after-it-ends/.

North Carolina Department of Health and Human Services. "Diseases and Topics: *Escherichia coli (E. coli)* Infection." Updated December 16, 2019. https://epi.dph.ncdhhs.gov/cd/diseases/ecoli.html.

Scutti, Susan. "Why What's Lurking in Leafy Greens Can Make You Seriously Sick." CNN, April 5, 2019. www.cnn.com/2018/05/02/health /e-coli-lettuce-explainer/index.html.

Upstream Impact

Consumer Reports. "Intelligence for a Better Marketplace." Accessed January 23, 2022. https://data.consumerreports.org/.

Safety in the Digital Age

Boghani, Priyanka. "What Has Happened to Boeing Since the 737 Max Crashes." *Frontline*, September 14, 2021. www.pbs.org/wgbh/frontline /article/what-has-happened-to-boeing-since-the-737-max-crashes/.

GSM Association. *2025 Every Car Connected: Forecasting the Growth and Opportunity*. February 2012. www.gsma.com/iot/wp-content/uploads /2012/03/gsma2025everycarconnected.pdf.

Moynihan, Tim. "Samsung Finally Reveals Why the Note 7 Kept Exploding." *Wired*, January 22, 2017. www.wired.com/2017/01/why-the-samsung -galaxy-note-7-kept-exploding/.

CHAPTER SIX: BUILDING A CONSUMER-FIRST MARKETPLACE

Consumer Rights Are Civil Rights

Roosevelt, Franklin. "Franklin Roosevelt's Re-Nomination Acceptance Speech, 1936." *American Yawp Reader*, accessed January 23, 2022. www .americanyawp.com/reader/23-the-great-depression/franklin-roosevelts-re -nomination-acceptance-speech-1936/.

#ConsumersDemand

B Lab Global. Home page. Accessed January 23, 2022. https:// bcorporation.net/.

Barry, Keith. "CR Engineers Show a Tesla Will Drive with No One in the Driver's Seat." *Consumer Reports*, May 27, 2021. www.consumerreports .org/autonomous-driving/cr-engineers-show-tesla-will-drive-with-no-one-in -drivers-seat/.

Beilinson, Jerry. "Glow Pregnancy App Exposed Women to Privacy Threats, Consumer Reports Finds." *Consumer Reports*, September 17, 2020. www.consumerreports.org/mobile-security-software/glow-pregnancy-app -exposed-women-to-privacy-threats/.

Carlson, Debbie. "ESG Investing Now Accounts for One-Third of Total U.S. Assets Under Management." MarketWatch, November 17, 2020. www.marketwatch.com/story/esg-investing-now-accounts-for-one-third-of -total-u-s-assets-under-management-11605626611.

Confino, Jo. "Paul Polman: 'The Power Is in the Hands of the Consumers.'" *The Guardian*, November 21, 2011. www.theguardian.com/sustainable -business/unilever-ceo-paul-polman-interview.

Deloitte. *The Deloitte Global Millennial Survey: A Decade in Review.* 2021. www2.deloitte.com/content/dam/Deloitte/global/Documents/2021 -deloitte-global-millennial-survey-decade-review.pdf.

Felton, Ryan. "Federal Lawmakers Push Bill to Tackle PFAS Contamination in Drinking Water," *Consumer Reports*, April 13, 2021, www .consumerreports.org/water-contamination/pfas-contamination-in-drinking -water-pfas-action-act-a7264470474/.

Forrester Research. "Values-Motivated Consumers Make Up 18% of the US Buying Population." October 27, 2021. www.forrester.com/blogs /values-motivated-consumers-make-up-18-of-the-us-buying-population/.

Harvard Kennedy School, Institute of Politics. "Harvard Youth Poll, 41st Edition, Spring 2021: Top Trends and Takeaways." April 23, 2021. https:// iop.harvard.edu/youth-poll/spring-2021-harvard-youth-poll.

McClain, Colleen. "56% of Americans Oppose the Right to Sue Social Media Companies for What Users Post." Pew Research Center, July 1, 2021. www.pewresearch.org/fact-tank/2021/07/01/56-of-americans-oppose -the-right-to-sue-social-media-companies-for-what-users-post/.

Murray, Alan, and Katherine Dunn. "CEOs Are Calling for More Regulation—of ESG Standards." *Fortune*, August 12, 2021. https://fortune.com /2021/08/12/ceos-are-calling-for-more-regulationof-esg-standards/.

Network of Executive Women and Deloitte. *Welcome to Generation Z.* Accessed January 23, 2022. www2.deloitte.com/content/dam/Deloitte/us /Documents/consumer-business/welcome-to-gen-z.pdf.

Wihbey, John P., Garrett Morrow, Myojung Chung, and Mike W. Peacey. "The Bipartisan Case for Labeling as a Content Moderation Method: Findings from a National Survey." Northeastern University Ethics Institute, October 29, 2021. https://papers.ssrn.com/sol3/papers.cfm?abstract _id=3923905.

A People-Powered Movement

Ablow, Gail. "Sign Here to Save the World: Online Petitions Explained." BillMoyers.com, September 26, 2016. https://billmoyers.com/story/sign-save -world-online-petitions-explained/.

Heimans, Jeremy, and Henry Timms. *New Power: How Power Works in Our Hyperconnected World—and How to Make It Work for You.* New York: Penguin Random House, 2018.

Lowery, Wesley. "Color of Change's Rashad Robinson Has Had Enough of Corporate America's Empty Platitudes." *Fast Company*, December 21,

2020. www.fastcompany.com/90584287/color-of-changes-rashad-robinson -has-had-enough-of-corporate-americas-empty-platitudes.

Melancon, J. Merritt. "Consumer Buying Power Is More Diverse than Ever." UGA Today, August 11, 2021. https://news.uga.edu/selig -multicultural-economy-report-2021/.

Nonprofit Megaphone. "Technology for the Public Good: Micah Sifry at Civic Hall." Accessed January 29, 2022. https://nonprofitmegaphone .com/civichall/.

Repko, Melissa. "As Black Buying Power Grows, Racial Profiling by Retailers Remains Persistent Problem." CNBC, July 5, 2020. www.cnbc .com/2020/07/05/as-black-buying-power-grows-racial-profiling-by-retailers -remains-a-problem.html.

SumOfUs. "Cecil the Lion Was Murdered—and Airlines Would Be Happy to Transport His Dead Body." Updated August 4, 2015. https:// actions.sumofus.org/a/cecil-airlines.

Index

recalls of products (*continued*)
Fisher-Price Rock 'n Play Sleeper, 193, 197–201
government sites information, 228–229
IKEA's Malm dresser, 210
Peloton Tread+, 204–205
Samsung Galaxy Note 7, 225–226
redlining, 144–145, 168
Rekognition software, 157
resource website, 13
reviews, online, 67–72, 91, 100
Richards, Ellen Swallow, 9
Richardson, Kimberly, 150–151
right to repair, 52
Rock 'n Play Sleeper, 191–201
romaine lettuce, *E. coli* in, 219–221
Romer, Paul, 54–55
Roosevelt, Franklin D., 237
Ross, Victoria, 132–133

safety
assigning blame for faulty products, 207–209
consumer demand for product safety, 241–242
designing products for, 212
E. coli in romaine lettuce, 219–221
Fisher-Price Rock 'n Play Sleeper, 191–201
gender bias in device design, 171–173
heavy metal toxicity in baby food, 216–219
individual action and advocacy, 228–230
manufacturers' use of consumer safety and quality data, 221–224
Peloton Tread+ death, 201–206
policy hurdles undercutting consumer safety, 209–213
reporting, 229
safety in the digital age, 225–227

seat belts, 187–188
as trust issue, 203–204
Sainsbury's grocery chain, 176
Samsung Galaxy Note 7 phones, 225–226
Samuelson, Judy, 205
Saunders, Lauren, 119
scams
hearse chasers, 103–105
internet health scams, 87–90
junk insurance, 106–108
scammers' reliance on trust, 61–65
through online reviews, 67–68
tricks and traps in financial sectors, 94–96
trust as grifters' technique, 106
See also data breaches
Schatz, Brian, 83
Schlink, Frederick, 10, 63–64
scientific research
clandestine experiments on Facebook users, 79
targeting deceptive advertising, 63–65
Scothon, Chuck, 198
seat belts, 187–188
Section 6(b) of the CPSC, 195–196, 209–213, 227, 242
Section 230 (Communications Decency Act), 82–83
security
personal debt threatening clearances, 99
protecting against data breaches, 42–44
protecting personal data from threats, 238–239
SeeClickFix, 246
segregation, 144–148
sewage treatment, 9
Shane's Foundation, 210–211
Shecter, Jen, 203

Marta L. Tellado is the president and CEO of Consumer Reports, America's foremost consumer organization, which advances truth, transparency, and fairness in the marketplace. In 2019, she led the creation of the organization's Digital Lab to develop new ways to test and report on digital products and services—from connected thermostats, to cars that collect data on their drivers, to online platforms such as Amazon, Google, and Facebook. She also created Consumer Reports' Digital Standard, an open-source set of benchmarks that can be used by companies and organizations to design digital products that are respectful of consumers' digital rights.

Prior to joining CR, she served as vice president at the Ford Foundation, executive director of the Domestic Policy Group at the Aspen Institute, director for national issues and outreach for US senator Bill Bradley, and vice president of the Partnership for Public Service.

PublicAffairs is a publishing house founded in 1997. It is a tribute to the standards, values, and flair of three persons who have served as mentors to countless reporters, writers, editors, and book people of all kinds, including me.

I. F. STONE, proprietor of *I. F. Stone's Weekly*, combined a commitment to the First Amendment with entrepreneurial zeal and reporting skill and became one of the great independent journalists in American history. At the age of eighty, Izzy published *The Trial of Socrates*, which was a national bestseller. He wrote the book after he taught himself ancient Greek.

BENJAMIN C. BRADLEE was for nearly thirty years the charismatic editorial leader of *The Washington Post*. It was Ben who gave the *Post* the range and courage to pursue such historic issues as Watergate. He supported his reporters with a tenacity that made them fearless and it is no accident that so many became authors of influential, best-selling books.

ROBERT L. BERNSTEIN, the chief executive of Random House for more than a quarter century, guided one of the nation's premier publishing houses. Bob was personally responsible for many books of political dissent and argument that challenged tyranny around the globe. He is also the founder and longtime chair of Human Rights Watch, one of the most respected human rights organizations in the world.

·   ·   ·

For fifty years, the banner of Public Affairs Press was carried by its owner Morris B. Schnapper, who published Gandhi, Nasser, Toynbee, Truman, and about 1,500 other authors. In 1983, Schnapper was described by *The Washington Post* as "a redoubtable gadfly." His legacy will endure in the books to come.

Peter Osnos, *Founder*